DAVE "POPS" MASCH:

FEARED BY FISH...

LOVED BY MANY...

KNOWS IT ALL!

On The Water • Suite 2 • 35 Technology Park Dr. • E. Falmouth, MA 02536.

www.OnTheWater.com

Printed in the U.S.A.

ISBN# 0-970 6538-4-0

10 9 8 7 6 5 4 3 2 1

written and illustrated by Dave Masch

Chris Megan, Publisher
Neal Larsson, General Manager
Gene Bourque, Editor
Elizabeth Scanland, Copy Editor
Bill Hough, Contributing Publisher
Andy Nabreski, Design & Cover Photography

Cooking The Catch

written and illustrated by
Dave "Pops" Masch

An **On The Water** Publication

about the author

● ●

I was born in 1937 in Detroit, Michigan, and came to Massachusetts in 1955 to attend Harvard College, kind of by accident.

I saw the ocean in 1955 and have not yet recovered from it. After Harvard I was in the biology department at the Woods Hole Oceanographic Institution for ten years, spending time at sea. I worked as a counselor, cook, instructor and "professional father figure" at the Penikese Island School for 29 years.

Since retirement three years ago, I spend my time reading, writing, cooking, eating, telling lies and some truths, and I fish.

Dedication

· ·

I dedicate this book to my young friend Seth Carey who died this autumn after a long, stubborn battle against amyotrophic lateral sclerosis (ALS, also known as Lou Gehrig's Disease). I knew Seth from the beginning of his life 42 years ago until his death. I taught him many things in his childhood and youth, and learned many things from him in his all too brief adult years. There are several of his recipes in this book.

I also dedicate the book to my lovely, usually tolerant wife, Jeanne, for putting up with strange creatures in the freezer (25 pounds of hagfish), long-lost bait in the car and many smoky kitchens.

Seth
a keeper

Acknowledgement

· ·

I want to thank the many people on the staff of *On The Water*: Gene Bourque, Neal Larsson, Chris Megan, Andy Nabreski, George Clondas and especially former editor Catherine Cramer (who hired me to write the cooking column in the first place) and assistant editor Liz Scanland, who slugged through all my stuff and made it presentable.

Introduction

I clearly remember the first striped bass I ever ate, almost fifty years ago, at the now long-gone Moors Restaurant in Provincetown, Massachusetts. It was grilled and served in a white sauce made from fish stock and garnished with black olives, and it was unforgettably delicious, the best fish I had eaten in my twenty years of life. This was a life-changing moment leading to this point – you reading this sentence in my cookbook.

Having grown up in the city of Detroit, far from any salt water, I did not see the sea until I visited Revere Beach in 1955, my freshman year of college. I had no idea that I would spend most of the rest of my life on, in, around and under the sea, pursuing knowledge, beauty and, last but far from least, food!

For ten years I worked as a research assistant at the Woods Hole Oceanographic Institution in the biology department, studying large fish, tuna and sharks much of the time. This got me to exotic ports to sample local seafood and culture.

I then was employed as a professional father figure, counselor and cook at the Penikese Island School. At Penikese we cooked and heated with wood and learned what "slaving over a hot stove" meant. I did this for 29 years.

At times during breaks from my regular employment, I cooked aboard research, fishing, and tug boats, enjoying almost every minute of it, except when the captain changed course as I was serving the chowder.

Cooking, cleaning and catching fish have fascinated me this entire time. I have taught hundreds of kids the rudiments of fishing and almost as many the rudiments of cooking fish.

On The Water magazine gave me the chance to share my recipes with you and now is publishing this book. I want to thank them here.

There are many fish cooking books but few, if any, about the fish and shellfish you and I can catch or gather ourselves. Almost every fish cookbook contains lengthy advice on how to tell if fish are fresh if you are buying them, so I will not repeat them all. My main criterion is smell; if it smells at all bad to you, do not buy it. In fact, the freshest fish should have almost no smell at all. Follow this simple rule and you cannot go wrong.

Many people, especially young people, consider cooking an art, and a difficult one at that, but it is not. It is a craft anyone can learn. One must first learn the basic techniques and then become creative; even Picasso went to art school for many years before he became a great creative force. I say try the recipes in this book, then develop your own. You will not be sorry, you will become a star to your family and possibly locally famous.

Go for it. Pleasure beckons!

David "Pops" Masch

Chapter One: SPRING

Chapter Two: SUMMER

Chapter Three: AUTUMN

Chapter Four: WINTER

Pops and the "Mad Irishman," Barrie Cooke.

Chapter One: Springtime

Spring – A Time of Hope and Renewal

Last week a few spring peepers were making lonely calls. In autumn, sometimes it gets unseasonably warm after a cold snap and a few of these tiny frogs emerge, and people who note such things refer to the autumn calls as "echoes." I hear them as promises of the resurrection of springtime, a promise that will come true, and as far as this cookbook goes, has come true.

In spring the herring return, fewer now than ever, but they still come. These fish saved the Pilgrims after their first disastrous winter here in New England. By the end of March the winter flounder, another fish way down in numbers, will be stirring and, if found, ready to take a bait after a long winter in the mud. The ice will fade away, and shellfish will be more accessible.

The tautog will appear along with the dandelions and soon thereafter the first bass and bluefish. We fishermen will have a cornucopia of fish available, and we cooks can revel in their variety. My cooking gear and fishing equipment are ready, I am ready, and I hope you are, too. So here we go again. Try something new, always a good idea!

What Do You Mean, Trash Fish?!

It has become fashionable to write about bravely preparing trash fish and extolling their culinary virtues. I am following that trend but resent calling perfectly fine fish "trash."

For many years dragger fishermen considered any fish, other than the readily marketable species they were targeting, as trash. If it was not cod, haddock or one of the various flounders, it was trash and was unceremoniously shoved, shoveled or hosed out of the scuppers and over the side. This was not only an unforgivable waste of natural resources, but also a loss of opportunities for fine gustatory experiences, like skate wings in brown butter, marinated ocean catfish (wolffish) deep fried (the Portuguese in Provincetown call this "galvanized fish") or goosefish "lobster" salad, and many, many more.

Fishermen, particularly fishermen of northern European origin, often do not like fish. More than one of these "Yankees" told me that two or three meals of baked haddock and one or two of fried yellowtail a year were plenty! They would not even consider any other species. The Scandinavians are often more conservative than that and want their fish salted, pickled, canned or salt treated with lye and then cooked. Wow!

We have caught so many of the most popular species of fish that they are depleted, and, out of necessity, we are expanding our culinary repertoire to include more and more trash fish. Several years ago the French government eased the pain of our cod and haddock fishermen, caused by limits on those species, by ordering as many skate wings as could be provided for their school lunch program. Can you imagine trying that here with our kids and their media-controlled appetites? The skate population is showing signs of overfishing. Goosefish is suffering a similar fate. The demand for fish grows throughout the world, as does the population. Fish and fishermen are troubled and so are we.

Last night I had sautéed yellowtail flounder for dinner. I noted an advertisement for yellowtail in the local market. I had not seen any for sale, as such, for many, many years so I decided to buy some. I hate to buy fish! Anyway, I dredged it in seasoned flour and sautéed it briefly in butter and oil. It was good, bland but good. It needs a sauce to liven it up for my taste, but it is this very blandness that appeals to the Yankees. Henry Klimm, a venerable Yankee fisherman, told me of regularly catching 23,000 to 30,000 pounds on trips to Nantucket Shoals. When this source "dried up," they steamed all the way to the Sable Island grounds and came back, more than once, with 80,000 pounds of yellowtail.

"We never thought we could catch them all up," Henry said with amazement. Well they almost did, along with the cod and haddock, but the sea is not exhausted yet, and we will continue to eat fish until that unlikely, but possible, event. So, let us cook and eat some trash fish, and hope that by doing so we will allow more of the usual fish to recover some of their former abundance.

SKATE IN BLACK BUTTER *(for 6)*

2 lbs. cleaned skate wings, skinned (leave whole or cut into bite-size pieces)
Seasoned flour

Dip skate in flour and sauté until browned. Keep warm.

Black Butter
1 stick butter
2 cloves garlic
Juice of 1/2 lemon
Salt and pepper
3 TBS capers (optional)

Lightly brown butter and add remaining ingredients. Sauté until garlic is transparent and pour over warm skate pieces. Oh boy!

SKATE RECIPE #2

3 lbs. skate wings
1 qt. water
1/2 tsp. salt
1/4 cup wine vinegar
1 medium onion, chopped
1 bay leaf
6 peppercorns

Simmer all ingredients, except skate, for 10 minutes. Add skate and cook gently for 15 minutes. Remove skate from liquid, pull meat from skin and cartilage; keep warm. Pour black butter over skate pieces and serve. These can be served on toast (anchovy toast is especially good), or over rice or boiled potatoes. Mmmmmm!

OCEAN CATFISH (WOLFFISH) GALVANIZED & FRIED *(for 4)*

1 ½ lbs. ocean catfish fillets
2 cups water
1 cup vinegar
4 bay leaves, crumbled
4 cloves garlic, crushed
1 medium onion, chopped
1 tsp. cumin seeds (or 1/2 tsp. ground cumin)

Combine these ingredients for a marinade. Add anything else you like – crab boil is good. Bring to a boil and cool. Pour cooled marinade over fish fillets, and soak for 1/2 to 3 hours. Remove from marinade. Coat with your favorite frying mixture and deep- or pan-fry. You will not be sorry.

LOBSTER SALAD (ALMOST)

Substitute 2/3 poached, chopped goosefish for lobster in your favorite lobster salad recipe. Most people will be unaware of your diluted generosity. I won't tell.

GOOSEFISH MARINARA *(for 4 lucky diners)*

Either buy or make a good marinara sauce. Many on the market are quite tasty, and none are bad. Poach cubed goosefish in the sauce until it is white all the way through. Use about a pound of fish to a quart of sauce. It will be better than good! Serve over pasta, or try garlic mashed potatoes.

I urge you to try these recipes for your own good.
When I say they are delicious,
I'm not talking trash!

Frozen Fish Favorites – What's Your Fancy?

The paper says it is going to reach 60 degrees in Boston today. It is already 50 here in Cataumet on Cape Cod this morning. I checked the ocean temperature in Woods Hole yesterday; it was 38. It is usually around 31 at this time of year. There is little ice in the bays and harbors this winter. This warm weather starts things stirring that usually wait until early spring.

Someone wrote that in spring a young man's fancy turns to thoughts of love. Well, in late winter an old man's fancy, I am told, is more likely to turn to thoughts of fishing. One of my mature friends asked me just last week if I would be interested in going down to the Thames River in Connecticut to try for an overwintering bass; two others asked me if the unseasonable warmth will make for earlier action this spring. So it's beginning.

I only travel for fish that will not come to me, such as salmon, tarpon, permit, bonefish and other noble creatures that almost never visit our New England shores. In midwinter my thoughts drift to how best to cook the fish frozen last fall that lurk in the freezer, or the fish that is offered by the local fishmonger and in supermarkets.

Winter is often a good time to find real bargains in frozen swordfish. It will vary in quality from very good to edible, depending on how long it has been frozen. It is safest to buy the steaks still frozen and thaw them in your fridge. This way you will at least know how long they have been thawed.

The master recipe and several variations I am going to give will be flavorful enough to make negligible whatever shortcomings our frozen fish have. This is about your last chance for last fall's bluefish; the bass will keep their quality longer. These recipes are good with any fish fillets or steaks but are best with white-fleshed fish.

SIMPLE MASTER RECIPE – BAKED FISH IN TOMATO SAUCE *(for 4)*

2 lbs. fish (steak or fillets)
3 cups tomato sauce (approximately)
Olive oil
Salt and pepper
Bread crumbs
2 TBS parsley, minced
Lemon

You may make your own sauce or use one already prepared. A Yankee might use plain stewed tomatoes. This is a good place to start for the non-adventurer.

Choose a roasting pan (Pyrex is good) big enough to hold the steaks or fillets and the sauce covering them. Preheat the oven to 400 degrees.

Oil your pan with olive oil. Lay your fish on the oil in a single layer. Sprinkle lightly with salt and however you wish with pepper.

Pour the tomato sauce or mixture around the fish. Cover the exposed fish lightly but completely with bread crumbs. Drizzle the crumbs with olive oil.

Bake this in the upper third of the preheated oven for about 10 minutes per inch of thickness of your fish. If you should cook it somewhat longer, it will not be the disaster it could be if you were not cooking it partly submerged. It is ready when it flakes easily when tested with a fork. If you would like to brown the top, broil carefully for a minute, as bread crumbs char easily. If this should happen, do not despair. Just throw out the burned parts, disguise the burned area with chopped parsley or lemon slices, and carry on.

Garnish your dish with sprigs of parsley in the corners and one in the middle. Sprinkle minced parsley wantonly. Add some quartered lemons and serve – simple but good.

I would serve plain boiled or mashed potatoes with this and barely cooked tiny frozen peas. Spinach would

---

be good. A salad would also be fine.

You can make several ethnic variations by following the above instructions. The supermarkets have many flavored stewed tomatoes and tomato sauces. I like to use canned tomato with jalapeño for Mexican-style baked fish, or basil, garlic and onion-flavored tomatoes for Italian-style fish. There are many available; none are bad.

PORTUGUESE BAKED FISH IN TOMATO SAUCE *(for 4)*

2 lbs. fish (steaks or fillets)
3 cups sauce
1 small onion, chopped
1/2 green pepper, chopped
1 stick celery, chopped
1 clove garlic, minced
1 tsp. cumin
1/4 tsp. (to taste) Tabasco
1/4 lb. chopped linguica or chourico
1/2 tsp. thyme
2 TBS olive oil

Sauté veggies in olive oil until soft. Add tomato sauce or canned tomatoes; simmer 10 minutes. Then proceed as in master recipe.

A Portuguese restaurant would serve plain boiled potatoes and white rice as sides, along with a salad. There should be oil and vinegar on the table and, maybe, crushed red pepper.

Use the same ingredients as in previous recipe, plus:
1/4 cup chopped olives (green, black or a mixture)
1/4 cup chopped fresh cilantro or 1 TBS dried
1 packet Sazûn Goya (coriander and annatto) or Sazûn Goya con Azafran (saffron)

The last ingredient, Sazûn Goya, is a premixed spice combination that seems almost magical. I use it in many Spanish-style dishes.

Proceed as in preceding recipe. Use chourico and a bit more hot pepper. Stir in the olives, cilantro and Sazûn just before baking the dish.

I would serve this with white or yellow rice, fried plantain or ripe banana. Garnish the platter with cilantro and sliced limes.

ITALIAN-STYLE BAKED FISH IN TOMATO SAUCE

Use the same ingredients as in the Portuguese recipe, omitting cumin and sausage. Use 1/4 teaspoon hot pepper flakes instead of Tabasco. Add 1 teaspoon oregano.

You could add a cup and a half of sautéed mushrooms to the sauce and 1/2 cup white (or red) wine. Bake as in the previous recipes. I would serve this with boiled spaghetti, lightly dressed in garlic-flavored olive oil and butter. Have plenty of grated Parmesan cheese available.

Sprinkle the dish with chopped Italian parsley. A green salad and crusty bread would be fine with this.

Try these things. Make your own variations: Throw in a half-dozen shrimp or scallops (double if you wish) for the final 5 minutes of baking. Have fun; get accolades. Go for it!

You Cannot Have Too Much Leftover Fish!

I am writing this in midwinter. My ice-fishing friends have not been active for lack of ice here in southeastern Massachusetts. My home port of Woods Hole no longer has a fleet of draggers except for some seasonal squid and fluke fishermen, a couple of lobstermen and one giant offshore dragger, so I have no easy source of cheap or free fresh fish. I cannot call the fish I catch free. Although I catch many, I spend a lot on gas, tackle, books and other sources of information. It would be cheaper to pay top dollar than to catch my own. True but dull, a silly idea. One cannot put a price on a strike on a surface lure at daybreak or on the "bulldogging" of a big blue after he has finished jumping or on the marvelous odor of a freshly caught false albacore. This is the stuff that songs, poems and paintings are made of by people more talented than I.

Fresh and free fish not being available, I am forced to the back of my freezer (for lurking fillets, pints of frozen quahogs and squid, another "eat the bait" possibility) and to the fish market to find fish for winter dinners. I always buy more fish than I need; one-half pound of filleted fish is a generous serving for one person. I buy one and a half pounds when I prepare dinner for my wife and me; that way I know I will have leftovers.

Last week I made baked haddock surrounded by chopped tomatoes, covered with bread crumbs dampened with olive oil. I served whole boiled potatoes, tiny frozen peas and salad with the fish in tomato sauce. It was fine and we had leftover fish, tomato and boiled potatoes, just as I had planned. This is not always so. From the leftovers I made a fine fish hash for lunch on the following day.

MASCH FISH HASH
(one of my myriad versions)
1/2 lb. leftover baked haddock (or cod or other white fish)
1 lb. boiled potatoes
3/4 cup chopped onion
1/4 cup chopped red or green bell pepper
Salt and pepper, to taste
2 TBS butter, olive oil or peanut oil

Heat butter or oil over medium heat. Sauté chopped onion and pepper briefly. Chop fish and potatoes into small cubes, add these to onions, stir well and sauté over medium heat until the bottom begins to brown. Add salt and pepper and stir; sauté until bottom begins to brown again. About 10 minutes of cooking are all you need. You can cook the hash to any degree of crispiness you desire. You can aid the crust-forming process by putting a couple of tablespoons of milk, cream or condensed milk into the sauté pan with the hash for a final browning.

The last version of this hash I made contained some leftover stewed tomatoes that I had cooked surrounding the haddock. I also added about a tablespoon of chopped parsley and a tiny grind of nutmeg. It was delicious!

I feel like I could write an essay on fish hash, which could easily advance into fish cakes, which are actually fish hash with egg and breading added. Fish hash and fish cakes can be made with virtually any leftover cooked fish. Fish cakes make for a more elegant presentation than does fish hash, but they do not taste any better.

Many ingredients can be tried in fish hash: celery, parsley, a little garlic, tomato, minced linguica or chourico in small doses. Various herbs and spices can also be used: adobo, Crazy salt, curry powder, cumin, chili powder, thyme and rosemary all work. Give fish hash a try – that's what I say! Serve it with poached eggs for breakfast or with a tossed salad for lunch. I always have ketchup or chili sauce and Tabasco with mine. (The gourmets are not always right, and ketchup is here to stay!)

You can use leftover cooked fish just as you use canned tuna. Some people make tuna salad with only mayonnaise; I like to add chopped green onion and celery and about a tablespoon of sweet pickle relish.

You can very easily make an elegant lunch salad using leftover fish.

FISH SALAD WITH EGG AND AVOCADO
(for 4)
1 head of lettuce (or 1/2 bag mesclun)
1 lb. cooked fish (chunked)
1 cup thinly sliced sweet onion (or red)
1 cup diced avocado
4 hard-boiled eggs, quartered
3 TBS capers
1/2 cup or more of vinaigrette

Divide lettuce or mesclun on four plates, or line a large shallow bowl with the greens, put the other ingredients on top and dress with vinaigrette, or let each guest dress his own. This is easy, impressive and elegant, kind of the way I like to think of myself.

JAMES BEARD'S (MY HERO) BASIC VINAIGRETTE
1 tsp. kosher salt
1/2 tsp. freshly ground black pepper
2 TBS wine vinegar (or balsamic)
8 TBS fruity olive oil (Pompeii is good or any Portuguese oil)

Mix these ingredients. You may flavor it further, should you wish, with mustard, garlic, green onions, chopped shallots or chopped fresh herbs, making it your own. Serve this and you will not regret it! Commercially bottled vinaigrette works, but I recommend making your own.

Serve this salad with warm crusty peasant bread and a glass of chilled dry white wine and my, oh, my! Life is good!

SEAFOOD FRITTATA (A LA BRUCE BECK)
(for 4 to 8)
2 TBS light olive oil
1 TBS butter
1 medium zucchini, sliced
1 medium onion, sliced
1 large clove garlic, minced
6 eggs
1 cup flaked leftover fish (or oysters or shrimp)
1 ½ cups cooked spaghetti or linguine
2 TBS chopped fresh herbs; parsley, basil or a
  combination to your taste
1/2 cup grated Parmesan
Coarse salt and pepper (freshly ground)

Heat the oil and butter together in an ovenproof, preferably nonstick skillet or large shallow casserole dish that can go in the oven. Sauté the onion and zucchini until translucent, add minced garlic for final 30 seconds (so it does not burn). Remove from heat.

Beat the eggs in a large bowl, season with salt and pepper. Pour other ingredients into casserole, add beaten eggs, mix well. Place in preheated 350-degree oven, bake for 12 to 15 minutes until slightly browned and barely cooked through. Remove from oven and allow to cool for 5 minutes. Cut into wedges and serve.

This is equally good at room temperature and can be served later.

A "Man Of Fish"

I have often used recipes from my friend Seth Carey, a fine fisherman, smoker of fish and preparer of fish both raw and cooked. There are many fishermen but few true "men of fish." I say Seth is one. He is the first one I have named. A "man of fish" must enjoy studying their habits, catching them, cleaning them, and cooking and eating them. Seth easily qualifies!

Sadly, Seth's fishing days are over. He is in the last stages of a most dreadful disease, amyotrophic lateral sclerosis (ALS, Lou Gehrig's disease), which causes gradual deterioration of all muscular function until life can no longer be maintained. However, during this implacable deterioration, the mind remains clear, making the awful process seem even crueler.

I was visiting Seth a couple of weeks ago. He can communicate using his computer and the one finger he can still move. I asked him if there was anything I could do for him in the time that was left. I thought he might need a legal favor or a message delivered, but I was wrong.

Seth thought briefly and asked if I would prepare a scup dinner for him on Friday night, using scup caught last autumn and frozen. With the help of Captain Tom Danforth, I spent an entire afternoon last fall filleting and skinning scup for the freezer. There were also some black sea bass in the mix.

Seth said his favorite breakfast was scup, double-dipped in milk and egg and seasoned bread crumbs, then pan-fried and served with hot salsa.

SETH'S FAVORITE BREAKFAST FOR 2 (ARMORED FRIED SCUP)

1 lb. scup fillets
1/3 cup seasoned (salt and pepper) flour
2 cups bread crumbs
1/4 tsp. cayenne pepper (optional)
1 egg
1 cup milk

Shake fillets in a bag of seasoned flour until coated.

Dip each fillet in a cup of milk in which you have beaten the egg. Now roll in bread crumbs and set aside on a plate.

Heat 1/8 inch of oil in a large frying pan as you bread the fillets.

For Seth's favorite method you would now dip some breaded fillets in egg and milk again and roll them in bread crumbs, making a heavy coating.

Fry these fillets over medium-high heat until golden brown and crisp on the bottom, turn over and brown the top. Serve with salsa. I like tartar sauce and Tabasco-laced ketchup as well.

This recipe may be adapted for a Chinese-style entrée. Substitute sesame seeds for the bread crumbs and proceed as instructed. Fillets prepared this way are good served with stir-fried vegetables in a sauce served over rice. I like broccoli with oyster sauce with sesame-crusted fillets.

You may substitute any fairly thin cut white fish fillet for scup. My meal with Seth included black sea bass; fluke, flounder, catfish, tilapia and haddock all may be used confidently.

Fillets cut into fingers, coated with sesame seeds and fried make a great appetizer served with an oriental dipping sauce. Outstanding!

When I asked Seth if I could do anything for him, I expected some somber duty, but Seth gave me the pleasure of preparing him a meal of fish. I taught him how to catch scup when he was a child, and he was teaching me about priorities now and thanking me as an adult. Seth also has a simple, wonderful recipe for squid.

MARINATED GRILLED SQUID

Cut squid bodies in strips of 1 inch by 4 inches or so, immerse in or coat with olive oil and lime juice to which you have added a little cayenne pepper.

Grill these strips for about 15 seconds on each side over hot coals.

Serve as is, or with dipping sauce.

This is easy, more than delicious, and will be tried (and often loved) by non-squid eaters.

Another contribution Seth made to my cooking repertoire that I use with large fillets of bass or bluefish baked and flambéed with gin.

GIN-FLAMED STRIPED BASS OR BLUEFISH *(for 8)*

1 fillet of bass or bluefish (about 4 pounds)
Juice of one lemon or two limes
1/2 cup of olive oil
Salt and pepper
2 ounces gin

Preheat oven to 425 degrees. Liberally salt and pepper the fish and put in baking pan in which you have mixed the oil and citrus juice. Roll fillets around until well coated and set aside for about an hour (you can bake immediately, but it is better to wait).

Put marinated (or oiled) fish in hot oven and bake 10 minutes for each inch of thickness at its thickest point. When nearly done, warm the gin. When fish is done, remove from oven, pour warm gin over fillet and ignite; be careful, it may do this by itself. When flames die, move fish to serving platter and surround with parsley, sliced lemon or limes, and you have a beautiful, delicious dish that will inspire love and respect.

I made a meal last night that I was so pleased with that I intend to make it for Seth next week.

SWORDFISH IN ITALIAN SAUCE *(for 2)*

1 lb. swordfish steak
(1) 14 ½-oz. can Italian stewed tomatoes
5 anchovy fillets
1/4 cup green salad olives
1/4 cup bread crumbs
Salt and pepper
3 TBS olive oil
1 lemon

Preheat oven to 425 degrees. Put 1 tablespoon olive oil in saucepan and heat; place anchovies in the oil.

Put 2 tablespoons oil and juice from 1/2 lemon in baking dish just big enough to hold swordfish and tomatoes without submerging the fish. Roll fish, which you have salted and peppered liberally, in oil and juice, add olives, sautéed anchovies and tomatoes to baking pan, mix and add steak. Sprinkle bread crumbs on fish and sprinkle with oil. Bake for 15 to 20 minutes and brown under broiler. Serve this with plenty of couscous (preferably Italian), rice, mashed potato or whatever – marvelous! A little salad, chilled white wine, and pears and Gorgonzola for dessert – wow!

I will add hot sauce to this and Seth will love it, as he loves friends, fishing, family in every form and fun. Here is to you Seth! And thanks!

Winter Blues Are Not Fish

* *

It is late January and my energy is low, my spirits lowish, and winter is heavily upon us. There are about 30 inches of snow outside my window, and, periodically, icicles of potentially lethal weight crash down from the eaves of my house. The sun is shining brightly, but my lethargy hangs on. So I think I will write some easy recipes for dead-of-winter cooking, the simplest, easiest recipes I know for the winter doldrums. Just because they are simple does not mean they cannot be delicious.

PLAIN BAKED FISH FILLETS *(for 2)*

1 lb. fish fillet (or steak)
1 TBS butter or olive oil
Salt and pepper

Preheat oven to 415 degrees. Butter or oil both sides of fish, liberally salt and pepper, and bake for 10 minutes per inch of thickness of your fish.

Remove from oven, put dab of butter on top and add any liquid in the pan, sprinkle with parsley, dust with paprika, place cut lemons alongside and serve. There is nothing more elegant.

I would serve this with mashed potatoes or rice with petit pois and a plain mesclun salad with vinaigrette. Some chilled dry white wine would not hurt a bit. Elegant and easy, and you will not be accused of laziness, you will be lauded.

SIMPLE POACHED FISH

1/2 lb. fish per serving
Enough liquid to barely cover
Salt and pepper
Parsley and lemon for garnish

Place fish in a pan barely able to accommodate the fish, and cover with cooking liquid. This liquid could be bottled clam juice, fish stock made from a bouillon cube, white wine, or white wine and water.

Fillets with the skin on will hold together better than will skinless. Bring liquid to a slow boil, reduce to simmer, and poach the fish for 10 minutes per inch of thickness. Remove cooked fish to a platter and keep warm in a 175-degree oven as you make the sauce.

To make sauce, boil down cooking liquid to about half, and swirl in as much butter as you need for it to thicken slightly. Pour this over warm fish, garnish and serve. The same side dishes recommended for simple baked fish will do here also.

You could follow these poaching directions using scallops or shrimp with fine results. If I cooked shrimp in this manner I would add some lemon juice and a touch of cayenne pepper or Tabasco as I stirred in the lemon. I would serve either of these over white rice.

I love, as you have probably noticed, petit pois with fish. These tiny, frozen, young peas are closer to fresh peas than any other frozen vegetable is to its fresh self and are delicious when not overcooked – merely thawing is nearly enough cooking. Shrimp poached and served with peas and rice is the basis of the classic risi bisi of Italian fame. I urge you to try this with shrimp and peas.

I have never eaten a frozen or bottled Alfredo sauce, but if they are any good at all they would accompany rice, scallops and petit pois with delicious results. The same could be said for bottled marinara. These dishes over pasta will be tasty, not as good as if you had started from scratch, or as ego-inflating, but your audience (unfortunately) may not know the difference – remember that they are lucky to have you cooking for them at all.

To make a quick, simple vinaigrette for green salad, put a tablespoon of balsamic or other vinegar of your choice in your salad bowl, add a pinch of salt, 1/2 teaspoon sugar, a few grinds of black pepper, a large 1/2 teaspoon of Dijon or dry mustard and 2 to 3 tablespoons of good olive oil. Beat this mixture with a whisk until emulsified, add your greens, and toss thoroughly just before serving. If you think you have too much dressing, save some for later use.

Scallops are a great boon for lazy cooks and thrive on simple treatment. In the fish market in winter you can sometimes find bay scallops (very pricey), sea scallops (not cheap but no waste) and small calico or "bay scallops" (only four or five dollars a pound). Local (Cape Cod) bay scallops are wonderfully delicious, sea scallops are delicious, and the calico is good but of a far lower degree of deliciousness than the other two.

Seviche is a way of serving raw shellfish or finfish by "cooking" (marinating) them in an acetic medium, using lemon or lime juice or sometimes high-quality vinegar – a great appetizer.

QUICK SEVICHE *(for 4)*

1/2 pound sea scallops
Juice of one lemon
1/4 cup (3 TBS) olive oil
Salt and pepper
3 TBS minced fresh basil

Cut scallops in 1/8-inch slices and divide among four plates. Drizzle 1/4 of a lemon's juice and olive oil on scallops on each plate, sprinkle with salt and pepper, and top with basil. Rest 5 minutes and serve.

These appetizers, based on Mark Bittman's *Fish* cookbook, are so easy and so good you will not believe how lucky your guests are.

Here is a recipe, not as simple, but not hard, using the inexpensive calico or southern bay scallops.

PASTA WITH SCALLOPS *(for 3 or 4)*

1/4 cup olive oil
1/4 stick butter
1 TBS garlic, minced
3/4 pound calico or other scallops
1/2 cup parsley, minced
1/4 cup toasted bread crumbs
1 pound linguine

Warm olive oil, butter and garlic over low heat until garlic turns pale tan, shake now and again. Add scallops and salt and pepper. Cook until scallops turn opaque; add half the parsley and all the bread crumbs and mix off heat.

The pasta could be boiling while you do all this. When pasta is nearly done, reheat the scallops, drain pasta, and top with scallop sauce, garnish with remaining parsley, and dribble with olive oil if it looks dry. I cannot imagine a better use for "lesser" scallops.

There you go – simple and delicious. The herring will be running soon. Hurrah!

Sea. Bay Calico

Scallops

On The Sorry State Of Chowder

Recently, as I was returning to the Cape from Boston around dinnertime, I decided to stop for an order of fish and chips and a cup of chowder at one of the seafood emporiums near the canal. I'm always looking for good chowder – clam or fish – and rarely finding it. The last truly fine fish chowder I had was in Damariscotta, Maine, in 1993, but hope springs eternal.

In the large restaurant I chose, the service was perfunctory at best, almost slipshod. Whatever was going on in the kitchen seemed of more importance than the needs of the few customers. When the waitress got to me, I ordered the evening special of fish and chips and a cup of fish chowder. I had to make a special request for silverware, which most restaurants consider helpful to diners.

My cup of chowder and scanty order of fried flounder arrived almost simultaneously. The chowder was not merely bad, it was terrible! Probably dangerous! It was beginning to sour, and the fish had been in there so long that there were no chunks, only browning shreds. The surface of the chowder was not horizontal or flat; it was so thick and pasty that it had peaks like beaten egg white. It was clotted, mucilaginous goop – not my idea of an adventure in dining.

QUOHAUG
CAPTURED '68
MEGANSETT
DAVID MARCH

When I finally saw the waitress again, I told her what I thought and sent my chowder back with an admonition for the cook. She was surprised at my reaction and dared to ask me if I'd like to try the clam chowder. She had to be kidding, but maybe not. Thank goodness this place is on the other side of the bridge and not really on Cape Cod!

After she pointed out that she had neglected to bring the coleslaw and tartar sauce to accompany my fish, she somewhat took the offensive thrill away. The fried flounder was adequate.

Most people who eat clam or fish chowder in restaurants have not experienced either of them as God meant them to be. They have not tasted the ambrosia that was immortalized by Herman Melville in Moby Dick. Then, clam or cod, chowder that is, were the only choices for meals offered to Ishmael and Queequeg in their boarding house on Nantucket, as they gathered strength to go off in pursuit of the great white whale. You can bet this "clam or cod" chowder was not some library paste concoction of margarine, flour, a bit of onion, over-boiled potatoes and the odd canned clam or bit of tired fish clotted together in one tasteless mass offering.

If the chef I visited were on top of his game, his chowder would probably be but a pale, insipid imitation of the real thing, which has all but vanished in recent times.

The late Gene Crocker of Sandwich, a tugboat captain and chowder aficionado, said the following recipe makes clam chowder "the way God meant it to be."

QUAHOG CHOWDER

3 dozen medium quahogs (aim to have at least half the volume of quahog meat as chopped potatoes in
  the finished chowder)
2 lbs. potatoes, cubed
1 medium onion
4 ozs. salt pork, diced
2 TBS butter
1 ½ cups whole milk
1 can evaporated milk or 1 cup whole cream
Salt and pepper, to taste
1/4 tsp. Tabasco
2 TBS flour (optional)

Steam the quahogs with 1 cup of water until they open. Save the broth. Boil the potatoes in the broth, adding enough extra water to cover. In a heavy-bottomed kettle, fry the salt pork in butter until brown. Add the onions and continue to sauté. If you like thick chowder, now is the time to add some flour to your butter, onion and salt pork mixture. Stir until smooth, making a roux. Now, add in this order: clams, potatoes, Tabasco and pepper; the taste should be quite salty. You can stop now as you have your base for chowder.

Never add the milk until you are close to serving, and once you add the milk, never boil the soup, or it will separate. If you are ready to serve, add the milk/cream and a pinch of thyme. The finished chowder should be cooled to room temperature before refrigerating and stirred occasionally as it cools. Chowder is good served immediately but can approach greatness with an overnight aging.

To serve, heat the bowls, put a bit of butter in the bottom of each and ladle in the soup. Sea biscuits, thick crackers, were traditionally served with chowder. The diner can thicken his chowder with crushed crackers; mashed potatoes can be used for the same purpose. I find the 2 tablespoons of flour to be quite adequate for thickening.

This chowder will not be white but a light gray with streaks of butter. A dash of paprika on top will add to its beauty. You can also make this recipe using steamer clams. Always make sure that your clams are free of sand.

I urge you to join me in the presentation of this "real chowder" by trying this recipe. Herman Melville and Gene Crocker would be proud of you if they yet lived.

The Not Quite Grand, Or Baby Grand, Paella

I have known some formidable cooks in my lifetime. Two of the most impressive are Louis Greenstein of North Reading, Massachusetts, who is a teaching professional, author and full-time culinary consultant, and Jean "Whitey" Densmore of West Falmouth, an accomplished home cook and food critic.

Both of these fine cooks preside over the construction of a grand paella on an annual basis: Louis on the 4th of July and Whitey on Bastille Day. These are grand affairs, indeed! These feats are prepared in the traditional manner over an open fire outdoors for 30 or more guests, and, as the kids say, "it's awesome!" It's done on a scale beyond the range of the average home cook but well within the scope of these paragons.

I am presenting a scaled-down version of the grand paella, a baby grand, and I urge you to try it. You will not be sorry. Do not be put off by the number of ingredients or their variety; the cooking techniques are simple. If you follow the instructions and include the essential, basic ingredients (chicken, spicy sausage, garlic, onions, rice and assorted seafood), you will not go wrong. This dish is truly greater than the sum of its parts! So let's get at it – a Cape Cod paella, roughly based on a recipe for Provincetown paella from Howard Mitcham's fine, funny and totally dependable book, Provincetown Seafood Cookbook.

CAPE COD PAELLA
(for 8 to 10)

(1) 4-lb. frying chicken in 10 pieces
1 lb. linguica or chourico, sliced
3 medium onions, chopped
1 sweet pepper (red or green), chopped
6 cloves garlic, minced
1/2 cup parsley, chopped
1 ½ cups olive oil
24 littleneck clams
24 mussels
(2) 2-lb. lobsters
2 lbs. shrimp
6 squid
1 lb. haddock or monkfish fillet
1/2 lb. chopped ham (prosciutto is great)
(1) 16-oz. can crushed tomatoes
(1) 8-oz can tomato sauce or purée
1 cup mushrooms, chopped
2 lbs. long-grain rice
3 or 4 quarts good stock (preferably fish)
1 package frozen tiny peas (1 pound)
1 small can or jar pimientos

STOCK

For superb paella, make your own stock.

4 lbs. fish trimmings (heads, backs, etc.)
4 quarts water
4 cloves garlic
3 onions (halved)
6 stems parsley
1 stalk celery
1 sliced lemon
1 pint dry white wine
1/2 tsp. basil
1/2 tsp. thyme
1/2 tsp. cumin
1 tsp. black pepper

Put all this stuff in a big pot, bring it to a boil, and boil gently for half an hour. You should cook your shellfish (except the shrimp and squid) in this magical brew. The lobsters take 20 minutes. Scrub the mussels and clams, and bag them in cheesecloth or an onion bag and cook until they open. The shrimp and squid will be done in the final assembly. Strain this broth through a colander and reserve. It will be superb!

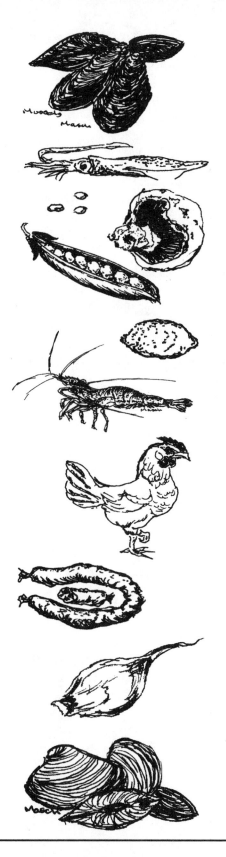

Now for the seafood: Cut each lobster tail into four slices, shell and all. Crack the separated knuckles and claws with a hammer and set aside. Remove the roe, fat and tomalley from the bodies, mash it up, and add it to the stock. Throw out the body and shell.

Pull the beards off the mussels and leave them in their shells. Set them aside along with the quahogs, also in their shells. Clean the squid and dice the bodies. Cut the heads off just forward of the eyes, leaving the tentacles intact. Mitcham says this gives a real Spanish look to the presentation. Set the squid aside.

Now brown the chicken pieces in 1/2 cup of the olive oil in a skillet large enough to take it all at once. This should take about 15 minutes over medium heat. Set the chicken aside. Now put ham, sausage (both kinds, sliced or cubed) and squid in the oil remaining in the pan and saute for 5 minutes. Set aside.

Now put 1/2 cup of olive oil in the same skillet and saute the peppers, onion, garlic and mushrooms until the onions are translucent. Stir in the parsley, tomatoes, tomato puree, pimientos, Tabasco sauce and green peas. Cook slowly for 20 minutes. Pour into a bowl and wash the skillet.

Put the last 1/2 cup of olive oil into the skillet over medium heat and saute the rice, stirring until somewhat translucent.

Now for the final assembly: Mix everything together in a pan that can be covered and will hold all the ingredients – a turkey roaster will do. Mix everything, including the raw shrimp and cubed fish, together gently. You can stop at this point and socialize a little, or a lot if you refrigerate the whole works.

An hour before serving time, preheat your oven to 350 degrees. Bring your stock to a boil. Pour in enough stock to cover all the ingredients by about 1/2 inch. If you need more, add white wine, water or chicken stock. Bring this to a simmer on top of the stove, cover the pan and put it in the preheated oven for 20 minutes. Uncover (the stock should be almost totally absorbed and the rice nearly tender; add more liquid if necessary) and bake for 10 minutes longer. You may garnish this with parsley, sliced lemons and pimiento slices. This is a wonderful dish!

I would serve this to any royalty on earth, even to my friends, Louie and Whitey, whom I think of as the king and queen of paella.

Early Spring Is Trout Time!

In my college years in the late 1950s, I eagerly looked forward to April and the beginning of trout season. On opening day I would fish, shoulder to shoulder, with other winter-weary fishermen, drowning worms to catch stocked trout. It was usually cold and miserable, but we felt like outdoorsmen in our waders and vests and hats and belt knives. We usually fished within hearing distance of a highway, but we loved it. We caught trout and we enjoyed eating them. Sometimes we cooked them right there at the pond. These trout probably cost a hundred dollars a pound, so they had to be deemed delicious.

In the few years between college and marriage, I fished with a classmate each spring, just after the ice went out in Maine. We fished for trout and landlocked salmon. One spring our 80-year-old guide arranged for us to be flown to a remote lake to fish for native brook trout – big ones, he promised. The catch was that it was a fly-fishing-only lake and we were poor fly-casters at best. He loaned us flies and rods and sent us on our way, promising us two-pound trout if we followed his directions. Just before we boarded the seaplane, he gave us each a pack of Marlboros. He made us promise not to open them until the plane had left us at the lake. We opened the cigarette packages as the plane took off. Both packages were full of moss and angleworms.

We caught many trout with these fly dressings, some over two pounds. They were delicious!

There are many ways to sauté freshly caught trout. Some involve complicated sauces, but once again I think the simplest recipes are the best with fresh native or hatchery trout.

SAUTÉED (PAN-FRIED) TROUT
(for 2)
2 whole trout of about 3/4 pound
4 TBS butter or olive oil
1 cup cornmeal (or seasoned flour or a mixture of cornmeal and flour)
Salt and pepper
Minced parsley

Rinse the cleaned fish, and dredge them in the seasoned coating. Melt the butter (or heat the oil) in a skillet until the foam subsides. The skillet should be on medium high to prevent burning the butter.

Sauté the coated trout in the hot butter until browned and cooked, about 5 minutes on each side. Sprinkle with parsley and serve. Oh boy!

SAUTÉED TROUT AMANDINE

Follow the instructions for sautéed trout. While the trout is cooking, melt a tablespoon of butter in a second skillet. When the foam subsides, add 1/2 cup of blanched, slivered almonds. Stir them often until they begin to brown, which takes a couple of minutes.

When the fish is done, sprinkle with the cooked almonds; squeeze the juice of half a lemon on top, and garnish with parsley. You have become an instant gourmet!

SAUTÉED TROUT WITH BACON

Prepare the trout for cooking as in the sautéed trout recipe. Cook 4 slices (preferably thickly cut) bacon in a skillet until nice and crisp. Remove the cooked bacon from the skillet and fry the coated trout in the bacon fat until it's cooked on both sides. Garnish with parsley and serve along with the crisp bacon. This is great! It is especially good cooked outdoors, right where you are fishing.

Dragged Muddler Minnow

Clams Casino – Money in the Bank

For many people on Cape Cod, the term "clam" means the soft-shell or steamer clam (Mya arenaria), but to me the word clam brings to mind the hard-shelled clam, as it is known in New Jersey and New York, or quahog, the Native American term for the round clam of New England (Venus mercenaria), a noble creature.

The clam (quahog) holds a revered position in my house and in my life; it is almost certainly my totem animal. A fine clam portrait hangs prominently in my dining room; a trophy quahog (remarkable for its great size) is mounted on a walnut plaque and hangs on the wall of my wife's studio; my room (den, lair, study or pit, as it is variously known) contains perhaps the only quahog ever taken on a surface lure, another with an attitude, shown by its Cagney-like sneer, and another behemoth soon to be hung beside my first trophy quahog.

I own several books devoted to their cooking, hundreds of dollars' worth of gear used to gather them, and many writings on their lifestyle and natural history. I even have a recording of a blues song about the quahog and its joys and sorrows. Obviously, this creature is very important to me. My reverence for this noble clam explains my violent reaction to the stuff that is served as clam chowder at many restaurants, but that is for another day.

I am going to discuss baked clams and clam sauce for spaghetti. I learned a new saucing technique last weekend and am excited about sharing it.

My wife, our dogs and I traveled to darkest Maine this past weekend to visit old friends from here on the Cape who now live among the beautiful woods and lakes but near enough the coast to enjoy the fine seafood. I once cooked on the swordfish boat run by Marty "Rocky" Bartlett who passed this spaghetti and clam sauce method on to me. He got it from his gracious and gifted wife, JoAnn.

BARTLETTS' SPAGHETTI IN WHITE CLAM SAUCE (WITH A SURPRISE FINISH) *(for 4)*

1 lb. spaghetti or linguine
2 cups of prepared quahogs (chopped)
3/4 cup onion, chopped
1/4 cup parsley, chopped
3 cloves (to taste) garlic, chopped
3 TBS butter
3 TBS olive oil
1 cup clam juice
1 cup white wine
Salt and pepper, to taste

Bring enough (I say 4 quarts) water to a boil to handle the pasta.

Shuck the clams, saving the liquid. Chop the clams coarsely and set aside.

Boil the pasta until al dente. If the box says, "Boil 11 to 13 minutes," drain it at 11 minutes.

While the pasta is boiling, prepare the sauce by melting the butter and oil together in a pan large enough to hold the cooked pasta. Sauté the onion until translucent, about 3 minutes, add the garlic for a minute more, then add the clam liquor and wine to the pan and bring to a boil. Boil about 2 minutes; now add the clams and return to a boil. Add the parsley and the al dente pasta, lower heat, cover the pan and cook gently until liquid is almost totally absorbed. You will not be sorry; in fact, you will be venerated by tasteful people.

Sprinkle with more chopped parsley and serve. I like crushed red pepper and Parmesan cheese with mine – some think this is anathema.

Finishing the pasta directly in the sauce was new to me. The result was outstanding – great, in fact! Bravissimo Bartletts!

On that Italian note, let's go on to Clams Casino, another dish that can be prepared with many different ingredients using the same basic method. Clams Casino is baked clams. Many people will say that their's is the only true one – so make up your own. I will give you a basic recipe and suggest some variations. Then you are on your own. Have fun!

SIMPLE CLAMS CASINO (BAKED CLAMS) (for 1 as main dish, 3 as appetizer)

12 littleneck clams (or cherrystones)
3 garlic cloves, minced or pressed
1 TBS dried oregano
2 TBS parsley, minced
1/2 cup fine bread crumbs
2 TBS (or more) olive oil

Quahog with attitude
MASCOT

Open the clams, cutting the bottom muscle so the meat is floating free on a half shell. Put these in a shallow baking pan, balanced so the juices won't spill out. This can be done by lining the pan with a 1/4-inch-deep layer of rock salt; or crush a large piece of aluminum foil (at least twice the area of the pan you wish to use) and then flatten it out to the area of the bottom of your pan. You will now be able to position your clamshells so they will not spill their juices.

Mix the garlic, herbs and crumbs and divide on top of the clams. Sprinkle each with oil. Bake in a preheated 400-degree oven for 8 to 10 minutes, or broil, watching carefully, until browned. Serve hot.

Variation: Put 1 teaspoon of cooked spinach under the clam, then proceed as above, putting a 1-inch slice of bacon on top of the crumbs. Bake or broil until bacon is crisp.

Variation: Do nothing at all, except for topping clam with a 1-inch piece of bacon. Bake or broil until bacon is crisp. Oh!

Variation: In the master recipe substitute scallion for garlic, Ritz cracker crumbs for bread crumbs, and butter for olive oil.

Variation: Use Italian bread crumbs and add 1 tablespoon of Parmesan cheese to the basic recipe.

Variation: Use 1/4 cup chopped green pepper, 1/8 cup Parmesan cheese, a sprinkle of dry sherry, 12 squares of 3/4-inch-square mozzarella, 12 square pieces of bacon and no bread crumbs.

I like to add a bit of cayenne pepper to any of the variations and to serve my baked clams with lemon sections and Tabasco. Try some of your own variations. You won't be sorry.

Here is a final method, somewhat different from the others, from The Fishmonger Cookbook by Dorothy Batchelder.

CLAMS BATCHELDER (for 3 as main dish; 9 as appetizer)

3 slices bacon
1/4 cup minced onion
1/4 cup minced red bell pepper
1/4 cup minced green pepper
2 sticks unsalted butter
2 TBS lemon juice
1 TBS Worcestershire sauce
2 dashes Tabasco
3/4 cup bread crumbs
36 littleneck clams on half shell
Lemon wedges for garnish

Fry the bacon until crisp and drain, saving 2 tablespoons bacon fat. Sauté the onions and peppers in this fat about 3 minutes or until soft.

In a bowl combine butter, lemon juice, Worcestershire sauce, Tabasco, crumbled bacon and sautéed vegetables. Mix thoroughly and refrigerate.

Open clams and arrange on baking pan. Top each with a heaping teaspoon of butter mixture, sprinkle with bread crumbs and bake for 10 minutes in a preheated 400-degree oven. Serve with lemon wedges. This stuff is messy, delicious and most wonderful. You will be a hero!

Native Americans made currency in the form of wampum, beads made from the beautiful cobalt blue sections of quahog shells. Modern Americans sometimes refer slangily to dollars as clams. Is there a connection? I don't know, but I do know that properly baked quahogs are better than money in the bank. Keep your "clams" in the kitchen and out of the casino. You will be richer for it.

What does panko have to do with fish, or what is panko anyway?

Recently I was sitting at my desk and thinking about recipes. The ground was covered with snow, the temperature outside was 16 degrees and fishing season still seemed far away. So I decided to write about fish from the market. I was not inspired, so I decided I was hungry and headed for the kitchen with lunch in mind.

I found about two cups of garlic mashed potatoes, left over from dinner, along with some Chinese cabbage that I had served wilted, dressed with bacon, vinegar and sugar, and thought of a cross-cultural Colcannon, an Irish mélange of onions or scallions, boiled potatoes and cooked cabbage mashed together and sautéed until hot and lightly browned, using Chinese cabbage. This thought easily led to one of my favorite foods, fish cakes, but I had no fish. What about that tall can of salmon that has lurked in the cabinet for years? Aha! I opened the salmon, drained it thoroughly, picked out the soft bones and skin, and mixed it with an egg, the leftover potatoes and cabbage, to which I added 1/4 cup of chopped sweet pepper and two tablespoons of minced celery. I mushed this all together, added some bread crumbs to make it workable for forming cakes, coated the cakes in bread crumbs and sautéed them over medium heat until brown and crispy, and "Bob's your uncle," fish cakes good enough to make you slap your grandma if she took more than her share!

SALMON CAKES (for 4 or 5)

(1) 14.5-oz. can salmon (or 1 or 2 cups leftover cooked salmon)
2 cups mashed potatoes (or more if you are a Yankee)
1 egg
1 medium minced onion (or 4 to 6 scallions)
1/4 cup chopped celery
1/4 cup chopped green pepper (optional)
1/4 cup minced parsley
Salt and pepper
1/4 tsp. Tabasco (optional)
Plain bread crumbs

Salmon Cake

Mix all ingredients thoroughly; add enough bread crumbs to make mix stiff enough to form into patties but wet enough to hold a coating of bread crumbs.

Form into patties, or cakes, dredge both sides in bread crumbs, and chill in refrigerator for at least 15 minutes. Heat frying pan over medium heat for 2 to 3 minutes; add oil (peanut, light olive, canola, whatever you like). Sauté cakes gently until golden brown on both sides and heated through, about 10 minutes in all, adjusting burner to prevent burning. Serve with lemon wedges, ketchup, hot sauce and tartar sauce. You do not have to serve the ketchup but I like it. Thank you!

You can get a bit more exotic with this dish by adding 1 teaspoon of minced or grated fresh ginger and 1 teaspoon of Dijon mustard to the mix, suggests Mark Bittman, in his cookbook *How to Cook Everything*.

Mr. Bittman also presents a simple recipe for cod or any other large white fish fillet (1 inch thick or so from striped bass, haddock, wolffish, mahi-mahi, whatever).

ROAST COD WITH POTATOES

(for 4 or 5)
2 lbs. of cod fillets (1 inch thick)
3 lbs. of boiling potatoes
Salt and pepper
6 TBS butter

Preheat the oven to 425 degrees. Put four tablespoons butter in a large baking dish. Preheat dish and melt butter in oven (be careful not to burn the butter). I preheat the baking dish, remove it from the oven and add the butter so that I will not forget it. I have burned a lot of butter.

Peel the potatoes and slice them into 1/2- to 1/4-inch slices. Thinner is better I think. Bittman and I both use a food processor or mandoline to do the slicing. Put the sliced potatoes in the melted butter, stir to coat them with butter, and bake them for 10 minutes. While they're in the oven, turn and stir them three or four times until potatoes are done and beginning to crisp. Salt and pepper both the potatoes and the fish liberally. Put cod on top of the potatoes, dot it with the last 2 tablespoons of butter, and return to oven 10 to 12 minutes, until opaque throughout. Serve with lemon slices, a salad or vegetable and my oh my, how good life is!

This recipe is similar to the recipe I call "The World's Best Bluefish Recipe."

You can vary this recipe by using olive oil instead of butter, adding 1 to 2 cups of sliced onions to the potatoes, or you can add garlic and chopped parsley, or a mixture of herbs or all of the above. Once you know and are comfortable with the basic recipe, you can go on to make it your own by your variations. Remember, cooking is first of all a craft that anyone can learn and only becomes an art after the basic techniques are mastered.

Any leftover fish and potatoes you may have, although you probably won't have any, can be easily made into fish hash or fish cakes.

Fresh white fish fillets, sautéed or deep-fried until crisp and still moist and succulent, present one of fish-eating's greatest pleasures when anointed with a spritz of lemon juice, tartar sauce or ketchup. I recently tried Japanese bread crumbs, called panko, for breading fish before sautéing. This stuff is available at some fish markets, all oriental groceries or online, and it makes a marvelously crispy bit of fish.

FISH SAUTÉED OR FRIED IN PANKO (for 4)
2 lbs. of white fish fillet (flounder, cod, haddock)
Flour for dredging
Salt and pepper
1 egg and 1/4 cup water
2 cups panko (Japanese bread crumbs)
Oil for frying

Cut fillets into 1/4-pound pieces, dredge them in flour seasoned with salt and pepper. Beat egg in 3 tablespoons water and dip floured pieces in egg and water mixture and then in panko, patting crumbs onto both sides of fillets, and set aside on a plate. Repeat this with remaining fish pieces and refrigerate until ready to sauté or fry.

Heat frying pan over medium-high heat for 2 or 3 minutes. Add oil (I use peanut oil) and when hot (flour will sizzle if you sprinkle it on oil hot enough to brown fish), add fillets, cooking until nicely browned and crisp on both sides, turning once. Drain on towels or brown paper and serve.

You may deep-fry these fillets in 2 cups of peanut oil heated to 375 degrees until just nicely browned. I was recently at a game dinner at which little finger-size pieces of various fish (striped bass, black sea bass and fluke) had been breaded and fried and served with lemon, ketchup and tartar sauce. It was a splendid appetizer! Swordfish is great cooked this way: buy those inexpensive chunks sometimes available in supermarkets. You can convince your guests that you are a gourmet by making a dipping sauce.

FRIED FISH DIPPING SAUCE
1/4 cup soy sauce
1 TBS dark sesame oil
1/2 tsp. cider or rice vinegar
1/2 tsp. minced or pressed garlic
1/2 tsp. vinegar
1/2 tsp. sugar
1 TBS chopped green scallion
Hot sauce (optional)

Mix all these together and serve with fish fingers. This is better than I can tell you. You have to try it!

Simple Stuff

• •

I am writing this in the middle of February. I heard my first red-wing this morning, the season is changing, the trout fishermen are busy and the stripers are on their way.

In spring, a young man's fancy lightly turns to thoughts of baseball or fishing at least as often as to love, but the way to a young or old man's heart is still through his stomach, so it is recipe time.

Recently, I made a quick simple dinner from a pound of cod, a couple of old vegetable-drawer lurker zucchinis, some aging mushrooms, some bottled Ragu and a little hot sauce. The result was a fine meal of spaghetti in fish sauce, something Americans do not think of.

I cut the zucchini in chunks, quartered some mushrooms to about the same size and added them to a canned tomato sauce in which I poached a piece of cod fillet.

LAZY MAN'S FISH AND SPAGHETTI DINNER (for 3 or 4)
1 bottle prepared spaghetti sauce (marinara or traditional)
1 ½ lbs. cod (or other white fish – haddock, hake, striped bass, wolffish, whatever)
2 cups zucchini, cubed
2 cloves garlic, chopped
Hot pepper flakes, cayenne or sauce
Parsley
2 TBS olive oil

Sauté mushrooms and zucchini in oil until beginning to brown, add chopped garlic, stir for 15 seconds and add tomato sauce. Simmer slowly about 10 minutes and add fish, cover with sauce and simmer about 15 minutes longer. Meanwhile, boil some pasta, drain, cover with sauce and fish, and serve.

There are many things you can do to alter this concoction and make yourself feel like a more serious cook. You could add herbs like oregano and basil, you could use different vegetables, you could add shrimp or scallops – you could leave out the fish and just use shellfish.

I like a kick to my sauce and always add hot pepper in some form. This can be done by each diner to his or her taste.

While I am talking about easy cooking, here is a quick and easy Italian weeknight dish.

TUNA AND NOODLES, SICILIAN STYLE (for 2)
4 TBS olive oil
2 cloves garlic, chopped or slivered
(1) 8-oz. can whole tomatoes
1/3 cup tiny frozen peas
(1) 6-oz. can tuna
1 small can black olives, pitted and sliced
1 box spaghetti or wide noodles

Heat garlic in oil until it is golden brown, remove it from oil, do not let it burn – burnt garlic will ruin any dish. Add the tomatoes, squeezed up, to the oil and simmer for about 1/2 hour, until thickened. Add peas, olive oil and flaked tuna, heat gently but thoroughly and serve over spaghetti or wide noodles. This may be topped with Parmesan.

QUICK MARINARA SAUCE

1/2 cup olive oil
2 cloves garlic, chopped
1 tsp. dried red pepper flakes
1 tsp. dried basil
1 tsp. dried mint
(1) 28-oz. can crushed or whole plum tomatoes
1/2 tsp. sugar (optional)
Salt and pepper
1 TBS chopped parsley

In a large skillet, very slowly heat the garlic, red pepper flakes, basil and mint. Cook for about 5 minutes until the garlic is golden. Now raise the heat to medium. When oil is hot, and before garlic burns, add the crushed-up tomatoes. Let this come to a soft boil and add a pinch more of pepper, basil and mint. Check for salt and pepper, add parsley and simmer uncovered for about 15 minutes, stirring occasionally with a wooden spoon and, wow, have you got a nice basic sauce.

This sauce can be served as it is, or you can fancy it up with sautéed mushrooms, black olives, a can of clams or crabmeat, or some cut-up squid – anything you like – and have a fine meal of spaghetti.

I get hungry and nearly drool just writing this – it must be close to lunchtime.
You can make a dish I will almost guarantee even your most experienced friends will not have tasted.
Here it is.

SARDINE FRITTERS

1 can small sardines in oil
1/2 cup flour
1 egg
1/2 cup milk
1 tsp. Worcestershire sauce

Mix all but sardines in a bowl. Heat 1/4 inch of oil, or lard or Crisco, in a small skillet. Dip each sardine in batter and fry at 350 to 375 degrees until golden crisp. Drain on paper and serve either covered in marinara over pasta or dip individually into marinara and eat as an appetizer. I write appetizer because hors d'oeuvre is too hard to spell and sounds a bit pretentious for a fried sardine.

Have some fun – try it – you will not be sorry! And you will be remembered.

Soon the bass will be back in our kitchens. Hurrah!

Simple stuff

Stripers, Trout And Weeds

My wife Jeanne and I spent the best weekend of March at the country home (in the Berkshire Hills) of our friends of many, many years, Bill and Toni Strassler. We, along with novelist David Plante and raconteur, editor and writer, Thomas Teal, and his wife, Anna, were gathered to make maple syrup from sap gathered from the Strasslers' own sugar bush. We would converse, and prepare and enjoy meals together. What does all this have to do with cooking fish? I will tell you. I know that when the mapling season ends, when the sap stops running, that the run of striped bass here in New England will soon begin. Winter is over, the crocuses are blooming – finest kind – and the daffodils have begun their show.

We had a meal of fish, rice and salad one night that will not soon be forgotten. This was a spring (or any season) menu I would recommend to anyone on earth. For appetizers we had cold, blanched asparagus, served with a mayonnaise-based dipping sauce, followed by oysters and littlenecks on the half shell.

The main dish was a thick Chilean sea bass fillet, braised with mixed vegetables; the accompaniments were rice cooked with clams, a green salad and a crusty bread for capturing the braising sauce. There were pears and cheese for dessert, along with apple pie and ice cream. My, my, but life is good! Good friends, good conversation and good food – what could be better?

OVEN-BRAISED STRIPED BASS
(for 6 lucky people!)

3 lbs. striped bass fillets or steaks (skin on)
(2) 10-oz. cans tomatoes with green chilies
2 cloves garlic, minced
1 medium onion, chopped
1 TBS ground cumin
1/2 cup green olives, chopped or sliced
1/4 cup raisins (steeped in boiling water)
1 TBS capers
1 cup dry white wine
1 cup bread crumbs
1 tsp. sugar
4 to 6 TBS olive oil
2 scallions (green only), chopped

Preheat the oven to 425 degrees.

Heat 4 tablespoons olive oil in an ovenproof pan that is suitable for sautéing and large enough to hold the fish. This could be a ceramic-coated iron casserole or a large frying pan. Dry the fish with paper towels, salt and pepper both sides lightly, and quickly sear on both sides in the hot oil. It is okay, even good, to blacken the fish a little. Remove the fish from the pan and set aside.

Now sauté the onions, celery and peppers in the same oil until they are soft and translucent, scraping browned bits of fish skin from the bottom of your dish. Add the minced garlic and stir briefly. Now add the rest of the ingredients, except the remaining olive oil, bread crumbs and scallions. Bring this mixture to a boil, reduce the heat, and simmer for at least 2 minutes.

You can prepare this ahead, up to this point. If you do, now put the seared fish into the dish with the sauce, spoon some sauce over it, cover it and refrigerate.

Remove the fish preparation from the refrigerator 45 minutes before doing the final cooking. Put the casserole in the preheated (425-degree) oven with its cover on. If your dish has no cover, use foil. The fish will cook properly if baked for approximately 10 minutes for each inch of thickness. About 10 minutes before the fish is done, remove it from the oven and sprinkle the bread crumbs (I like Italian-flavored) over the surface, drizzle with the remaining olive oil, and return to the oven. If the mixture seems dry, add more white wine. When the fish flakes easily, it is done. If the crumbs brown too fast, lower the oven temperature to 325 degrees. Garnish with the chopped scallions and serve with some lemon slices on the side. You will be famous!

This dish can be served with rice, pasta or boiled potatoes. Follow the directions, pay attention and you cannot go wrong.

Any white-fleshed fish will work in this recipe: haddock, cod, halibut or swordfish, to name a few worthies. The Chilean sea bass I used was a resounding success. Soon, with any luck at all, I will prepare it with my first large striper of the season. So should you!

The month of May will also provide trout from the ponds here on Cape Cod and from the streams and ponds throughout New England. My friends, the Strasslers, have a trout stream passing through their maple bush that has often provided us with fine meals. If you should be fortunate enough to get some trout this spring, try the following simple French classic recipe.

TROUT ALMONDINE

6 fresh trout
1 cup milk
Flour
1 tsp. salt
1/4 tsp. black pepper
Vegetable oil (for frying)
1/4 cup butter
1/3 cup slivered almonds
Parsley and lemon (for garnish)

Soak the trout in milk for a half-hour. Put the flour, salt and pepper in a plastic bag. Take the trout, one or two at a time, and shake them, still wet, in the seasoned flour. Put aside.

Heat 1/4 inch of oil in a skillet, and brown the trout in the hot oil on both sides, about 3 minutes per side. Put the browned trout on a platter and keep it warm.

Pour the oil out of the skillet and wipe the skillet with a paper towel. Now put the butter and almonds into the still-hot skillet and heat until the butter is browned. Pour this over the trout, garnish with parsley and lemon, and, as they say in the United Kingdom, "Bob's your uncle!" A grand simple dish it is. Omit the almonds and you have trout meuniere, a French classic meaning "in the manner of the miller's wife" – coated in flour and sautéed.

Serve this dish with buttery mashed potatoes and a wilted dandelion or spinach salad and you will have a noble spring meal and a growing reputation as a culinary magician. This dish is delicious made with yellow perch should trout prove elusive.

WILTED DANDELION (OR SPINACH) SALAD

2 quarts coarsely chopped dandelion greens
8 strips of bacon (cut crosswise in 1/2-inch strips)
1/2 tsp. salt
1/2 tsp. black pepper
1/2 tsp. dry mustard
1 TBS sugar
5 TBS mild vinegar

Wash dandelions, remove tough stem bases, coarsely chop and measure two packed quarts. Put into a salad bowl.

Fry the bacon until crisp, add the remaining ingredients to the pan containing the bacon and its rendered fat, and stir until the sugar is dissolved. Pour this mixture over the greens and toss well. Wow!

I harvest dandelions from my lawn in springtime. They remain mild in flavor until the flowers open, at which time they become too bitter for my taste. You can substitute lettuce, spinach, arugula or a combination of any or all for the dandelions in this salad. All are good – in fact, delicious.

Spring is here. The bass are back, the dandelions are growing, and the trout are rising. Go and get some for yourself – you will not go wrong!

Three Signs of Spring:
The Herring, the Osprey and the Flounder

The herring are running and the bass will soon follow, if they are not here already. The winter flounder season is about to open. Fresh fish are once again readily available for man, osprey, and us fishermen, and for those lucky enough to share our catch.

In the early days of the Massachusetts Colony, the Pilgrims shared the early spring bounty of winter flounder and herring with the osprey, often called the fishhawk, a very large raptor nearly extirpated from New England 25 years ago but now back in large numbers.

Bartholomew Gosnold, the first English visitor to our shores, gave Buzzards Bay its name because of the abundance of ospreys, which resembled the buzzards of England. Now the "buzzard" of Gosnold, the osprey, is doing better than either the alewife (spring herring) or winter flounder on which it feeds in spring. Both the herring and the oyster are suffering from overfishing and environmental degradation. I hope we can bring them back as we brought back the flounder. The numbers may be down, but we can still take a few and leave enough for the ospreys.

Many of us use herring for bass bait. We can get a grand meal from our baitfish and still have our bait by taking the roe from our female herring and making a traditional, rich New England dinner. Herring roe is every bit as good as the shad roe prized by gourmets. The shad is, after all, no more than a big alewife.

SAUTÉED HERRING WITH BACON AND ONIONS (for 2)

6 to 8 pairs of herring roe
1 large onion, sliced
6 slices of bacon
Seasoned flour (salt and pepper)

Fry the bacon until crisp, and drain it on a paper towel or brown paper grocery bag. Save 2 tablespoons of bacon fat. While the onion sautés in the rendered fat, coat the roe sacs with seasoned flour. I put a cup of flour, a teaspoon of salt and 1/2 teaspoon of pepper in a Ziploc bag and shake the roe in the sack to coat it with the flour.

When the onions are transparent, move them aside in the frying pan and add the floured roe. Cook over medium heat, turning after about 3 minutes; brown the second side and serve with the onions and bacon.

Accompany this dish with mashed potatoes and some asparagus or, better yet, fiddleheads that have been boiled or steamed to crisp-tender and dressed with butter and lemon. The food will not be much better in heaven.

While I am not going to present a recipe for the second sign of spring, the osprey, I will say that winter flounder are a welcome blessing. I like to get a flounder that just fits in my cast-iron frying pan, coat it with seasoned flour and pan-fry it whole. I love the crispy skins and other crispy bits. I like to have both tartar sauce

Osprey   Herring

and ketchup with my fried fish, despite the pompous protestations of my gourmet friends. This recipe is very simple and very delicious.

WHOLE PAN-FRIED FLOUNDER
(for 1 or 2)
1 flounder (or whatever), 1 ½ pounds
Seasoned flour
1/2 cup cooking oil (peanut preferred)
Parsley and lemon (for garnish)

Gut and scale your fish, and shake it up in a bag with seasoned flour. Fry the coated fish over medium heat for about 5 minutes on a side.

The fish will look beautiful on a platter garnished with parsley and lemon slices. It will taste even better than it looks.

You can coat flounder fillets the same way and fry them. Herring fillets are good done this way as are scaled whole herring, if you are not serving "bonophobic" people. Bonophobic is my own word.

Last week I had a yen for fish, a frequently recurring phenomenon, so I bought a 1-pound fillet of haddock for my wife and myself. I planned to bake it with seasoned bread crumbs and olive oil and serve it with mashed potatoes and steamed broccoli. I then thought of stewed tomatoes, which my mother served as a side dish when I was a child. I liked them on my mashed potatoes. So I came up with this recipe.

BAKED HADDOCK FILLET WITH CHILI TOMATOES AND WHITE WINE *(for 2)*
1 haddock fillet (1 pound)
1/2 cup bread crumbs
1 cup canned tomato with chili
3 TBS olive oil
Salt and pepper
Parsley, chopped

Preheat the oven to 425 degrees. Heat an ovenproof casserole just large enough to hold the fish. Put 1 tablespoon of olive oil in the casserole, moisten both sides of the fish piece with oil, and place it skin-side down in the casserole. Salt and pepper the fish. Sprinkle the bread crumbs over the fish, covering it completely. Drizzle the remaining olive oil over the crumbs. Pour the cup of tomatoes with chili around the fish. Pour in the white wine, and return the casserole to the preheated oven. Bake until the fish flakes through and the crumbs are nicely browned. Garnish with chopped parsley and serve. Beautiful!

Several companies now can tomatoes with chili. The ones marked "jalapeños" are quite hot and delicious; the ones marked "mild" are indeed mild. I had not seen this product until recently and recommend it highly for quick tomato sauces. You do not have to be Hispanic to enjoy chilies.

This dish turned out splendidly and I am proud of it! It will be part of my standard repertoire. I know it will be good with striped bass. The recipe can be expanded at will. Just keep the same proportions of ingredients.

I will not give a recipe for osprey, though I heard of a guy who was arrested for eating a spotted owl. The judge, who fined him heavily and gave him a suspended sentence, asked him how it tasted. He said, "Somewhere between osprey and bald eagle, Your Honor."

Blazing Tuna

Last evening my wife and I were guests for dinner in a beautifully refurbished Victorian summer cottage on Squeteague Harbor in Cataumet. This "cottage," actually a near mansion, was equipped with as fine a kitchen as money can buy, so I was pleased when our hostess, who was house-sitting there, asked me if I would prepare some tuna steaks she had purchased. They were so tempting that she decided to have them rather than the pasta dish she had planned. I was happy to agree, if only for a chance to use the magnificent restaurant stove in the kitchen.

I decided I would briefly marinate the tuna, pan-sear it, and serve it with a mayonnaise, mustard and anchovy sauce I had recently come upon but not tried.

To pan-sear fish steaks, you heat your skillet as hot as possible so that the meat will sear and caramelize almost instantly when it hits the pan, thus sealing in the juices and flavor. You heat your skillet as hot as an ordinary stove will heat. The stove I was using was no ordinary stove. I usually use peanut oil as a frying medium; clarified butter is also good. I had neither, so I used the olive oil that was available.

The restaurant-grade stove heated the pan so well that the marinade remaining on the steaks and the olive oil I coated them with immediately burst into flame when the steaks hit the pan. The flames shot three feet – yes, three feet – into the air but, thank God, only briefly. The stove's hood prevented disaster even with the fan off. The magnificent house filled with smoke, alarms sounded and lights went on. The flames subsided, I reduced the heat under the steaks and cooked them for two minutes on each side. While I was doing this, the exhaust fan was turned on, doors were opened and the fire department was called to tell them the fire was out, as we were afraid the alarm system in this well-appointed house was hard-wired to the fire department. In minutes the steaks were done to near perfection, the house was smoke-free, the fire department was absent and we sat down to dinner. Whew!

PAN-SEARED TUNA STEAK *(for 4)*

2 lbs. tuna steaks (about 1 inch thick)
2 TBS peanut oil (or clarified butter)
Salt and pepper
1/4 cup lime juice
1/4 cup soy sauce

Marinate the tuna in a mixture of lime juice and soy sauce for 1/2 hour at room temperature, or up to 4 hours in the refrigerator.

Remove the steaks from the marinade to drain while preheating your skillet to as hot as you dare. Rub the steaks with oil, salt and pepper. Sear them briefly (about 30 seconds on each side), lower the heat to medium, and cook for 2 minutes on each side for steaks of the thickness usually cut by fishmongers (a little less than 1 inch thick). The steaks should be pink in the middle, even a bit raw.

They may be served as is with lemon and butter or with a sauce of your choosing. I recommend the following anchovy-mayonnaise concoction.

ANCHOVY-MAYONNAISE SAUCE FOR TUNA STEAK

1/4 cup dry white wine
2 TBS capers, drained and chopped
4 anchovy fillets, mashed (I often use more)
1 cup mayonnaise (recipe below)
2 tsps. minced garlic
Parsley (for garnish)

After removing the steaks from the skillet, add wine, garlic, anchovies and capers, and simmer for 1 minute. Remove from heat and stir in the mayonnaise; pour this over the steaks, garnish with parsley and serve, or serve sauce in a separate bowl. You won't be sorry.

MAYONNAISE (EASY)
2 egg yolks
1 tsp. Dijon mustard
1 ½ TBS fresh lemon juice
1/2 cup olive oil
1/4 cup corn oil
1 tsp. boiling water

Everything (except the water) must be at room temperature. Put the egg yolks, mustard and lemon juice in a food processor with a metal blade, and blend for 10 seconds. Mix the oils together and add 1 tablespoon of oil at a time to the running blender until 1/2 cup of oil is used (6 tablespoons). Add the remaining oil in a slow, steady stream. Add boiling water to stabilize, and stop the blender.

Your sauce will be great if you make your own mayonnaise. It will be very good if you use commercial mayonnaise. I recommend Hellman's.

Serve this with pasta dressed with butter and Parmesan, some asparagus and a small green salad. Your virtue will not be questioned, nor will that of Dorothy Batchelder's cookbook *The Fishmonger Cookbook*, upon which these recipes are based. Try it!

I am writing this on the first day of spring, March 20. My calendar says that spring will arrive at 2:16 this afternoon. Boy, am I ready.

The first alewives are already in the runs. In a month the bass will be arriving to eat them. I will be ready for both. I often use cut herring (alewives) for my early bass fishing. I almost invariably get my first legal-size fish by this method. When I am cutting my bait, I save the herring roe, as great a delicacy as the prized shad roe eagerly awaited each spring by gourmets. Herring roe is every bit as good as that of its much larger cousin, the shad.

HERRING ROE WITH BACON (for 2)
12 pairs of roe
2 TBS butter
2 slices thick toast
4 strips bacon
1/2 lemon
2 TBS capers (optional)

Shake roe in a bag containing a little flour seasoned with salt and pepper. Stick each section with the point of a knife. Melt the butter in a skillet over medium heat, add floured roe, and gently cook for about 1½ minutes per side. Don't overcook.

Serve these on toast garnished with bacon and the optional capers. Squeeze lemon over everything, toss a piece of parsley on top, and "Bob's your uncle," as the Brits would say. This stuff is goooood!

You could also serve this with anchovy-mayonnaise sauce, which, by the way, makes a great potato-salad dressing! I add chopped sweet red pepper and a chopped boiled egg or two to some boiled waxy potatoes and revel. Serve this with breaded striped bass fillets and enjoy. Cooking is fun, eating great, life is good and spring is here!

Other Fish To Fry?

I think all cooks should have a few basic recipes in their repertoire using each of the five most common methods used for cooking fish. The basic techniques are frying, broiling, roasting, boiling and steaming.

When I, and I believe most Americans, think of eating fish, the fish visualized is usually floured, battered or bread-crumb-coated and then deep- or pan-fried until golden brown and crispy on the outside and moist, sweet and succulent on the inside. This is the ideal, and perhaps my favorite way to eat fish and other seafood such as clams, oyster, scallops and shrimp. My taste here is shared with most Americans, so let us find out how to do this at home.

Deep-frying at home (unless you are one of those who deep-fries whole turkeys) is somewhat daunting, but it can be done safely and easily, at least on a small scale. I use from two to four cups of oil (canola is best) in a heavy saucepan to get at least two inches of oil. Put the saucepan on a back burner so you are less likely to bump it accidentally. Do not ever fill your frying vessel more than half full. Always use a tool to put fish pieces into the hot oil. A slotted spoon works; tongs or chopsticks are even better. Put in only a few at a time because the oil will froth up. Keep a box of baking soda handy to put out grease fires.

Mark Bittman says that rules for deep-frying are simple, in his book How To Cook Everything; first you must get your oil to the proper temperature to brown the outside of the fish without burning it and to cook the inside. This temperature is between 350 and 375 degrees; 365 degrees is a good compromise for most frying. A frying thermometer is necessary, but if you do not have one, you can dip a cube of bread in the oil. At the proper temperature it will brown nicely in about one minute. If the oil smokes, it is too hot.

Once your oil is at the proper temperature, add your fish pieces, a few at a time. Things being deep-fried must never be crowded or they will not brown properly. You must avoid lowering the temperature by adding too much fish at once. When the fish is nicely browned, remove, drain well on paper towels or brown paper bags, and keep warm in a 200-degree oven until serving. Bring the oil back to the ideal 365 degrees before doing the next batch. When the oil temperature is right, the coating will absorb very little oil and the fish's flavor will be sealed. Done properly, it will not be at all greasy.

Here is a simple recipe for deep-frying small fillets not more than one inch thick or small whole fish, such as smelt, snapper blues and tinker mackerel.

DEEP-FRIED SMALL FILLETS
Small fillets or small whole fish
1 cup milk
Fish (1/2 lb. per person)
Enough crushed Saltines to coat fish (2 cups for 4 people)

Heat enough oil (two inches in a pan) to 365 degrees. Dip the fish in milk, then roll them in crushed crackers to coat. Allow to dry for a couple of minutes on a plate. Fry until golden brown (3 to 5 minutes); drain and serve immediately, if possible, with lemon and tartar sauce. I like hot sauce and ketchup also. Drop whole (dry) parsley sprigs in oil for 5 seconds as a garnish. Simple and very fine!

There are many coatings and batter recipes. Batters are best when deep-frying rather than pan-frying, for a seal is formed around the piece immediately upon immersion in the hot oil. Batters are messier than crumb coatings when pan-frying and become thin on the surface; not so in the hot oil.

To pan-fry small fillets or small whole fish, put 1/4 to 1/2 inch of oil in a skillet and heat to 360 degrees or until a bread crumb begins to sizzle instantly when put in oil. Do not heat oil to the smoking point. Put the coated pieces in the hot oil carefully, making sure not to splash oil onto yourself, or anyone else for that matter, and not to overcrowd the fish pieces. After 2 to 3 minutes, carefully lift the edge of one piece to see how it is browning. If it is browning too much, lower the flame. Turn all the pieces carefully and, as my friend Seth says, "always away from you." When the second side is nicely browned and the fish flakes, remove from heat and serve, after draining thoroughly.

If you must keep the fish warm for a time, place them in a single layer on a baking sheet in a 200-degree oven.

My favorite coatings for deep-frying fish fillets are flour and bread crumbs. Japanese bread crumbs are especially good (called panko or Hanayuki). Fresh bread crumbs make a very crisp and delicious coating.

I mix a cup of flour with 1/2 teaspoon of ground black pepper, 1 teaspoon of salt and 1/4 teaspoon of cayenne pepper. I shake my pieces of fish in a bag with the seasoned flour. Then I dip the floured pieces in a cup of milk in which I have beaten 1 egg. I roll these damp pieces in the bread crumbs or in a mixture of cornmeal and corn flour and proceed with the frying. You may allow the coated fish to dry on a plate before frying.

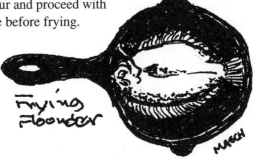

A simple batter can be made by stirring 3/4 cup of club soda or beer into 3/4 cup of flour to make a smooth paste. Now gently stir in another 1/4 cup beer or soda and you are ready to go.

Another light and crispy batter can be made by mixing 3/4 cup of flour with 2 teaspoons of baking powder. When ready to fry, whisk 1/2 cup of cold water into the flour to make a paste. Stir in another 1/2 cup of water until smooth, and Bob's your uncle! Fry away.

There are many more batter recipes, but these are perhaps the simplest!

FRIED COCONUT SHRIMP

1 lb. medium shrimp, shelled
Batter (from recipes above)
1/4 cup dried coconut (or to taste)

Shell and dry shrimp. Add dried coconut to batter, and proceed to fry the shrimp. Chinese duck sauce or plum sauce is a good dip for these shrimp, especially with added lemon juice.

Remember that if you keep your frying oil at 360 degrees, you will not have greasy fried fish, and it will be delicious. There are two dangers in frying fish: one is burning yourself, and the other, to some of us more serious, is overcooking your fish or seafood.

Be brave, be careful, and give fish frying at home a try, and remember Seth's words: "Always flip the pieces away from you."

Hooray, Hooray, Bass And Blues Arrive In May!

May, spring is here, the bass are back and so are the blues; that could be the title of a blues song. The only time blues give me blues are when they cost me a fortune in plugs and eat up my eels when I am looking for bass. I actually prefer them for culinary purposes when they are handled properly; that is, bled and chilled quickly. Bass, which are far more tolerant of minor neglect when caught, do not have to be bled or gutted immediately, though they should be kept as cool as possible. In fact, I believe a cleaned bass actually improves in flavor with 24 hours in the refrigerator. Spring blues benefit from being leaner than those of September and from the fact that they have not been feeding on oily menhaden, the only truly inedible fish in our local waters. Dining on menhaden increases and worsens the flavor of the already high fat content of blues. Autumn blues are best smoked or served with a tangy sauce, but we do not have to worry about that now, for the blues of spring are at their most succulent and delicious. I recommend filleting them and cooking them as simply as possible at a high temperature.

I have one favorite recipe taken from More Classic Italian Cooking by Marcella Hazan. I believe it is the best recipe out there and is worthy of repeating.

BAKED BLUEFISH WITH POTATOES, GENOESE STYLE *(for 4)*

2 bluefish fillets (about 1 lb. each)
1 ½ lbs. boiling potatoes
A 16x10-inch bake-and-serve dish (an enameled cast-iron pan or a Pyrex is good)
2/3 cup olive oil
1 TBS (or more) garlic, chopped
1/4 cup parsley, chopped
Salt
Freshly ground black pepper

Preheat the oven to 450 degrees. Peel the potatoes and cut them into thin slices (no more than 1/8 inch thick). Rinse and pat dry. Put all the potatoes, half the olive oil, half the garlic, half the parsley and a liberal amount of salt and pepper into the baking pan and mix thoroughly, then spread them evenly over the bottom of the pan.

My family likes the potatoes so much in this dish that I often cook two baking pans, each with one of the fillets, and a whole recipe worth of potatoes. I lean a layer of potatoes against the vertical sides of the pan to become especially crisp. I have witnessed near fights over these tasty pieces – be careful!

Put the pans in the top third of the preheated oven. Bake until half cooked, 12 to 15 minutes. Remove the pans from the oven and place the fish fillets, skin-side down, over the potatoes. (I usually skin my fillets, but this works with the skin on or off. Many people believe the skin adds flavor; they are probably right.) Mix the remaining oil, parsley and garlic, and spread over the fillets, basting well. Sprinkle with a generous amount of salt and pepper. Return the dish to the oven.

Bluefish
Parsley
Potatoes
Garlic olive oil

After 10 minutes remove from oven, and with a spoon scoop up some of the oil in the dish and baste the fish and potatoes with it. Loosen some of the crispy potatoes from the sides of the pan and replace them with less crispy ones from the bottom, return to oven and bake for 5 more minutes.

Serve directly from the pan, being sure to scrape up all the potatoes stuck to the pan. Marcella Hazan agrees with my family, saying, "These are the most delectable bits, so save them for yourself or for someone you like nearly as well." I am with her. This dish is truly "smack your grandma good" and will make you a loved hero – that is, if you are fair with the crispy potatoes!

This is a quick and easy dish; all you need is a green salad to complete it. Portuguese vinho verde, very cold, goes nicely with this dish. I can hardly wait; after all, it has been over six months since I last had this treasure of a dish – too long.

I talk to many fishermen who say they always "throw" the bass fillets on the charcoal or now, more often, the gas grill, pointless devices as far as I'm concerned because they impart no flavor to foods cooked on them. I urge you to grill your fish over hardwood charcoal, better than briquettes in my not at all humble opinion. I think many men cook only on grills because cleaning up is easier and the food cooked is usually uncomplicated. I will suggest a few simple techniques for grilling large striped bass fillets. Most people grill fillets to a dry, tasteless death. Better undercooked than over, I say. Leave the skin on fillets that are to be grilled. This helps hold them together when turned on the grill. You should hope for leftovers, which can be used for a fish salad just like tuna or made into fish cakes or eaten cold with flavored mayonnaise.

Make sure your grill is rust-free and clean to help keep the fish from sticking. I was told this winter that rubbing the grill with the cut side of a potato will aid in preventing sticking. I have never tried it, but it cannot hurt.

SIMPLE GRILLED STRIPER (for 4)

2 lbs. or more of fillet of bass
2 TBS olive oil
1 TBS chopped garlic (optional)
Salt and pepper
Lemon wedges

Start a hot fire, arrange grill about 3 or 4 inches above hot coals. Coat the fish with olive oil, rub with chopped garlic, liberally salt and pepper.

Grill the fish flesh-side down, slipping a metal spatula under it every couple of minutes to prevent sticking. After about 5 minutes, carefully turn the fish over and grill for about another 5 minutes.

The fish should now be translucent, white throughout. Serve skin-side down and eat while hot with lemon – pure and delicious food.

This is good on a dressed salad while hot. Try it. You can also serve butter on the side as you would with a boiled lobster. I like the leftover fish marinated in vinaigrette to eat cold the next day. Commercial Italian dressing is good for this job if you are impure, as I am.

We all should be catching fish now, that is, if we can get out fishing. The bass are here on the south side of Cape Cod, and soon the bluefish will be blitzing the beaches. Bass are chasing herring, and the scup should be plentiful for bottom fishermen before too long. These are three of my favorite fish, along with fluke, tautog and black sea bass. There is hardly a fish that I do not like if handled properly when caught, cleaned and cooked with care.

I worry more and more about mercury contamination in the fish we eat, not so much for an old guy like me, but for the children of all of us. If anything, new, more lenient federal laws are making the problem worse – "help the corporations and harm the children" seems to be an acceptable approach.

I intend to keep eating fish until there is enough mercury in me to tell the temperature by looking in my eyes, and I intend to eat them with great pleasure.

I always harp about bleeding bluefish immediately upon boating them, and gutting them as soon as possible. The bleeding should be done even if you are putting them on ice. Captain Charley Soares, striped bass guru, always bleeds the bass he is taking home as well. Any fish will benefit from prompt bleeding, but it is critical with bluefish.

BAKED BASS AND POTATOES – *in the style of the World's Best Bluefish (for 4)*

2 lbs. bass fillet
2 lbs. potatoes, sliced ½ inch thick
1/2 cup parsley, chopped
3 large cloves garlic, minced
1/3 cup olive oil
Salt and pepper
Lemon quarters for garnish

Preheat oven to 415 degrees. Put 3 tablespoons olive oil in a casserole big enough to be lined with potato slices in a single layer, 8x13 inches should do, add 2/3 of the minced garlic and 2/3 of the chopped parsley. Mix potatoes with garlic, parsley and oil until thoroughly coated, salt and pepper them liberally, and arrange like tiles on casserole bottom and standing on edge along the sides. Bake this arrangement for 15 minutes or until vertical potatoes begin to brown, and remove from oven.

Salt and pepper fish fillet and coat with remaining oil, garlic and parsley, and return to oven for 15 to 20 minutes or until fish flakes when tested with a fork.

Serve garnished with lemon, accompanied by a green salad dressed with vinaigrette and a dry white wine for a great meal of bass or a splendid meal of bluefish. This simple dish of fish and potatoes can make you renowned in your own circle and loved, even more, in your family.

You men should make this – if you clean the pan afterward it will guarantee you more fishing time, and make you, at least briefly, a hero at home.

Over the years I have prepared many easy-to-prepare recipes with few and common ingredients; well, it is time to get a little more esoteric – not more complicated – with some new flavors. Limes are not too esoteric to begin with.

MARK BITTMAN'S BROILED BLUEFISH WITH LIME MUSTARD *(for 3)*

1/2 cup Dijon or coarse grain mustard
Juice and grated zest of 1 lime
Salt and pepper
1 TBS olive or peanut oil
1 ½ lbs. bluefish fillet
1 large ripe tomato, skinned, seeded
    and chopped
Lime wedges

Mix the lime juice, zest, mustard, salt and pepper. Preheat the broiler, oil a roasting pan, broiler pan or cookie sheet, and lay the bluefish on it. Brush the fish with the mustard-lime mixture.

Broil for 6 to 8 minutes about 6 inches from the heat. The thickness of the fillet determines cooking time; the fish is white all the way through when done. Sprinkle with tomato and broil 1 minute more. Serve immediately with lime wedges. You could skip the tomato, but it is a great addition.

The final recipe is simple, delicious and only slightly exotic, or at least something you have never tried before. I read that it should be a good scup year. Spring and early summer are the times to catch the big one you should have for this recipe.

HERB-ROASTED SCUP (PORGY)

2 lbs. scup (porgy) whole
Salt and pepper
1 tsp. garlic, minced
2 TBS herbs, fresh or dried sage and rosemary mixed or mint
3 TBS bread crumbs
3 TBS olive oil

Preheat oven to 415 degrees. Mix all ingredients into a paste. Cut two or three vertical slits on each side of fish, fill slits with paste, put extra in cavity. Bake for half an hour or until meat is white to the backbone. Garnish with parsley on a platter with lemon wedges. A lovely sight to a fish lover like myself. You can spoon the meat off the bones.

You could substitute fluke for porgy. Use whatever herbs you prefer. The only way you can ruin this sort of recipe is by overcooking the fish.

The first two recipes will work well with salmon. I rarely write salmon recipes because I do not approve of the damage to the environment and the threat to the wild salmon caused by their culturing. If you can get wild salmon, use it by all means; it is far superior to the farm-raised variety.

Roast Scup

Man Doesn't Live By Fish Alone — So What Else?

Man does not live by fish alone. (I think that is a biblical paraphrase; even in the loaves and fishes miracle, the bread was central.) So, let's consider some side dishes. I will write of my personal favorites and those of my hero, dead alas, James Beard. The dishes described will be suitable for serving with any simply prepared, grilled, baked or breaded and sautéed fish.

We are all familiar with the often-soggy french fries served with fish and chips in many restaurants; sometimes we get lucky and get hot, crisp delicious "chips." However, for me, the potato is not quite, but almost, necessary in a fish dinner. I like them best mashed with garlic, or roasted with garlic, olive oil and parsley.

GARLIC MASHED POTATOES (for 6)
8 medium potatoes
6 TBS butter (4 TBS olive oil may be used instead)
1/2 cup heavy cream (or milk)
4 cloves garlic, peeled
Salt and pepper

Peel and boil the potatoes and garlic until tender. Drain and mash them thoroughly with the garlic. Add the butter and salt, and mash again. Heat the cream or milk, and beat it into the potato garlic purée.

Put this manna in a serving bowl and sprinkle it with black pepper. I just love potatoes this way with fried fish!

You may fancy these up a bit by beating some chopped scallions, chives or parsley into the potatoes. You can keep this all warm over boiling water if you wish to do them in advance.

I like either fresh green peas, rarely available, or frozen tiny peas, always available, cheap and nearly as good as fresh. This is hard for me to admit because I have been growing my own peas for 30 years.

ROAST POTATOES WITH PARSLEY AND GARLIC (for 4)
2 lbs. boiling potatoes
2/3 cup olive oil (not necessarily the best)
1 to 2 TBS garlic, minced
1/4 cup parsley, chopped
Salt and pepper

Preheat the oven to 450 degrees. Peel, if you wish, the potatoes and slice thinly (thicker than a potato chip, thinner than a LifeSavers candy). Put the sliced potatoes in a bowl, add the parsley and garlic, pour on the olive oil, and add a generous amount of salt and pepper. Mix this all together until the potatoes are coated with oil. Now line a glass, enamel-covered steel or other heavy pan with a single layer of potatoes, maybe overlapping them slightly. Bake for about 25 minutes until brown and done. Check during the last 10 minutes to prevent burning. Be careful: People have been known to fight over these.

You may baste with oil a fillet of any kind of fish that weighs about a pound, and put it on top of the potatoes for the last 15 minutes. You may have to add a little time if you do this. You won't be sorry.

I would serve with this meal a tossed green salad dressed with lemon vinaigrette.

LEMON VINAIGRETTE

2 TBS lemon juice (or balsamic vinegar)
6 TBS virgin olive oil
1 tsp. coarse salt (or any salt)
1/2 tsp. ground black pepper

Mix these all together and taste. Add more of anything you think it needs.

Spinach would go well with these roasted potatoes and fish, just as canned stewed tomatoes go good, as my mother would say, with garlic mashed potatoes. Canned stewed tomatoes are good!

STEAMED SPINACH (for 4 or 5)

2 lbs. spinach
Salt and pepper
Butter

Wash the spinach and put it in a pot. Do not add additional water; sprinkle with salt and cook gently, stirring occasionally until the spinach leaves are wilted and tender. Drain, and dress with butter, salt and pepper. You could add some sautéed mushrooms to this or mashed hard-boiled egg, or both, if you want to tart it up a little. A little garlic would not hurt either. James Beard said, "Ah, garlic, a great friend to fish!"

This leads us to a simple and delicious side dish of pasta with garlic and oil.

PASTA WITH GARLIC, OIL AND CHEESE
(for 4)

1 lb. pasta (spaghetti, linguine, etc.)
1/2 cup olive oil
3 cloves garlic
Salt and pepper
Grated cheese to taste (Parmesan, Pecorino
   Romano or whatever you like)

Crush and peel the garlic cloves. Crushing with the side of a knife will almost pop the clove out of its tight skin. Gently cook the crushed garlic in the oil until it is browned. Press the garlic now and again to squeeze out its flavor. Discard the garlic cloves.

Boil the pasta the way you like it while the garlic gives up its flavor. Drain the pasta, pour the garlic-infused oil over it, stir in some cheese, salt and pepper, and you're golden.

I keep remembering more fish accompaniments as I go along.

I cannot neglect boiled new potatoes with parsley and butter. I know, new potatoes are hard to find in winter, but red-skinned potatoes will do nicely.

BOILED RED POTATOES WITH PARSLEY AND BUTTER

Enough red potatoes for your guests
Enough parsley to flavor potatoes (1/2 cup chopped parsley to 2 lbs. potatoes)
Enough melted butter to coat them well

I like potatoes just a bit larger than a golf ball. I usually peel a bare midriff around them. I think it makes a prettier dish; my grandchildren say I think it is sexy. Boil the potatoes until just done, pour melted butter over them, add salt and pepper, stir in the chopped parsley and they are ready.

There are many more possibilities. There is rice (plain or boiled and mixed with tiny peas and butter), pasta, coleslaw, tartar sauce, asparagus with hollandaise, and hush puppies, beloved in our South.

Olive Oil Garlic Spaghetti

A few photos of the author
back in the days he worked
aboard a research vessel.

Chapter Two:
Summer!

Summer – The Shortest Season

Summer begins suddenly here on Cape Cod about the third week of June. After a long gray period of cool rain with a few sunny warm days that we call spring, suddenly it is summer. Everything is green, the summer fish are here and fishing is at its early summer peak. In a couple of weeks, around the Fourth of July, the family will start arriving, so get out the grill. It is easier and less messy to feed them outside whenever possible.

Now is the time for fish salads, including squid salad or cold cooked bass instead of tuna. Cold fried fish marinated in vinaigrette is good to take on a beach picnic, this "escabeche" is delicious made with tinker mackerel or snapper blues.

Whole fish or large fillets can be delicious grilled – but be careful to avoid overcooking! These can be served with grilled vegetables. Unfortunately, tomatoes and corn are more late-summer and autumn crops, but zucchini will abound. However, tasteless store tomatoes improve greatly when split, coated with olive oil and grilled – grand with simple grilled fish and a grilled onion!

Summer should be fun, make it so, catch and eat those fish. Joy will be yours!

What's at steak here? Mango salsa?

By the middle of spring, just before the migrating coastal fish return, I begin to eye the mildly suspect frozen, partially frozen and thawed swordfish steaks that appear on sale, at suspiciously low prices, in the fish display at my local supermarket. Some of these fish have traveled farther out of the water than they ever did in it, yet if they were frozen soon enough after being caught, they remain not only edible but also sometimes good. Unfortunately, you cannot tell how good they will be until you cook them. You can tell if they are bad, for they will stink when thawed. The clerks will be of little help in learning the provenance of the steaks, so you are on your own. This is where mango salsa comes in, or any of the exotic tropical condiments that accompany mediocre swordfish in many restaurants. These accompaniments may seem like putting Carmen Miranda's headdress on a Quaker lady from West Falmouth – remarkable, but somewhat inappropriate, yet possibly exciting and certainly memorable.

BAKED MARINATED SWORDFISH STEAKS WITH MANGO SALSA

2 lbs. swordfish steaks
1/2 cup lemon juice
1/4 cup olive oil
1 TBS ground black pepper
2 cloves garlic, pressed

Marinate steaks overnight (12 hours minimum) in oil, lemon juice, pepper and garlic mixture. Preheat oven to 450 degrees. Bake fish in marinade for 10 to 15 minutes until barely cooked through. Serve with cold mango salsa.

MANGO SALSA

2 firm ripe mangos (peeled and chopped)
1 clove garlic, pressed
1 medium green pepper, diced
1 jalapeño pepper, diced
1 medium onion, diced
1/2 cucumber, peeled and cubed
1 tomato, chopped
1 tsp. balsamic vinegar
1 tsp. sugar
1/2 cup cilantro, chopped
1/2 tsp. ground cumin
Salt and pepper

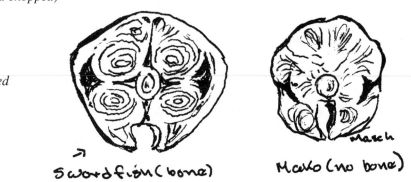

Swordfish (bone)   Mako (no bone)

Mix all ingredients and store overnight in refrigerator. Taste for seasoning (salt, pepper, hotness) before serving with baked swordfish steaks. It will be interesting and probably good – and it may be excellent. Give it a shot. The marinade will liven up a long-frozen fish and will not harm a fresher one.

My eight-year-old grandson Owen and I went striper fishing last evening for the first time this year. I usually get my first bass during the last week in April. This proved true again this year. I hooked and landed a bright, shining, 22-inch striped bass. My grandson was not as fortunate but shared my joy in our first fish of the season. It was April 28. We released the legally undersized fish somewhat reluctantly, for it was the perfect size to bake and stuff or to steam, Chinese style. The perfect size for four or five people – but, alas.

I think it would be good to have a one-fish, of any-size, per day limit put on striped bass so that more people could enjoy dining on fish they have caught. It might even result in lower mortality because people would not catch and release as many undersized fish before getting their "keeper."

In the spring the first keepers are usually pretty thin, so with the head and tail cut off they might be small enough for the following recipes. You may have to buy a farm-raised striper to get a 4- or 5-pounder, or you could substitute a small scrod (cod or haddock).

PORTUGUESE BAKED BASS *(for 4 to 6)*

(or haddock or cod)
(1) 5- to 7-pound fish (whole or beheaded)
1 ½ cups (or one large) green pepper, chopped
2 large cloves garlic, chopped
1 #10 can plum tomatoes
1 tsp. cumin, ground
1/2 tsp. saffron (optional, or substitute turmeric)
1 cup white wine
4 TBS olive oil
1 medium onion, sliced
1 tomato, sliced
Salt and pepper
Parsley, chopped

Preheat oven to 375 degrees. Sauté the peppers, onion and garlic gently in the olive oil until they are transparent. Stir in wine and optional saffron or turmeric, add canned tomatoes, squash them with a potato masher, and simmer (simmer means simmer, not boil) for 20 minutes. Rub the fish inside and out with salt and pepper and olive oil (a little lemon couldn't hurt), and put into an oiled baking pan. Pour wine over the fish. Put sliced tomato and sliced onion on the fish; ladle the sauce over everything. Bake for about 45 minutes, basting occasionally with the sauce. Sprinkle with parsley, garnish with black olives and serve with plain rice or boiled potatoes.

STEAMED BASS

(cod or haddock)
1 whole 3-pound bass or 1 3-pound chunk
 of bass (bones and all)
2 tsps. salt
1-inch piece of ginger (julienned)
3 cloves garlic
3 TBS fermented black beans (or black bean sauce,
 available in ethnic section of supermarket)
3 whole scallions
2 TBS soy sauce
2 TBS dry sherry
Pinch of sugar
1 ½ TBS peanut oil
3/4 tsp. dark sesame oil

Put fish on a platter that will fit in a roasting pan, sprinkle it with salt and shredded ginger. Chop garlic and black beans (bean sauce), shred (chop) scallions, and cover the fish with this stuff. Mix sherry, soy sauce and sugar, and pour over the fish.

Stand a trivet, or improvise one with two tuna-fish cans with the lids cut off, in a roasting pan big enough for the fish platter. Put the platter on the trivet. Now pour boiling water into the pan to just below, not touching, the fish platter. Cover the whole works tightly with a tent of aluminum foil. Put over a low burner or in a preheated 400-degree oven for about 10 minutes for each inch of thickness of the fish. When the fish is done, remove the platter from the steamer. Heat peanut and sesame oil together until nearly smoking, and pour over the fish. Beautiful! Eat with rice. The thin sauce in the platter is ambrosia!

Joseph Mitchell, thought by many to set the standard for writing at The New Yorker, *wrote "McSorleys Wonderful Saloon" and many other stories. The following is an excerpt from Old Mr. Flood, himself a seafoodetarian, as he discusses a restaurant review with a friend. "God defend us, son," he said. "Read this." In the column, Mr. Beebe described a dinner that had been "run up" for him and a friend by Edmond Berger, the chef de cuisine of the Colony Restaurant. He gave the menu in full. One item, the fish course, was "Fillet de sole en Beteau Beebe." "The sole, courteously created in the name of this department by Chef Berger for the occasion," Mr. Beebe wrote, "was a delicate fillet superimposed on a half-baked banana and a trick worth remembering."*

"Good God Almighty!" said Mr. Flood.

"Sounds nice, don't it?" asked Mr. Murchison. "A half-baked bananny with a delicate piece of flounder superimposed on the top of it. While he was at it, why didn't he tie a red ribbon around it?"

"Next they'll be putting a cherry on boiled codfish," said Mr. Flood. "How would that be, a delicate piece of codfish with a cherry superimposed on the top of it?"

I wonder what they would have to say about my swordfish and salsa. God save us from an answer.

Good Fish Cooks – Is Being Old And Mean Enough?

The following quotation was first printed in The New Yorker magazine in the mid-1940s and was then reprinted in the book Old Mr. Flood, published in 1948 and written by Joseph Mitchell. Mr. Mitchell was a graveyard humorist and the finest portrayer of New York City characters who ever set pen to paper.

"I've made quite a study of fish cooks," Mr. Flood says, "and I've decided that old Italians are the best. Then come old colored men, then old mean Yankees, and then old drunk Irishmen. They have to be old; it takes almost a lifetime to learn how to do a thing simply. Even the stove has to be old. If the cook is an awful drunk, so much the better. I don't think a teetotaler could cook a fish. Oh, if he was a mean old tobacco-chewing teetotaler he might."

I can meet some of Mr. Flood's requirements for a good fish cook, having drunk my share of booze and being adequately aged, and if I take up tobacco chewing, I may even qualify as an acceptable old Yankee, but I hate to think of myself as mean. However, given the choice of being either a good fish cook or kind, I'd probably go for the "good fish cook" title, take up tobacco chewing and learn to be mean.

In the meantime I will share some simple recipes from Cape Codders who cook fish well enough for me.

I spoke with Dave Mutti, an accomplished cook here on the Upper Cape, who makes a fine, pure fish chowder.

Dave says, "I'm not old, but I have been accused of being mean, and I am Italian." Dave gave me this recipe for fish chowder.

SIMPLE FISH CHOWDER
(for 6 or more)
2 TBS butter
1 gallon fish stock
1 large cod fillet (I'd guess 1 ½ lbs.)
6 good-sized boiling potatoes, skin on
1 good-sized white onion, chopped
Salt and pepper, to taste
Thyme (leaf, not ground)
1 to 1 ½ cups light cream

Dave makes his own fish stock by getting racks, backs and heads of fish from his fish man and boiling them up with onions. He starts with 2 gallons of water and about 4 pounds of heads and bones and one large onion. He boils this mixture until reduced by half, strains it and proceeds with his chowder.

Heat the strained stock, add the butter, the minced onion and the washed, unpeeled, cubed potatoes and about 1/2 teaspoon of thyme. (Be sure to use whole leaves and not powdered thyme, the latter can clot up and taste bitter). Boil these things gently until the potatoes are barely done.

When the potatoes are just tender, add the cod fillet in one piece, and simmer until cooled through. Now add the cream, check the seasoning, and add the pepper and salt, if necessary. Do not boil the chowder after adding the light cream.

Dave says to make this in the morning if you are going to serve it for dinner, or better still, the day before serving. Chowders, like cooks, improve greatly with a little aging.

"Do not forget to cook the fillet of cod whole," says Chef Mutti. "If you cut it up before cooking, it will fall apart and you won't have nice big chunks of fish in your chowder. Serve it hot!"

This final sentence did not sound like a request.

Dave gave me another recipe that could become a classic.

BLUEFISH WITH BACON
(for 4)
2 lbs. of bluefish fillets
8 slices of bacon
Bread crumbs
Salt and pepper
1 TBS butter

Bluefish rolled with bacon

Roll 4 single-serving-size fillets or fillet sections. Wrap each roll with bacon strips. Dip the ends of the rolls in bread crumbs moistened with butter. Bake these rolls in a 400-degree oven until the bacon is crisp and the fish is cooked through. Salt and pepper, and serve. This is outstanding and easy.

One only has to look at the photograph of Howard Mitcham on the back cover of his Provincetown Seafood Cookbook to know that he meets Mr. Flood's requirements for a good fish cook. The posture and the glare, reinforced by the knife, seem mean enough, and the face shows signs of possible sobriety avoidance. Mr. Flood was right.

Here is how Mitcham broils bass or bluefish fillets.

BROILED BASS OR BLUES
Allow 1/2 lb. fish per serving
Butter
Salt and pepper
Lemon
Parsley

Bass or Blue Fillets

Put unskinned bass or bluefish fillets, skin-side up, on an oiled broiling pan. Brush fillets with butter, salt and pepper. Place the pan four inches below the broiler flame. When the skin has crisped and begun to brown, turn the fillets skin-side down, baste with pan juices, and broil for about 5 minutes more, until the fish is opaque all the way through. Baste and serve with melted butter, parsley for a garnish and sectioned lemon. What could be better?

If you have a huge bass, substitute steaks for fillets – this, too, could be a classic!

PAN-FRIED FLOUNDER FILLETS
1/2 lb. flounder per person
Yellow breader flour, used for fried clams
Milk

Dip flounder fillets in milk, then in clam breader (seasoned flour may be used, or cornmeal and flour mixed).

Melt the butter in a skillet over a medium flame until it's foaming. Lay breaded fillets in the butter and sauté gently until light brown on one side, shaking the pan occasionally to prevent sticking. Turn and brown the other side. Remove the fillets from the pan, sprinkle with salt, pepper, paprika and parsley, and serve with lemon sections and melted butter. It's wonderful!

Mitcham says, "Anybody who would put ketchup or cheap tartar sauce on a beautiful flounder fillet should be burned at the stake." I wouldn't mess with him.

The Octopus And The Striper? Why Not?

I put an octopus on the stove to simmer until tender before I sat down to write this. Why? Because it is good and it is exotic, which makes it interesting to talk about. It is also vaguely menacing and, to some, ugly. Octopus is not expensive, compared to shrimp, scallops or even halibut. It is often available in supermarkets and always available in Portuguese groceries in New Bedford or Fall River where I sometimes shop – you should, too!

I like octopus, especially simmered and then grilled and served with garlic-flavored olive oil, lemon juice and hot pepper as an appetizer, or simmered, marinated and served in a salad. It is outstanding in a tomato sauce and will always get a reaction from your guests. Give octopus a go. Serve it as an appetizer, and follow it with striped bass.

GRILLED OCTOPUS (for 4)

1 octopus (2 to 3 pounds)
1 bay leaf
3 crushed cloves of garlic
2 TBS lemon juice
*1 TBS plus 1 tsp. herbs (oregano, thyme,
 marjoram, crab boil – your choice)*

Simmer the skinned octopus in water, to which you have added the bay leaf, two cloves of garlic and a tablespoon of herbs. After about an hour, a sharply pointed knife should easily pierce the beast. Remove from heat.

Cut the octopus in large pieces. Combine olive oil, remaining clove of garlic and lemon juice; add salt and pepper and the herbs (1 teaspoon). Warm the mixture and pour over the octopus pieces.

Grill these pieces until slightly crisp, brush with the oil mixture and serve accompanied by bottled hot sauce or pepper flakes and the remaining basting sauce. Oh yeah!

OCTOPUS SALAD (for 4)

1 lb. simmered and chopped octopus
1/4 cup chopped sweet onion
1/4 cup chopped celery
1 TBS chopped parsley
*1/4 cup of oil and vinegar (1 TBS vinegar and 2 TBS
 oil) or bottled vinaigrette (Italian dressing is good)*

Mix all the ingredients and serve on a bed of lettuce or mixed greens, accompanied by or garnished with quartered tomatoes and olives. Yes!

After simmering the octopus until tender and chopping it, you can add it to a clam sauce or a marinara with laudable results. Try it.

June is when the number of "keeper" striped bass reaches the springtime peak here in New England. I know some people resent the use of the term "keeper" as an implication of greed or competitiveness, but as long as there is a size limit on fish, there will be "keepers" and "shorts." One major reason I fish is to get fish to eat; "keeper" makes sense to me.

I would like to see a "one fish, of any size, per day" limit for striped bass. Such a law would allow us to keep a 4- or 5-pound fish, which is just the right size to stuff and bake for a family of four, or to steam with scallions and ginger in the classic Chinese manner, but, alas, under the current law such fish are forbidden.

As the law stands now in Massachusetts, the fillets of a legal bass will, together, weigh at least 3 ½ pounds and will often be much larger. Many people are daunted by such large chunks of fish and consequently fear serving fish to large groups of people. By giving you a modification of another recipe, I will relieve you of this fear.

BAKED BASS FOR TWELVE

6 lbs. of striped bass fillets
4 (14 ½-ounce) cans diced tomatoes with chilies
  (mild, medium or hot)
2 cloves garlic, minced
1/3 cup olive oil
1 cup dry white wine
1/2 cup parsley, chopped
1 cup or more bread crumbs (seasoned, if you like)
Salt and pepper

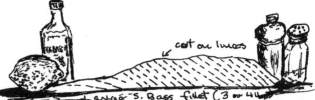

Coat with olive oil the bottom of a shallow, ovenproof pan that is big enough to hold the fillets and the canned tomatoes without submerging the fish. Add the chopped garlic. Place the fillets on top of the garlic, salt and pepper them, and cover them with the bread crumbs. Pour the canned tomatoes and white wine around the fillets, leaving the crumbed upper surface high and dry. Moisten the bread crumbs with the remaining olive oil. Put this creation in a preheated 375-degree oven for 30 to 45 minutes, until the fish flakes when tested. Garnish this with lemon wedges and parsley, serve with mashed potatoes and salad, and sit back and enjoy – after you have eaten – the accolades.

I have some advice on preparing large bass fillets for frying. People have told me that steaked fillets fall apart while frying. The trick to prevent this is to cut the fillet on the bias, or on a slant.

Make your pieces slightly over a half inch thick. These pieces will hold together when pan- or deep-fried and will cook through before the coating burns.

CRISP, FRIED STRIPER FILLET

Striped bass fillets (1/2 lb. per person)
1 cup plain flour
2 cups seasoned flour (ingredients below)
1/4 cup cornmeal
1 tsp. dried thyme
1/2 tsp. cayenne pepper (optional)
Salt and pepper
1 egg
1/2 cup milk

Put 1 cup of plain flour in a bag; a plastic grocery bag will do. Put 2 cups of seasoned flour, made by mixing the dry ingredients, in a separate bag. Beat the egg in the 1/2 cup of milk.

Now shake the fish fillets in the bag of plain flour, remove them, and dip them in the milk and egg mixture. Now put these drenched fillets in the bag of seasoned flour, shake to coat, and arrange on a dry platter. Leave them until you are ready to fry them.

Fry these coated pieces in hot oil (I like peanut oil) until nicely browned on both sides. Serve with tartar sauce and lemon wedges; add some salad, and you may not need anything else but protection from your delighted diners. I like hot pepper in the coating; you may not. Try it my way or develop your own.

Two of my grandchildren and I made pizza for lunch. Part of one pizza was octopus pizza (the octopus section was carefully delineated with black olive slices so they would know where it lurked). I ate the "contaminated" section, but they told their cousins they had "had" (not "eaten") octopus pizza – not quite a lie.

Octopus + Pepperoni Pizza

Possibly Magnificent Chowder (For A Multitude)

I recently had the honor of being asked to make clam chowder for the banquet celebrating the marriage of my friend Seth Carey (outstanding fish cook) and his fiancée Shannon Rafferty (outstanding observer of fish cooks). So last week I prepared clam chowder for 100. It was good on the day I made it and would have been better the next day if any had been left over. Chowder, even already good chowder, improves if kept overnight.

I used two bushels of quahogs, fifteen pounds of potatoes, six large onions and two pounds of salt pork in the construction of the chowder base. I snuck in a couple of cloves of garlic for luck, and about a teaspoon of Tabasco. To this I added six cans of evaporated milk, a gallon of whole milk and half a pound of butter. I stirred in a tablespoon of thyme shortly before serving. It was consumed in 30 minutes flat.

I made half this recipe on the following day with yet another bushel of chowder clams. This was almost totally eaten by 25 people. I did manage to save four servings to age overnight so I could have some the next day. It was nearly magnificent!

If you are ever faced with preparing chowder for 100, here is one way to do it.

QUAHOG CHOWDER FOR 100 OR SO

2 bushels chowder clams
15 lbs. potatoes
6 large onions (2 lbs.)
2 lbs. salt pork
1/2 lb. butter
1 cup white flour
2 cloves garlic
6 cans evaporated milk
1 gallon whole milk
1 tsp. Tabasco
1 TBS thyme
1 TBS black pepper

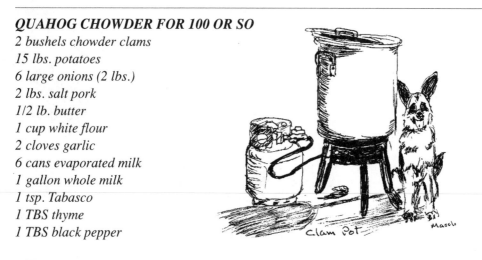

Clam Pot

Find a pot big enough to hold a bushel of washed (hosed) clams. Put about an inch of water in the pot. Dump in the clams and put over a heat source. I use an outdoor propane-burning gas ring on metal legs. You can cook your clams in several batches in a smaller pot.

I have a pot big enough to boil a German shepherd. It holds over three bushels of quahogs but is too heavy to lift alone. So I cook only a bushel at a time.

Boil the clams until they open. I allow them to cool considerably before draining and shucking them. Be careful; the broth is hot. Save the broth!

While the clams are cooking, you can peel the potatoes and chop them into pieces of the size you like to find in your chowder. Cover the cubed potatoes with the clam broth reserved from steaming the clams, and boil until done but not mushy.

While the potatoes are cooking, chop your onions and two cloves of garlic (don't tell Yankees about the garlic). Chop the salt pork into 1/4-inch cubes. This is perhaps the hardest job of all in making this chowder. It helps to have the salt pork thoroughly chilled, but not frozen hard, when you cut it.

Now render your salt pork in a large skillet, along with a half pound of butter. Do this on low to medium heat. You do not want to brown the salt pork, just turn it golden. When the pork is golden, add the onions, and sauté until nearly transparent. Add 1 cup of white flour to the onion-and-butter mixture, and sauté for 2 minutes, stirring constantly.

Now put as much hot potato-clam water as you can into the skillet with your salt-pork-and-onion roux, and stir. Add the whole works to the boiled potatoes and broth, and stir until it is all incorporated.

Now you must hand-grind or chop your clams, or chop them in a food processor, before adding them to the potato-and-onion mixture. Grinding or machine mincing somehow releases more flavor than chopping clams by hand. Believe me, this is so!

After you mix in the ground clams, you have your chowder base, a grand amalgam of goodness, so intensely flavored that it must be tamed by the addition of whole milk and evaporated milk. Some people use cream (as the lady on Nantucket said, "maybe summer people"). I use a gallon of whole milk and six cans of evaporated milk.

To finish the chowder I add a teaspoon of Tabasco sauce, a tablespoon of black pepper, and a tablespoon of ground or whole thyme – kind of like sprinkles on a sundae, not truly necessary but well worth having.

Ideally you would now keep this chowder overnight and serve it tomorrow. This is hard to do, even with a large cooler. You must bring the whole works to room temperature before refrigeration, otherwise the fat congeals on top, the interior stays warm and goes anaerobic, and bacteria grow and ruin the whole thing. This is a tragedy that I have experienced. If you age your chowder overnight, remember to stir it frequently until it reaches room temperature before refrigerating.

Warm this up on the day you construct it and you will be lauded when it is served. Do it after a successful aging and you will be praised until you lose your modesty. It happened to me.

Mark Rose, shellfisherman extraordinaire and chowder critic of long standing, said it was "pretty good," high praise indeed from that half-Yankee.

If you should be catching bass big enough to provide you with large fillets, a 30-pound fish should give you at least 10 pounds of fillets. If you have these large fillets, you may use them instead of clams in the chowder recipe. You will not have clam broth to boil your potatoes in, so you will have to make fish broth.

FISH BROTH

5 lbs. bass heads and bones
7 large onions
3 stalks celery
3 carrots
12 sprigs parsley
1 tsp. peppercorns
Salt to taste (make it salty)
2 cups dry white wine (optional)

Put all ingredients in one large pot. Bring to a boil, and simmer for at least 30 minutes or, even better, for 45 minutes. Strain, saving the broth. Taste for seasoning. It should be quite salty because it will be diluted with milk.

Follow the recipe for clam chowder, using the fish broth to cook the potatoes and fish. Leave the fish fillets whole when you cook them, only breaking them up when it is time to serve this ambrosia.

I simmer the fish fillets for 15 minutes in the broth. Remove the fish from the broth, carefully breaking it up as little as possible, and put it aside. Now use this broth to boil the potatoes. You should have broth left over from the boiled heads and bones.

Finish the chowder, return the cooked fish, heat the whole works, and your fame is assured. Go for it.

I cut the last 6 inches from the thin ends of the bass fillets to coat with flour or cornmeal and fry them for a snack while the chowder construction is proceeding. You will earn your rewards, and it is easier than it sounds.

Out Of The Frying Pan And Into The Oven!

Baking is perhaps the easiest way to prepare fish for the table.

My culinary hero, James Beard, writes, "Too much fish is overcooked until it becomes flavorless and uninteresting," in his book of fish cookery, published in 1954. This is the first fish cookbook I ever bought; it is worn but still whole. James Beard also wrote, "The Fishery Council of New York has one basic rule that I feel all of us who love fish should follow, 'Fish is cooked to develop flavor, not to make it tender.' No amount of cooking will ever make fish tenderer than it is when it comes from the water."

SIMPLE BAKED FISH #1

Whole fish (3 to 5 pounds), cleaned and scaled
3 slices bacon or salt pork
1 bay leaf
1/2 sliced onion
Salt and pepper

Preheat oven to 425 degrees. The fish may be baked with or without stuffing. The head and tail may be removed or left on. Clean the fish, dry, and rub salt in the inside. Stuff if desired, and sew or skewer. Put a sheet of heavy aluminum foil or parchment paper in a baking pan; make the paper large enough so it can be used to lift the fish when done. Place the bay leaf and a few slices of onion and bacon on the paper, and lay the fish on top. (I would put another bay leaf and some onions in the fish's cavity as well.) If the fish is lean (cod or haddock), cut a few slashes down its sides and place a strip of salt pork or bacon in each slit. Bake for 10 minutes per inch of thickness at its thickest point. It should flake easily when tested with a fork. If it does not, bake 5 minutes longer.

The Fishing Board of Canada came up with what is known as the "Canadian Rule" for fish cooking; at high temperatures (400 degrees plus, or on a grill, or in a hot frying pan), cook fish 10 minutes for each inch of thickness. The rule applies to whole fish, fillets or steaks. If you stay close to this rule's advice, you will not go wrong cooking fish. I promise.

SIMPLE BAKED FISH #2

3 to 5 lbs. fish, cleaned and scaled
1/2 cup each finely chopped celery, onion and carrot (more is fine)
3 slices bacon or salt pork
Salt and pepper

Preheat oven to between 400 and 425 degrees. Oil the bottom of a baking pan, or place minced vegetables on bottom of pan (I would do both). Place the fish, salted and peppered inside and out, on the vegetables, lay salt pork or bacon strips over the fish, or oil it well. Add between 1/2 to 1 cup white wine or broth to pan for basting. Baste every 10 minutes. Bake for 10 minutes for each inch of thickness or pound of weight. Test for doneness; fish will flake when done.

PORTUGUESE BAKED SWORDFISH (for 2 to 3)

1 lb. swordfish steak
(1) 14-oz. can stewed tomatoes (Italian style)
1/4 cup olive oil
1/2 cup diced onion
1/2 cup diced green pepper
1/4 cup diced celery
1 clove garlic, minced
1/4 cup green or black olives, halved, or salad olives
1/2 cup linguica or chourico, diced
2 tsps. powdered cumin

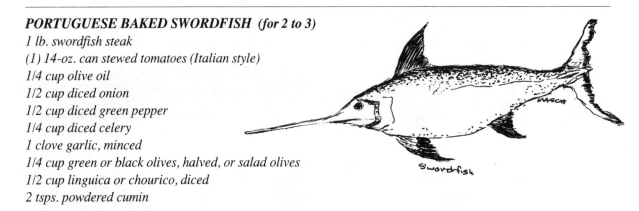

Swordfish

1/4 tsp. cayenne pepper (optional)
Salt and pepper, to taste
Parsley and sliced lemon for garnish

Salt and pepper the steak liberally and place in an oiled baking pan just big enough to hold the fish piece and sauce without submerging the steak.

Brown the minced sausage in 3 tablespoons olive oil. When the meat begins to brown, add the celery, onion and pepper. Sauté over medium heat for about 2 minutes, and add minced garlic and cumin. Sauté 1 minute longer. Now pour in crushed-up stewed tomatoes. Bring all to a boil while stirring. Pour sauce around, not on top of, the steak. Put the whole works into an oven preheated to 425 degrees, and bake for 10 to 12 minutes. Do not overcook.

Serve this with white rice or boiled potatoes. A Portuguese chef might serve both, some peas and a salad, some vinho verde and crusty bread.

Some people like to add 1/4 cup of white wine or a tablespoon of vinegar to the sauce before baking. I do!

This recipe can be used very successfully with a whole 3- to 5-pound freshwater black bass. Be sure that the gills and all the blood along the backbone are removed before proceeding with recipe. Spoon a little sauce in the fish's cavity, and pour the rest around the beast. Make three or four cuts in each side of fish, salt and pepper, and baste with olive oil. Bake for 30 to 45 minutes or until fish flakes.

Substitute 1 teaspoon of oregano, 1 teaspoon of thyme for the cumin, Italian sausage for the Portuguese sausage, and serve with spaghetti, salad, crusty bread and Pinot Grigio. Mama mia! Prepare this for your wife and family, and fishing time will grow easier to come by.

Large fillets of striped bass can be used in place of the fish in the previous recipes, or they can be prepared very simply on their own. Remember 1/2 pound of fish is a normal amount per diner when using fillets; at least twice that weight is necessary when using whole fish.

SIMPLE BAKED FILLETS
1/2 lb. fish per person
Salt and pepper
Bread crumbs
Olive oil (my preference) or butter

Preheat oven to 425 degrees. Liberally salt and pepper the fillets. Coat them with olive oil or melted butter. Put seasoned and oiled fillets in a baking pan. They can be baked just like this. I like to sprinkle them with bread crumbs and drizzle the crumbs with more oil or butter. You may sprinkle them with herbs of your choice as well. Put them in the hot oven, and bake for 10 minutes per inch of thickness.

Serve these simple and delicious fillets with lemon slices, garnished with parsley and plain or flavored additional melted butter or olive oil. Rice or mashed potatoes and sautéed spinach go well with this. A plain, delicious meal.

Bass, salmon, bluefish or cod fillets can be baked on a bed of half-cooked sliced potatoes, dressed with garlic, parsley and oil or butter, making a terrific dish. Bass and bluefish fillets baked without crumbs can be flambéed with a couple ounces of gin before serving for an added fillip of flavor.

Can A Fish Be "Wicked Good"?

I recently was served an outstanding dinner by my soon-to-be son-in-law, Scott Britton. I dislike the use of the words "awesome" and "marvelous" for everyday events that are very pleasant; the first implies fear, the second, divine magic. So as not to sound too pedantic or proud, I will use the oxymoron "wicked good" for Scott's dinner.

This dinner was simple, elegant and prepared meticulously, not overcooking the fish or the asparagus. The meal consisted of charcoal-grilled (in this case in the fireplace) swordfish, asparagus and saffron rice, followed by a green salad dressed with Gorgonzola vinaigrette.

The swordfish was cut fairly thick, about an inch through. Thick is better than thin for grilling because you are less likely to dry the fish out. Buy 1/2 pound of swordfish steak for each person you will serve.

GRILLED SWORDFISH

1/2 lb. swordfish per diner
Olive oil
Salt and pepper

Salt and pepper the fish generously on both sides, and coat with olive oil. Allow to sit at room temperature while you prepare the coals. Redwood charcoal is best for this recipe, though briquettes can be used, or even a gas grill.

Grill the steaks for a total of about 10 minutes; if the steaks begin to darken too quickly over the coals, turn them over and brown the second side. To avoid burning, it is easiest to finish steaks in a preheated (415-degree) oven.

Scott dressed the steaks before serving with herb butter and presented them at the table as the butter melted. The platter was garnished with parsley and lemon quarters – splendid and delicious!

HERB BUTTER FOR 2 POUNDS OF SWORDFISH

4 TBS butter at room temperature
2 tsps. single or mixed herbs (tarragon, sage, rosemary, parsley – I like tarragon here)
Freshly ground black pepper
Juice of 1/2 lemon

Cream butter with herbs and seasonings, and roll into a cylinder in kitchen wrap. Chill until ready to use.

Herb butter is good on many things – grilled meat, steamed vegetables and poultry, as well as baked, grilled or steamed fish. Not bad on noodles or rice either.

Prepared butter can be kept frozen for months, or in the fridge for days, though the herbs will lose flavor over time.

SAFFRON RICE

1 cup white rice (I like basmati, but Uncle Ben's works fine)
2 cups chicken stock
1 medium onion, chopped
2 TBS red sweet pepper, chopped (optional, but looks great)
1/4 teaspoon saffron threads or 1 packet Goya's Sazon con Azafran (cheaper and delicious)
2 TBS olive oil

Sauté the onion in the olive oil until transparent. Add rice and stir until well coated with oil and turning translucent. Add hot chicken stock and bring to a boil, reduce to simmer, add seasoning, cover, and simmer for about 20 minutes or until rice is done.

ASPARAGUS WITH OIL AND LEMON

2 lbs. asparagus
2 TBS virgin olive oil
1/2 lemon
Salt and pepper

Boil or steam asparagus just until it will bend from its own weight when picked up in the middle and is still bright green. Dress with oil and lemon, and serve with rice and swordfish.

The whole thing makes a pretty plate that is also so, so delicious.

Scott followed this with green salad with Gorgonzola dressing; you can also use blue cheese or Stilton or any other moldy cheese of your choice. It is convenient to buy half pints of crumbled Gorgonzola at the supermarket rather than crumbling your own – a messy job at best.

GORGONZOLA SALAD DRESSING

1/2 pint crumbled aged cheese
2 TBS plain yogurt
1 TBS mayonnaise
2 TBS olive oil
1 tsp. vinegar or lemon juice
Salt and pepper

Save a tablespoon of cheese for sprinkling on dressed salad. Put all other ingredients except olive oil in the blender and blend; drizzle in olive oil until you get the consistency you want. Taste, and adjust seasoning. Pour this over any combination of greens you desire and – Bob's your uncle – happiness!

Serve all of the above with a nice dry white wine (even though connoisseurs say no wine is right for asparagus, do it anyway) and some crusty bread for soaking up the delicious juice on the fish platter.

This meal is already "wicked, wicked good!" but could be put between raw oysters or littlenecks as an appetizer, and pears and cheese for dessert. Scott served crackers with herb cream cheese and smoked salmon as an hors d'oeuvre, and cookies and ice cream for dessert, or was it homemade sherbet – you cannot beat him for a wicked-good cook!

My stepdaughter and Scott were discussing writing vows for their wedding ceremony. I told them I knew what my vow would be should I be asked to make one. It was no problem: I vowed to come to dinner or any other meal whenever they asked me. It was the least I could do.

asparagus
swordfish
rice
mash

The Percentages Are With You

••

I made a simple, delicious meal last week that I would proudly, or at least confidently, serve to anyone on earth. It would not qualify as a "gourmet meal" because of the side dishes of delicatessen coleslaw and oven-baked frozen french fries. The stars of the meal were baked fillet of haddock and pan-seared sea scallops.

PAN-SEARED SCALLOPS

1 lb. sea scallops
1 TBS butter
2 TBS light olive oil
2 slices ginger
2 cloves garlic
Salt and pepper

Melt butter in olive oil in a sauté pan large enough to hold scallops without them touching each other.

Crush the unpeeled whole garlic clove, and separate skin from bulb. The skin will separate easily – this is a chef's trick for quickly peeling garlic. I use the side of my chef's knife as a crushing tool.

Put ginger and crushed garlic cloves in the heated oil and butter, and sauté until garlic is golden brown on both sides. Do not burn the garlic, or the dish will be ruined. Remove the garlic, leave the ginger. I dry the scallops a little with paper towels so they will brown and caramelize more readily and put them in the hot oil. Arrange so they are not touching and leave undisturbed until the bottoms are nicely browned. You can check by tilting one scallop. Do not shake the pan or disturb the scallops until browning has occurred, now turn them over and repeat on unbrowned side. Sprinkle with salt and pepper and "Bob's your uncle!"

Serve these splendid morsels on a platter, surrounding the baked haddock of the next recipe.

SIMPLE CRUMBED AND BAKED HADDOCK

1 lb. haddock fillet
1/4 cup bread crumbs
Salt and pepper
2 TBS light olive oil
2 TBS butter

Preheat your oven to 415 degrees. Put olive oil in baking pan and put fillet in oil, turn it over so that both sides will be oiled. Salt and pepper fillet, and cover with crumbs. Dot the crumbs with butter and bake for about 15 to 20 minutes until it flakes easily. While the fish is cooking, you can prepare the scallops.

I prepared frozen french fries in the oven while cooking the fish. I served the fish on a platter surrounded by the browned scallops and garnished with parsley and a quartered lemon. The combination looked beautiful.

I served the fries in a towel-lined basket and the coleslaw in a bowl. I also melted 4 tablespoons of butter to which I added the juices and oils from the baking and sauté pans to make a dipping sauce for the fish and scallops, just as one would use for a lobster. This made a simple and truly delicious meal . . . good enough for anyone on earth. I urge you to take on this minor amount of work and prepare a major marvelous meal for four, three of whom are fortunate enough to know you.

You could substitute striped bass, tautog, black sea bass or even fluke for the haddock and produce a meal as good or better, especially if you caught the fish yourself. I believe men should prepare the fish they catch and encourage their wives to come along so they can cook some, too.

The former recipes reminded me of a fine dish I had once of monkfish served with melted butter. The monk-fish, or goosefish, or, as some call it, "poor man's lobster," can be cooked in a couple of ways. You may, but are unlikely to, catch one yourself, and if you do, keep your hands away from its enormous snaggly-toothed mouth. This beast is somewhat hard to dress, so I suggest you buy some already cleaned fillets and strongly recommend that you try the following simple recipes.

SAUTÉED MONKFISH FILLET (for 4)
2 lbs. monkfish fillet in one or two pieces
Bread crumbs
Flour, seasoned with salt and pepper
1 egg
1/2 cup milk
2 TBS butter
2 TBS light olive oil

Beat the egg in the milk. Roll the fillets in the flour, now dip them in the egg and milk mixture, and roll in the bread crumbs until well coated.

Melt the butter in the oil in a sauté pan over medium heat. When the butter bubbles for the second time, put in the fillets and sauté on all sides (monkfish fillets are usually kind of round) until light brown. If the crumbs are browned before the fillet is cooked through, lower the heat. Monkfish will not flake easily even when cooked. It is done when opaque all the way through. Serve this with melted butter, and you have one version of poor man's lobster. Salad and potato chips go well with this, or serve the old standby, coleslaw.

BAKED POOR MAN'S LOBSTER (for 4)
2 lbs. monkfish fillet
Flour, seasoned
2 TBS dry sherry
1 stick melted butter
1 sleeve Ritz crackers, crushed
1 egg
1/2 cup milk

Preheat oven to 415 degrees. Follow directions of first recipe for coating fillets, this time with crushed crackers. Put fillets in baking casserole.

Melt butter with sherry. Pour melted butter over fillets until all crumbs are dampened. Bake for about 10 minutes per inch of thickness of fillets or until opaque throughout – about 20 minutes. If crackers brown too quickly, turn down oven.

Serve with leftover sherry butter, if you have any, or additional melted butter. Tastes like baked stuffed lobster.

If you have any leftovers, mix three to one with lobster meat in a salad, and not many will know the difference. My friends always suspect me of fraud when I serve a big lobster salad. Sometimes they are right.

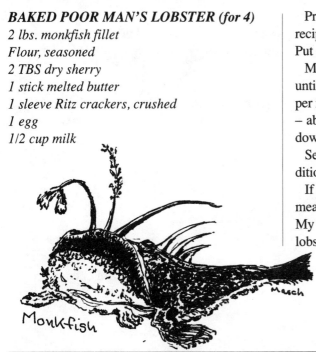
Monkfish

Bass Braising And Bluefish Baking

It is July again and, believe it or not, there are more striped bass and bluefish around than there are tourists. Tourists are more easily seen, but fish are more fun to catch! I am happy to see the crowds of fish and people return each year, and they arrive on similar schedules. The bass and blues have been increasing in number since the middle of May. The summer lull in fishing action has not yet begun, so I think recipes for preparing blues and bass are appropriate. These recipes, however, are not appropriate for preparing tourists – they are probably harder to clean, anyway.

I have always been an admirer of James Beard, a giant in late-twentieth-century American cooking. In his voluminous writing, he often presented master recipes for various dishes and then suggested variations. I am using his approach here, with striped bass as the main ingredient and braising as the technique. To braise is to cook in a moist atmosphere in a covered pan. The juices from the fish combine with the other ingredients to flavor the sauce, which may be thickened or served as is.

BRAISED BASS IN TOMATO SAUCE (for 4)

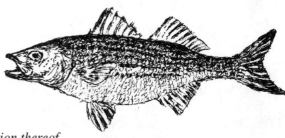

2 lbs. bass fillets or steaks
(1) 14-oz. can diced tomatoes
1 medium onion, chopped
1/4 cup green pepper, diced
1 clove garlic, chopped
1 TBS fresh parsley, chopped
1 cup white wine, clam juice, fish stock or any combination thereof
2 TBS olive oil or butter

Preheat oven to 375 degrees. Sauté vegetables in olive oil until limp. Put fish in an ovenproof pan that can be heated on top of the stove. Pour sautéed vegetables and stock or wine over the fish, and heat on the stovetop until simmering. Cover the dish and put in oven. Check after 12 minutes. If the fish flakes easily at the thickest point, it is ready to serve. Garnish with parsley and serve with mashed potatoes and tiny peas – or anything you wish. This is good, but I prefer things more highly seasoned and suggest the following variations.

Portuguese Style

Use the above ingredients, increasing the diced green pepper to 1 cup. Add 1/3 cup chopped linguica, 1 teaspoon of cumin and 2 cloves of garlic. Add a shot of Tabasco. Serve with boiled potatoes or rice, or both, and garnish with black olives.

Italian Style

Use the above ingredients plus 2 cloves of garlic, 1 teaspoon of oregano, 1 bay leaf and 1/2 cup of chopped olives (green). Thicken with 2 tablespoons tomato paste and 1 teaspoon sugar. Serve with pasta and Parmesan cheese. Crushed red pepper adds that certain zip.

Creole Style

Use the above ingredients, increasing the green peppers to 1 cup and adding one stalk of chopped celery, 1 bay leaf and 2 cloves of garlic. Garnish with 3 chopped scallions (green as well as white). Serve with rice and Tabasco on the side.

Greek Style

Same as above, except increase the parsley to 1 cup, and cook it with the sauce. Squeeze the juice of 1/2 lemon over the fish. After baking for 10 minutes, uncover and sprinkle with 1/4 pound crumbled feta cheese, and return to oven until cheese begins to melt. Serve with noodles or rice and Greek olives on the side.

I could go on and on – and probably will sometime. You do not have to be precise in your measurements with these recipes. Make your own variations, serve the sauce thickened or not, add a few clams or some shrimp, or even mussels. As long as you do not overcook the fish, the sauce will be delicious at the very least. Serve with crusty bread and green salad, cold white wine and a dessert of ripe pears and moldy cheese. (Try Roquefort, Gorgonzola, Stilton, Danish blue, etc. The last costs only 1/3 of what the first does but is 2/3 as good.) Do this and you will become famous!

Bluefish is often maligned as "too fishy, too oily, too strong." This is because many people do not bleed bluefish immediately when they catch them or even ice them down, and, as blues are oily fish, the quality declines rapidly. Well-handled fresh bluefish is perhaps my favorite fish, which is like saying that Ava Gardner is my favorite beauty, one of many that are more than worthy of regard.

I call the following recipe from Marcella Hazan's book, More Classic Italian Cooking, *"the world's best bluefish recipe" – simple and grand.*

BAKED BLUEFISH WITH POTATOES (for 6)
2 bluefish fillets (about 1 lb. each), skin on
1 ½ lbs. boiling potatoes
2/3 cup olive oil
1 TBS chopped garlic (at least – I double this)
1/4 cup chopped parsley
Salt and pepper

Preheat oven to 450 degrees. Slice potatoes thinly (3 times the thickness of a potato chip; do not worry if some are thicker). Put potatoes in a baking dish (13 by 9 inches or bigger) with 1/2 the olive oil, garlic and parsley mix, and arrange on sides and bottom of baking dish. Place potatoes in upper 1/3 of heated oven for 15 minutes. Remove dish and place bluefish fillets on the potatoes; pour remaining oil, garlic and parsley mix over the fish. Liberally salt and pepper. Baste after 10 minutes with juice accumulated around potatoes; move the potatoes to keep them from burning. Bake another 5 minutes. People have been known to fight for the crisp potatoes in the corners of this dish. You must try this recipe – and do not spare the salt. Serve with a green salad and a sharp vinaigrette dressing and you will become more famous!

Cook Some Seafood You Long For – For A Long Time

I have long advocated the cooking of fish until barely opaque and denounced overcooked fish. However, last night I prepared a recipe for swordfish (or tuna steak) that I found in a fine, informative and entertaining cookbook by Susan Harriman Loomis called the Great American Seafood Cookbook, *which recommends cooking the steak for over 45 minutes, and it was delicious! Can you believe it? It is the first new recipe, let alone new technique, that I've found in a long time that will be included in my favorite recipe repertoire. Here it is.*

SALTY SWORDFISH FOR THREE

1 swordfish or tuna steak (1 lb.)
1 TBS peanut oil
1/2 cup fish sauce (nuoc mam)
1 large jalapeño chili, seeded and chopped, or 1/4 tsp. pepper flakes
2 TBS sugar

Heat the oil in a skillet that will just hold the fish. Brown the steak for about a minute on each side.

Mix the fish sauce with 3/4 cup of water and pour over the fish; add the chopped pepper. Bring the liquid to a boil, reduce it to a simmer and cover. Cook for 25 minutes. Turn the fish over and cook covered for 20 minutes more.

About 5 minutes before the allotted cooking time is up, combine a tablespoon of water with 2 tablespoons of sugar, and heat until caramelized to a golden color in a small saucepan. Stir 3 tablespoons of sauce from the fish skillet into the caramel.

Remove the steak to a heated platter.

Stir the sugar-sauce mixture into the sauce remaining in the skillet. Pour this over the fish. I garnished my presentation with chopped scallion and quartered limes. Serve with rice and a vegetable, and wow! It is a treat! My guests (guinea pigs) were delighted.

Nuoc mam, or fermented fish sauce, is perhaps the only thing of value we Americans gained from our unfortunate adventures in Viet Nam, except for modesty. This sauce is available in most large supermarkets and in all oriental groceries. Get some!

I am going to try this method with salmon steaks and striped bass steaks, and if I get a gorilla blue, I will try its steaks, too; so should you. I may try cutting the cooking time in half. I am excited by the possibilities. I'll bet it would be a great way to prepare big scup, whole.

My friend Seth Carey called the other night to tell me he had netted a large eel in a local stream while collecting alewives for bass bait. He wanted to know how to clean it and prepare it for the table. Eels are considered delicacies in much of the world but are usually ignored or abhorred by most Americans.

Seth brought over the eel, and I skinned and gutted it for him and advised him to cut it into no more than 3-inch lengths before cooking it because they writhe in the pan. This can be alarming for a neophyte fish cook or one of mystical bent.

Eel is cooked for a longer time than most fish. This long cooking releases excess oil and does not cause the flesh to shred as it does in most fish. In the following recipe the eel is cooked like fried chicken.

BREADED, FRIED EEL

1/2 lb. eel per person (big eaters will eat a whole pound)
Breading for fried chicken
Enough oil to cover skillet bottom to 1/4 inch
1/2 cup milk
1 egg
Lemon and parsley

Beat the milk and egg together. Dip the eel sections in this mixture and then in breading mix. (Shake and Bake can be used; I like to use equal amounts of white and corn flour, salt, pepper and a little cayenne, but use any breading you like.) Set the pieces aside to dry slightly.

Heat the oil over a medium-high flame, add the eel pieces and sauté gently on every side until uniformly brown and crispy. This should take about 30 minutes. Drain the pieces on paper bags or paper towels, and keep them warm in a 200-degree oven until all your eel is cooked.

Serve the eel with quartered lemons and tartar sauce. A parsley garnish is nice; a fried parsley garnish is a treat. Just toss some whole parsley stems in the hot oil in which you cooked the eels. They will, if dry, fry crisp almost instantly without changing much in appearance. Try it!

QUICK TARTAR SAUCE

1/2 cup mayonnaise
1 TBS lemon juice
2 squirts Tabasco (or a pinch of cayenne)
1 TBS sweet pickle relish
1 scallion, chopped finely
1/4 tsp. sugar

Mix them all together and you have quick tartar sauce. It's not bad – not great, but not bad.

Another recipe for breaking my own rule of brevity in fish cooking is for squid stew, a Portuguese delight, which brews for hours. My rule for cooking squid is under a minute at high heat, or over an hour at low heat.

SQUID STEW

3 dozen squid with tentacles
Potatoes, diced, equal in volume to the squid
1 quart red wine (cheap)
1 quart fish stock or water
(1) 28-oz. can tomatoes, squeezed
1 small can tomato paste
1 onion, chopped
6 cloves garlic, minced
3 TBS olive oil
2 TBS Worcestershire Sauce
1 pinch allspice
1 pinch cumin (I use 1 tsp.)
Salt to taste (I use a tsp. of sugar also)
Enough powdered cayenne or Tabasco
 to make it hot, hot, hot

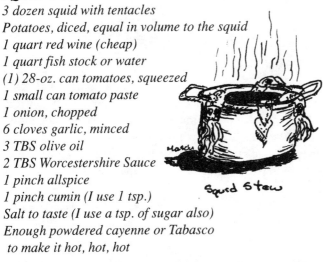
Squid Stew

Sauté the onion and garlic in the olive oil. Put everything but the squid into the pot with the sautéed onion and garlic, and simmer for 1 hour. Then add the squid meat (cut in rings); raise the heat to a boil, then lower the heat to a simmer and cook for 1, 2, 3, 4 or 5 hours, according to the amount of time you have on your hands. Stir it now and then, adding more liquid if necessary. Serve this with crusty bread and a good salad and you need nothing else . . . maybe a glass of wine.

There, three exceptions to my brevity rules. Rules need to be broken sometimes, so try them. Cook some seafood you long for –for a long time – and you will long no more for a while. I promise!

Remember the Red, White and Blue!

I try to come up with something amusing to include with my recipes, if not amusing, at least clever. At least I think they are vaguely amusing or clever, but just now I've been feeling dull, stumped, uninspired.

Independence Day is approaching, the Fourth of July, time to wave the flag and "remember the red, white and blue." So how about red and white clam sauces and a couple of bluefish recipes? The sauce is from the kitchen and the blues are on the grill. The bluefish are here, the water and air are warm enough for clamming, and the evenings are warm enough for cooking and eating outdoors. This idea may not be all that clever, but the dishes will be delicious! I promise! We may even cheat a little in the interests of convenience and speed for preparing these meals in summer.

EASY RED CLAM SAUCE
(for 4)

*2 cups of chopped clams or quahogs
(even canned clams)*
1 quart prepared marinara sauce
1/2 cup white wine (optional)
Parsley and lemon

Steam clams or quahogs, and chop; a food processor is the best way to go. Warm the prepared sauce to simmering, add the optional wine if you wish, and the clams. Simmer together and serve over a pound of cooked pasta. I like linguine with clam sauces. Garnish with parsley and lemon. Offer crushed red pepper on the side. I like Parmesan cheese with this, thus losing my gourmet classification – so what! Try it – a crusty bread, a salad and a glass of wine . . . ah, summer.

EASIER WHITE CLAM SAUCE
(for 4)

*2 cups of clam meats, chopped (canned will be good; fresh
will be much better), with their juice*
3 TBS olive oil
3 TBS butter
3 cloves garlic, chopped
1 tsp. oregano
1 TBS parsley, chopped
Black pepper
A pinch of crushed red pepper
1 lb. thin spaghetti or linguine

Warm the olive oil and butter, add the chopped garlic, and sauté it gently until it is soft and just beginning to brown. Add the clams, their juice, the hot pepper, and simmer for 5 minutes. Cook the spaghetti al dente, drain, and put in a warm platter or bowl; pour the sauce over the pasta, and add parsley. Stir the whole works thoroughly; serve with black pepper on the side. I also like grated Parmesan with this – lowering my gourmet qualifications even further. Crusty bread is a necessity with this to sop up any possible juices.

There are many variations that can be made on these simple clam sauces that may improve them, but they take a lot of effort for only a little improvement. It is like improving your golf game after becoming competent. The effort is worthwhile, but let's save it for autumn.

For our third patriotic color, let's try the simplest bluefish broiling method I know of, short of throwing a whole fish in a fire.

SIMPLE BROILED BLUE FILLET
1/2 lb. bluefish fillet per person (skin on)
Enough bottled Italian salad dressing to coat fish on both sides
Parsley and lemon wedges

Dip fillets in salad dressing; grill about 3 minutes on each side, about 4 inches above hot coals. Serve with lemon. What could be easier?

I like to slip a spatula under the fillets about every 45 seconds to prevent them from sticking to the grill. I usually do the skin side last. If you have one, use a broiling cage, a fine utensil.

This recipe is also good with striped bass. One must be more careful not to overcook bass, which, being less oily than bluefish, dries out more quickly.

There are many simple things one may do with simple broiled fillets. They may be rubbed with olive oil, garlic, and salt and pepper and served on top of, yes directly, a mixed green salad dressed with a sharp vinaigrette. This is very nice!

The fillets may be rubbed with oil and spices of your choice. You might try chili powder and oil, broiled and served over rice with heated salsa; or curry powder and oil, grilled and served in a curry sauce, with rice and chutney on the side. The possibilities are endless! Grilled fish chopped and added to prepared tomato sauce makes a fine, quick sauce for pasta. This may be sacrilege, but I sometimes deliberately (O.K., sometimes accidentally) overcook grilled fillets. I then salt them too heavily and eat them with some sort of dipping sauce like cocktail sauce or even, God forbid, ketchup laced with Tabasco. Delicious! Great with cold beer! Gourmets be damned!

Now for a more exotic recipe, but one that is made with easily available ingredients. This recipe can be used with bass, bluefish or bonito. Bonito steaks should soon be available, if we are lucky. In the meantime, try this with striped bass or blue fillets.

FILLETS WITH CHINESE SOY MARINADE
(for 4)
2 lbs. fish fillets (skin on) or steaks
1/4 cup soy sauce
2 TBS cheap dry sherry
2 TBS white vinegar
1-inch piece of fresh ginger root, sliced thin
1 TBS garlic, chopped
1 tsp. cornstarch dissolved in 1 TBS water
Sprigs of cilantro, optional garnish
Toasted sesame seeds, optional garnish

Mix the soy, sherry, vinegar, ginger and garlic. Marinate the fish in this mixture for at least 1/2 hour at room temperature or up to 6 hours in the refrigerator.

Remove the fish from the marinade and strain. Put the strained marinade liquid into a small saucepan and heat to boiling; stir in dissolved cornstarch mixture and remove from heat. The sauce should have thickened and become opaque. Now broil the fish over hot coals for 2 to 3 minutes per side, basting frequently with sauce during the final minutes. Garnish and serve.

Serve this wonder with rice and stir-fried vegetables and the remaining marinade on the side, and you and your guests will be more than pleased.

Remember you will be happier if you leave the skin on when you broil fillets. They hold together better. Happy Summer!

Was Blackened Bluefish Caused By Contact With Mussels Marinara?

I have recently been privileged to have some very simple but absolutely delicious, nearly exquisite seafood dishes involving locally available and often abundant shellfish. The first was a simple white clam sauce for pasta, the second was a red sauce for pasta that in this case was adorned with newly caught, never-frozen squid. I feel I owe it to you to try to provide recipes to prepare these fine dishes.

The first, the clam sauce, was served by my friend Vickie Merrick of Woods Hole. She lived in Italy for more than a decade before returning with two fine children and many nearly equally fine recipes. She told me that upon returning, she thought at first that none of our clams could possibly match the tiny, delicious butter clams of Italy. She has since changed her mind and a part of my life with this simple dish.

She left this message on my answering machine after I asked for a recipe:

"Let's see. Sauté some garlic, plenty of that, and some red pepper, flaked or whole in plenty of olive oil. Throw the clams in there and let them do their thing [cooking and opening must be 'their thing']. Then, just toward the end, throw in some parsley, and plenty of that, too! Oh, no. I forgot: Throw in a half glass of white wine with the clams. This is optional, but I think it adds."

Don't you love recipes like that? Here is my interpretation of Vickie's "recipe":

VICKIE'S WHITE CLAM SAUCE *(for 2 to 4)*

48 (or more) smallest legal quahogs
  (or 1 cup of chopped quahogs)
5 cloves garlic, chopped
3 small hot red peppers or 1/2 tsp. red pepper flakes
5 TBS olive oil
1/2 glass (1/2 cup) white wine
1/2 cup parsley, chopped, lightly packed

Sauté the garlic gently in the olive oil over medium heat until it just begins to color. Pour in the clams (if you are using whole ones – the best way to go!). Add the white wine and simmer gently in a covered pan until all the clams are open. As the last clam opens, add the parsley, stir, and pour over a pound of cooked pasta.

I like to use linguine, cooked al denté. Serve this with crusty bread, some cracked black pepper on the side and nothing more. You will be revered. This will serve four people, but two like me could destroy it happily.

If you are using chopped clams, add them with the wine. Sauté them briefly, about 2 minutes. Add the parsley, and serve.

You could follow the same procedure using ground or chopped squid, cooking them in the olive oil, wine and garlic mixture for no more than 2 minutes before adding parsley. If you use squid, you will have to add about 1 teaspoon of salt.

The second recipe is my attempt to duplicate a dish I had in an unpretentious, small restaurant in Boston.

SQUID, PEPPER AND OLIVE MARINARA

1 lb. prepared squid (cut in rings, tentacles chopped)
1/4 cup sliced canned pepperoncini peppers (mildly hot, pale green)
1/2 cup pitted Kalamata (or other) olives, cut in quarters
1 quart of marinara sauce

You can cheat – I've done it – and use a good, even a less good, prepared marinara from the supermarket for a very good result. For a great result, you should make your own marinara. You will be prouder.

If you use ready-made sauce, merely heat it until gently bubbling, add the other three ingredients, and heat for no more than 2 minutes after the sauce has returned to a simmer. Serve over spaghetti or any pasta of your choice with additional pepper flakes on the side. Parmesan is also good with this red sauce. Warm crusty bread should accompany this as well.

BASIC MARINARA SAUCE
6 slices bacon, cut in small bits (1/4 inch)
3 onions
4 cloves garlic, chopped
1/4 cup olive oil
2 cans (No. 2 ½) good-quality tomatoes
4 anchovies
3 cloves
4 sprigs parsley
2 tsps. dried basil (1/4 cup packed, fresh)
Salt and pepper

Fry bacon until almost crisp; add the oil, garlic and onions. Sauté gently until lightly colored and soft. Do not burn the garlic! Never serve a dish in which you have burned the garlic! Start over. Sorry.

When onions are soft, add the remaining ingredients. Cook gently, stirring occasionally for about an hour. Now either strain the whole works by forcing it through a ricer, or purée it in a blender or food processor. Return this to the stove and simmer for another hour over very low heat, stirring to prevent sticking – always a good idea.

This sauce can be used as is over pasta, or it can accommodate many additional ingredients: browned Italian sausage, shrimp added 5 minutes before serving, cooked lobster meat, mussels, cooked fish, a raw fillet simmered in the sauce, or cut-up scallops barely heated through. These are all good. You could even use canned tuna. Go for it! Cook a 2-pound bass fillet whole in this sauce, cut into 4 portions as you serve it over pasta, and you will have three improved guests and will be better for it yourself. A bottle of dry white wine, a warm loaf of crusty bread, a green salad, and you can skip the wilderness. Try these simple recipes, you can only gain by doing so.

You would not go wrong by serving this marinara sauce alone on pasta, accompanied by blackened bluefish fillets.

BLACKENED BLUEFISH (for 4)
1 bottle Paul Prudhomme's Magic Seasoning Blend labeled "Blackened Redfish Magic" or make your own seasoning. Mix:
1 TBS paprika
2 ½ tsp. salt
1 tsp. onion powder
1 tsp. garlic powder
1 tsp. ground red pepper
1 ½ tsp. black pepper
1/2 tsp. thyme (dried)
1/2 tsp. oregano (dried)
1/2 lb. butter or 1/2 cup olive oil
Four 1/2-lb. bluefish fillets

Mix the seasoning ingredients. Melt the butter. Dip each fillet in melted butter; coat each buttered fillet generously with seasoning, patting it in. Set aside.

Heat heavy, preferably iron, frying pan as hot as you dare. Put fillets in hot skillet. Pour a teaspoon of butter on top of each. Cook uncovered for 2 minutes or until almost charred. Turn over and repeat on second side. Remove and serve while hot. This is a smoky, sometimes dramatic process (the oil or butter may flare up), but well worth the risk! The results are beyond delicious!

Vickie told me that some Italians thicken their clam sauce with bread crumbs. This will work like crackers crushed in clam chowder. The blackening process can be done with any fillet or fish steak. The fillets should not be thicker than 3/4 inch.

You must try these recipes!

Out Of The Water And Onto The Barbecue

Summer is here and cookout season is in full swing. In recent years more people are branching out from the usual menus of hamburgers, hot dogs, sausages, ribs and steaks by adding fish and shellfish, which can be delicious when prepared carefully on a barbecue grill.

The word barbecue itself is of American origin, derived from the Caribe Indians' name for the wooden frame they built over a fire for drying, smoking and cooking fish, the barbacoa. They used this same frame for preparing an occasional fallen enemy. I do not advocate the latter use, having been raised in the Christian persuasion, but I heartily endorse the former.

Barbecuing, or grilling, is an especially good technique for cooking the oilier, richer fishes: salmon, bluefish, mackerel and striped bass. Striped bass is the least rich of the fishes listed but contains more fat than haddock or cod, which tend to dry out and disintegrate when grilled.

Grilling is a grand method for preparing the three- to five-pound fillets one gets from striped bass that weigh between 15 and 30 pounds. For preparing fillets for grilling, I recommend scaling but not skinning the fillets. The skin will help prevent the fillets from falling apart in the cooking process, especially if you grill the meat side first.

Barbacoa

Remember, one-half pound of fillet will satisfy most guests, so the fillets from a 20-pound striper will serve 10 to 12 people. Serve this simply broiled fish with melted butter and lemon, a potato salad, a green salad or coleslaw and grilled tomatoes; you will be revered. A cold dry white wine such as an inexpensive Portuguese vinho verde would be a fine accompaniment. Mmmm!

GRILLED STRIPER FILLET FOR A DOZEN

6 lbs. of fillet
Olive oil
Herbs of your choice or a commercial seasoning mix
Salt and pepper
Parsley and lemon for presentation

Prepare your grill for cooking. Liberally salt and pepper (freshly ground is best) fillets, and rub all over with olive oil. Place on grill, meat-side down. Grill for about a minute and a half or until color is developing. Turn carefully, using two large spatulas, and cook, covered, skin-side down for 12 to 15 minutes.

Remember, these large fillets will continue to cook after being removed from the heat. Take them off when they are opaque almost all the way through to prevent overcooking. Gourmets say that if it flakes easily when still on the grill, it is overcooked. Even if it does, it will be better than good!

Remove the fillets carefully, using two spatulas, and put on a platter; garnish with parsley and lemon, and serve. Beautiful!

I was fortunate enough in my seagoing years to twice visit Portugal, where seafood is treated with great respect and care. Every evening in Lisbon, small grills are brought out on the walks in front of many private homes and most local bars in working class neighborhoods to grill small pieces of meat, sausages and especially the positively delicious sardines. These wonderful fish, each about eight inches long, are cleaned and salted overnight in coarse sea salt. Most of the salt is rubbed off the fish, and they are anointed with olive oil.

They are then unceremoniously tossed on the grill over high heat until charring barely begins; they are turned over and cooked until the second side begins to blacken. They are then placed on half of a split crusty roll long enough to accommodate the fish. You then eat the fish, holding it by the head and tail and nibbling the meat off its sides like corn on the cob. You carefully hold it over the roll so that the roll's soft center can absorb the oil and juices from the succulent fish. After eating three or four fish, so delicious in themselves, you eat the saturated half roll – wonderful! You then proceed to the other half roll and do it again. This is so ambrosial that it is almost painful for me to remember, almost like first love.

You can rarely get fresh Portuguese sardines in New England, although I have found some at Stop & Shop. They are available on certain days in fish markets in Cambridge, Fall River and New Bedford. They are flown in from Portugal. It is worth the trip.

I have found that snapper blues and tinker mackerel can be prepared in the same manner with outstanding results. Follow the directions for sardines; get some good Portuguese rolls, and go for it! The bread will not get as succulent, but this still may be the best you have tasted. I promise.

My soon-to-be son-in-law, Scott Britton, whose skill on the grill I greatly admire, recommends the following treatment for grilling large bluefish fillets and fillets (or steaks) of farm-raised salmon, or wild salmon should you be lucky enough to get some. Salmon, once a costly delicacy, has become readily available and inexpensive.

GRILLED SALMON OR BLUEFISH *(for 4)*

2 lbs. fillet of fish
Salt and pepper
Olive oil
Fresh herbs, your choice (thyme, basil, tarragon or a mixture)
Garlic or shallot
Parsley and lemon for presentation

Marinate fillet in flavored oil. Scott chops about one tablespoon of garlic or shallot and up to 1/4 cup of fresh chopped herbs (parsley, basil and thyme are good) to flavor 1/4 cup of olive oil. Marinate fish for at least 1/2 hour but no more than an hour, or it will get too soft.

Now take off excess marinade and save to anoint fish at the end of cooking time.

Place fillet on grill, meat-side down, for about 1 minute; turn over carefully with two spatulas and cook, skin-side down, without moving for 10 to 12 minutes with grill cover on. Scott often throws a couple handfuls of water-soaked hardwood chips on the coals to add a smoky flavor. About a minute before the fish is done, anoint it with the saved marinade.

Carefully remove to a platter, decorate with lemon slices and parsley, and Bob's your uncle!

Scott serves a corn salad with this, combining cooked fresh corn with chopped mango, celery, sweet red pepper and scallion, dressed with vinaigrette, and cold couscous or orzo with chopped vegetables, or orzo with pesto. Serve it with anything you want, you will not be sorry if you follow his directions – another promise.

Smaller bluefish fillets lightly coated with horse-radish-flavored mustard are grand; so is marinated squid. I think these ideas will lead to another recipe. I have heard of barbecued oysters. Hmmmm. . . .

Sardine on a roll

Roe, Roe, Roe Your . . .

I was recently asked to dinner at the home of my former mentor and still hero, and now my dear friend, Dr. Richard Backus, who is retired from the Woods Hole Oceanographic Institute, an ichthyologist of world renown, a gardener of local renown and a shark expert.

Dick has done many impressive things with the study of fish, but may have done nothing better with fish than the preparation of the perfect sautéed shad roe he served as part of a splendid dinner I was lucky enough to attend.

Dick sautéed this delicacy gently, and fairly briefly, in butter and served it with crisp bacon. It was superb! I was supposed to bring a lemon to gild this lily of a dish, but I forgot. My conscience was eased when the roe's pure flavor needed no lemon. I guess I will have to add fine roe cooking to Dick's lengthy list of accomplishments.

Phil "The Predator" Stanton, also a retired biologist, was present at this dinner. Phil sent me a fillet from his first striped bass of legal size this season, caught on May 16, which I had for dinner last night. He had to send me some because he knew I had not caught one yet, so he could be both generous and exultant at once; I thank him anyway.

Fresh shad roe is only available for a short time in the spring, though it may be available frozen throughout the year. I have never had it frozen so I will not comment on its quality. Shad roe, however, is not the only fish roe commonly eaten. The many varieties of caviar are prized almost universally, but we are speaking of more pedestrian fare here. The roe of alewives is prized on Cape Cod but also has a limited season. However, in summer, one sometimes finds gravid (full of eggs) fluke, cod, striped bass (rarely) and black sea bass. Any roe can be eaten and is prized. Dolphin (mahi-mahi) roe is precious in the Caribbean. I had yellow perch roe last winter; it was mild, but good.

I urge you to try roe and follow the advice of cook and author Mark Bittman: "As with any fish, there are two keys to a great dish: Buy it fresh (or catch it yourself) and don't overcook it!"

BACKUS'S SHAD ROE (for 1 or 2)

One pair shad roe (6 to 8 ozs.)
4 TBS butter
Salt and freshly ground pepper

Melt butter until foaming, add roe and sauté over medium heat for about 3 minutes a side until lightly browned. The roe should remain slightly soft when pressed. Sprinkle with salt and pepper, and serve.

I recommend crisp bacon served alongside. Lemon wedges are optional, but good. You can sauté the roe in bacon fat instead of butter, but butter is better.

Serve this on a white plate with asparagus and whipped potatoes. Garnish with parsley sprigs, and you have one of life's great experiences at hand – beautiful and delicious.

There are many fancier preparations you may want to try, but start here. You can use this method for any roe that you can get your hands on.

I stopped writing to call "Predator Phil," thinking he might be out on his boat, fishing. He was, with two friends; they had a 32- and a 36-inch bass in the box, caught on jigs in Woods Hole, and were heading for the Weepeckets to, as he put it, "get another."

Phil caught his first legal fish of the year on Sunday after going to church with his mother who is 89. "If I go to church with her, she comes fishing with me," he explained. Phil thinks his virtue was rewarded with this fine early bass. We all worship in our own way.

BAKED BASS FILLET WITH VEGETABLES (for 2)

1 lb. bass fillet
(1) 14 ½-ounce can tomatoes with zesty jalepeños, chopped
1/2 stalk celery, chopped
1/2 sweet red pepper, chopped
1/2 medium onion, chopped
1/4 lb. mushrooms, sliced
2 cloves garlic, minced
1/2 tsp. thyme
Salt and pepper
1/4 cup bread crumbs
2 TBS olive oil

Sauté the chopped vegetables in oil (or oil mixed with butter) until limp; add garlic when the other vegetables are half cooked or it may burn and damage the sauce.

Put vegetables and canned tomatoes in a baking dish slightly larger than the fillet. Now moisten the fillets on both sides in the sauce and lay them in the dish. Cover fillets with bread crumbs, drizzle oil on crumbs, and bake in a preheated 415-degree oven for 15 minutes, and there you have it. This recipe can be expanded to serve a crowd, 1/2 pound of fish per person.

You can use oregano instead of thyme and serve this on spaghetti without fear.

I served mine with whipped potato, lightly flavored with truffle-flavored olive oil, and barely cooked cauliflower with melted Parmesan. Splendid!

In July all of the summer treasures are available. You'll find scup, clams for digging and plenty of bluefish. Here is a hint for using big and inexpensive chowder clams, which are almost free compared to littlenecks. I open them, cut them in three pieces and fry them as you would soft-shell clams – chewy, delicious and easy to do. Serve with Tabasco-laced ketchup and tartar sauce. This is worth trying and is less trouble to do at home than soft-shells.

FRIED CHOWDER CLAM PIECES

1/2 cup all-purpose flour
1/4 cup fine cornmeal or corn flour
1 tsp. salt
1 tsp. paprika
1/4 tsp. black pepper
1/8 tsp. cayenne
12 chowder clams, cut into thirds

Coat clam pieces in flour mixture. I shake them up, a handful at a time, in a doubled plastic grocery bag. You do not have to deep-fry these, though you may. Heat about 1/2 inch of oil in a frying pan until quite hot, put in clams, separated, and fry until golden. Now, turn and do the second side, and goodness is at hand.

A Significant Chowder

··

My friend Seth is very near death from ALS, and although he has not been able to talk for some time, he can still communicate, and last week he asked me to make him a striped bass chowder as soon as I could. I am writing this in May, and the large bass are just arriving.

I have quoted Seth's recipes several times over the years and find it fitting to write of him now. I helped teach him to fish, dress a swordfish, clean a squid and open a hard clam. He was a friend of my children from infancy. He was with my son when my boy drowned in a boating mishap 25 years ago. He became a surrogate son for me when his father died 12 years ago, and we had fine times together fishing, eating and happily ragging each other.

A couple of days ago a friend of Seth's gave me a large chunk of striper fillet another friend had caught that morning, probably a 20-pound fish from the size of the fillet. I had let the word out that Seth wanted a striper chowder, and three days later the fish was there and it was caught in Woods Hole, Seth's favorite fishing spot. It could not be more appropriate.

STRIPER CHOWDER FOR SETH

2 lbs. striped bass
2 lbs. cubed potatoes
1 medium onion
4 cups fish stock or clam broth
4 to 6 ozs. salt pork
4 TBS butter
1 can unsweetened condensed milk
Whole milk as needed
2 to 4 TBS flour
Salt and pepper
1/2 tsp. thyme
4 dashes Tabasco or 1/4 tsp. cayenne
1/4 cup diced celery, optional
I could write an essay on chowder preparation, but I will try to keep this simple.

Cut the salt pork into small cubes. This is done most easily if the pork is chilled, even frozen.

Put the diced pork into a heavy-bottomed, 3-quart pot along with the butter, and slowly render the fat, no more than lightly browning the remaining cubes.

Peel and cube your potatoes and place them in another pot, and boil in clam or fish broth or both until tender but not mushy.

I used a Knorr fish bouillon cube for 2 cups of my stock and augmented it with 2 cups of frozen clam broth from 2001. It was still good.

As the potatoes are boiling, add the chopped onion to cooking pork fat, optional celery goes in now also, and sauté until the onion is transparent.

If you wish to have a fairly thick chowder, add 4 tablespoons flour to pork and onion mixture, and stir for at least 2 minutes to cook the flour. If you want a thinner chowder, reduce the amount of flour or omit it.

When the potatoes are cooked, pour them and their liquid into the pork pot all at once, and stir until the liquid is smooth.

Now put your fish on top, do not cut up the fish, cover the pot and simmer until fish is cooked through.

While the fish is cooking, stir and scrape the bottom of the pot, it must not burn. Try to keep the fish whole as you do this.

When the fish is done, add the condensed milk and whole milk, stirring until you have the consistency you want. Taste for seasoning, add some Tabasco and a large pinch of thyme, and stir, and "Bob's your uncle." It should be delicious today and delectable tomorrow.

I like to serve this in warm bowls with a dab of butter and a sprinkling of paprika, oyster crackers and sweet pickles on the side. There are few things better.

Seth will have his puréed, but it will still be the real thing. Everyone should make this at least once to have a full life.

This past week, I made a meal of which I am proud and will pass on to you.

SPAGHETTI WITH SCALLOPS, FISH AND ANCHOVY SAUCE (for 2 or 3)

1/2 lb. white fish (haddock, cod, striper, etc.)
1/2 lb. sea scallops
1/4 cup chopped flat-leaf parsley
4 cloves garlic
1/3 cup virgin olive oil
2 TBS butter
1 can anchovies or bottled equivalent
1/2 lb. thin spaghetti
Salt and pepper
Cayenne pepper, optional
6 ozs. white wine

Melt the butter in 3 tablespoons of olive oil over medium-low heat. Peel and crush the garlic, and cook in butter and oil until browned but not burned. Add the anchovies as garlic is cooking, and mash; it will dissolve in the developing sauce. Add the parsley and stir, cooking gently, now place fillets on mixture (I floured and salt and peppered them) and cook, turning once until cooked through. You can remove the garlic and chop and return it to pan or not.

While the above is simmering away, melt 1 tablespoon butter and 1 tablespoon olive oil in another sauté pan over medium-high heat. Put the sea scallops in the pan until you fear they are burning on one side, do not disturb them until this point, now turn them and caramelize the other side.

Put cooked fish and caramelized scallops on dish and keep warm in a 175- to 200-degree oven.

Pour 1/2 the white wine into each sauté pan, scrape the scallop pan to dissolve brown bits and add to sauce in larger pan.

Meanwhile, you have cooked the spaghetti and drained it. Add the spaghetti to sauce in pan, and stir to coat evenly. Serve on a platter with fish fillet on top and scallops on the side. Garnish with parsley and serve a grand dish of simple ingredients, a tossed salad and bread and some beer or white wine and my, "life is good."

I would have loved to serve this to my exuberant, lovely, fish-loving friend Seth who would agree that life is good!

Seth
a keeper

The Clam And I

I have an affinity for clams of all kinds, but particularly for quahogs of all sizes, from the smallest legal littleneck, through cherrystones, to the biggest chowders, the ones said to reach six inches in width. Any quahog larger than five inches is a trophy. I have one on my wall that measures 5 3/8 inches. I have another that's nearly as large that I am mounting. A quahog may be the only animal that can be stuffed twice – once to eat and the second time as a trophy.

STUFFED QUAHOG MASTER RECIPE

1 part (2 cups) chopped or ground quahog meat
1 part (2 cups) crumbled white bread
1 part (2 cups) mixture chopped onion, sweet pepper
   (green or red) and celery
2 TBS parsley, chopped
2 cloves garlic, chopped
Tabasco (optional)
Salt (careful) and pepper
1/2 stick of butter
1 TBS lemon juice

Mix chopped clams with crumbled bread and enough clam liquid to make a dry paste. Melt the butter, and gently sauté vegetables until onions are transparent.

Mix the whole mess together with parsley and lemon juice and a little shot of Tabasco, if you like. Fill the shells, or use half a shell. If you leave them uncovered, sprinkle them with paprika before you bake them in a 350-degree oven for 35 minutes. Serve with Tabasco and lemon and additional melted butter. This should provide 8 to 12 stuffers, depending on their size.

You can vary this recipe to your taste, changing the amounts of vegetables or adding 1/2 cup or so of chopped linguica or chourico sausage. You might use a bit of salt pork, or try cracker crumbs instead of bread crumbs. Just one caution: Don't oversalt, over-Tabasco or burn this dish. Anything else you try will not only be edible, it might also be magnificent!

When my grandchildren spend the day, we often make bread, turning it into fanciful shapes of snakes and animals. Lately the kids have been into rolling out pizzas. Yesterday we made a clam (quahog) pizza, and it was a triumph!

QUAHOG PIZZA

Two 12-inch pizza shells
18 chowder clams (cooked)
1 medium onion, chopped
2 cloves garlic, chopped
1/4 cup sweet red or green pepper, chopped
10 strips of bacon, chopped raw
8 ozs. cheese, shredded

Either make or buy your pizza shells.

Preheat your oven to 450 degrees. Put a little oil and cornmeal on your baking sheet, and pile on your ingredients, adding the cheese last. (I buy the four-cheese shredded combination made for pizza.) Bake 30 minutes or until slightly bubbly.

This stuff is terrific, both for a grand meal or cut into small squares for a fine canapé. Serve with crushed red pepper, green salad and a cold beer! "Let grandpa sleep – he needs his rest, at least till we have had our fill!" This could happen, believe me! Once again, you could vary this recipe. Four fully ripe, chopped and seeded fresh tomatoes and some fresh basil would be a good idea.

I remember the first quahog I ever found, which was also the first one I ever ate. It was a great revelation to me, as was the following dish from Mary-Jo Avellar's fine Provincetown Portuguese Cookbook.

PORTUGUESE CLAMS AND RICE

1 cup long-grain rice
1/2 cup olive oil
2 small onions, chopped
1 green pepper, chopped
4 dozen littleneck clams
4 cloves garlic, minced
3 cups whole tomatoes
1/2 tsp. saffron (I use the Sazon con Azafran package – it's cheap)
1/2 pound linquica, chopped and skinned
Salt and pepper, to taste

Steam the clams in very little water until they open; cool and discard any ones that did not open. Reserve the broth, and don't forget to strain it through a coffee filter to get the sand out. Sauté the rice in the oil till just golden brown. Add the onion and green pepper, garlic and linguica, and continue to sauté for 5 minutes. Break the tomatoes up with the back of your spoon and save the juice. Add tomatoes to the rice mixture. Cook over a low flame until the rice is soft (20 minutes). Add some of the reserved clam juice if it appears dry.

Remove the clams from their shells, keeping 8 to 10 for a garnish. Add the clams and the saffron, mix well. Serve with Portuguese bread – instant ambrosia!

If you try one or all of these recipes, you will never use a quahog for bait again, though sometimes they are just what a striper wants on a summer night. Try putting them (shucked, of course) on a circle hook on a fishfinder rig, and fish them on a sandy bottom. You will be pleasantly surprised. But I know you will be clamoring for more clam recipes.

My wife likes clam dishes even more than I do, but luckily she does not like them more than she likes ME!

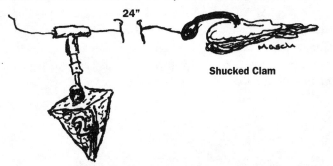

Shucked Clam

The Three Bs

No, not Bach, Beethoven and Brahms, but bass, blues and bonito, and the lowly scup – the fish of summer here on Cape Cod.

It is already August, the summer is half over and the living is easy. Bass, the first B, are harder to find than they were in June, but they are present and catchable, especially if you fish at night. They are even more catchable if you fish casting live eels at night near rocky shores. This is great fun, mysterious and exciting. Sometimes dealing with the eels is as exciting and adventurous as the fishing. "How can that be?" you ask. Try it, and you will find out.

Blues, the second B, are here and may turn up in feeding bursts almost anywhere at any time, though the best action is often at dawn and dusk. Keep a rod armed with a surface lure and ready at all times, no matter what you are fishing for. The blues will turn up sometime, so be ready.

Remember to bleed your bluefish immediately upon boating them. Ideally, you would gut them and ice them down at once, but this is usually not possible. I keep a couple of burlap bags in my boat, which I wet and store my bled bluefish in. Evaporation keeps them cool. How you handle your bluefish is more important than any recipe I can give you. Many people dislike bluefish. This is usually because the fish they have eaten were mishandled and partially spoiled before they even got to the dock. I prefer bluefish to striped bass, both as a gamefish and as a cooked dish.

Bonito, the third B, are blasting through the surface, breaking hearts and tackle with boisterous behavior. They are either jumping just out of casting range or abruptly right beside the boat. Your heart jumps into your throat and bonito fever makes even a cast impossible.

If you should be fortunate enough to hook one of these speedsters, you are in for a thrill, for they, along with their close relative the false albacore, are the fastest, strongest fish, pound for pound, that you can meet in Southern New England waters. They do differ in that the bonito is delicious and the false albacore is not. Go get them! These are the finest gamefish for local light-tackle and fly-fishers.

MARINATED BAKED STRIPED BASS *(for 4 to 6)*

2 lbs. striped bass fillet
1 cup vinaigrette (Italian salad dressing is good)
1 cup seasoned bread crumbs
2 TBS olive oil
Salt and pepper
Lemon and parsley

Marinate the bass pieces (cut about 1 inch thick) in vinaigrette for at least 2 hours (overnight is better). Preheat the oven to 400 degrees. Salt and pepper the fish in an oiled serving casserole. Cover with bread crumbs, then moisten the crumbs with olive oil. Bake for 12 to 15 minutes or until the fish flakes fairly easily. Garnish with chopped parsley and lemon wedges. Serve this simple dish with mashed potatoes, tomatoes dressed with fresh basil, oil and vinegar, and a glass of wine, and you will be loved. Delicious!

You may skip marinating the fish and still have a fine dish. You may bake the fish covered with a commercial marinara sauce and serve it over pasta. Serve this with a green salad and crusty bread and enjoy. In fact, you may use striped bass in any recipe calling for white-fleshed fish. Go for it.

WORLD'S BEST BLUEFISH RECIPE *(for 4 to 6)*
2 bluefish fillets (about 1 lb. each)
1 ½ lbs. boiling potatoes
1 TBS chopped garlic (I double this)
1/4 cup chopped parsley
Salt and pepper

Preheat the oven to 450 degrees. Slice the potatoes thinly (about 1/8 inch thick). Mix the sliced potatoes with half the olive oil, parsley and garlic. Line a 13x9-inch or larger casserole, bottom and sides, with the potatoes. Salt and pepper them. Bake for 15 minutes, then remove from the oven. Put fish fillets on top of the potatoes, and salt and pepper generously. Put remaining oil, parsley and garlic on top of the fish. Return the casserole to the oven and bake for 10 minutes. Baste fish with accumulated juices. Bake 5 minutes more. Garnish with chopped parsley and lemon wedges. Serve with a green salad, and sit back and wait for the applause.

For the third B, the beautiful bonito, we have a classic recipe from Spain, where it is highly prized.

BONITO SPANISH STYLE, CALA AUSTRIANA *(for 4 to 6)*
6 bonito steaks (about 2 lbs.), 3/4 inch thick
Salt and flour
7 TBS olive oil
1 lb. sliced onion
2 cloves chopped garlic
2 TBS chopped parsley
1 tsp. vinegar
1/2 tsp. paprika or cayenne pepper
1/2 cup chicken broth
About 1/4 cup canned red pepper strips or peeled roasted pepper

Season the steaks with coarse salt, coat with flour, and fry in hot oil until golden on both sides. Place the seared steaks in an ovenproof dish. Use the same oil (strain it if the flour has burned) to lightly brown the onion, garlic and parsley. Now add the vinegar and chicken broth, and pepper and salt to taste. Bake in a preheated 350-degree oven for 25 minutes. Garnish with the red pepper strips and serve. I would serve rice and either fresh or frozen tiny peas with this dish. Olé! You might want to fight a bull after this meal.

So much for the three Bs, and now for the lowly S. S is for scup, another summer fish. If you can't get any of the big three, don't scoff at the lowly scup. Your kids could provide them for you.

FRIED SCUP
Enough scup to feed the family, scaled and gutted, head on or off
1 cup milk
1 egg
Mixture of 1/2 flour and 1/2 cornmeal, seasoned to your taste with salt, pepper and any seasoning you like

Dip the scup in the milk and egg, beaten together. Then dredge in seasoned flour, and fry in oil until nicely browned and crisp on both sides. Serve with lemon, tartar sauce and ketchup laced with Tabasco. You won't taste a sweeter fish. This may be my favorite fish of all, but then the fish I have on hand is the one I prefer. Life is good!

August: Sun, Clams, Snails And Stuff

•••

I recently went quahogging with my wife and two of my grandchildren. We were armed with clam rakes, in three styles, two shellfish baskets, one with a life ring around it to keep it afloat and the other with a tennis ball on a 3-foot tether attached to its rim so we could find it when we abandoned it on the bottom.

Everybody got clams. I use the term "clams" for both quahogs (Mercenaria mercenaria) and steamers (Mya arenaria), the former also known as a hard clam and the latter as a soft-shell clam. All this can be confusing, but today I am talking about quahogs.

The kids soon gave up their rakes and used their feet to find and tread out the clams, which they then dove excitedly to retrieve.

Grandma is persistent and experienced and soon fills the top of her bathing suit with clams until it is distended beyond the point of embarrassing the kids, to a point of humorous grotesquerie.

I work steadily for half an hour; grandma empties her suit, returning her contours to normal, into my floating trove of clams. The kids empty their buoyed bucket into mine and we have our limit, our peck of quahogs for the week.

The tide has risen enough that the youngest must swim part of the way to the beach. We feel competent and pleased with ourselves, having met some unconscious atavistic food-gathering need. A family group, much like ours, may have had an almost identical experience here, or very near here, several thousand years ago. To me, this is a rare, delightful and satisfying notion.

On another beach-centered occasion, parts of my family group have harvested enough steamer clams for a meal, using no tools at all except their eyes to spot the clams' breathing holes and their hands to dig them. We have gathered oysters (in season), blue mussels and slipper shells (Crepidula fornicata), moon snails, conchs and periwinkles. These harvests have often been unplanned by-products of a day at the beach or a walk through the marsh, serendipitous opportunities for free feasts. If you and your family hang around the water long enough, this bounty will come to you. So once you get the stuff, how do you deal with it? Read on.

If your bonanza consists of quahogs (hard clams), I strongly suggest that you eat the ones under 3 inches wide raw, with pepper and lemon or cocktail sauce. I make the same recommendation for oysters.

To ease the opening of clams and oysters, chill them thoroughly and handle them gently. Do not scare them. These beasts can be dangerous to open, so be careful. They are worth the effort. Raw clams are perhaps the finest gourmet treat to originate on this continent. They are often exquisite!

If you gather soft-shell clams, or steamers, you will not face the difficulty of opening them, for they are not eaten raw, but you will have to purge them of the sand in their digestive tract before you can enjoyably eat them. I do this by suspending them in an onion bag, or other mesh bag that allows circulation, in the sea from a dock, a float or a boat. You may also soak them in a bucket of seawater, changing the water frequently. After six to eight hours, possibly sooner, they should be free of sand.

Many people have the mistaken notion that they can best keep lobsters, crabs, clams, snails and the like alive by submerging them in water. If the water is circulating, this is true, but if not, it is not; you will kill the creatures you are trying to keep alive, for they will soon use up all of the available oxygen and die by suffocation.

Clams and oysters can be kept for longer than two weeks in the vegetable drawer of a refrigerator. Lobsters and crabs will keep far longer alive if kept cool and moist in the air than if submerged in a bucket of water. The crabs and lobsters can get some oxygen from the air if their gills are damp; they get no oxygen from oxygen-depleted water.

When soaking steamers, some people add cornmeal to the soaking water. I do not because I prefer my clams free of soggy, raw cornmeal.

Another gourmet treat prepared unadorned, except for butter and clam broth, is now at hand.

SIMPLE STEAMED CLAMS

(for 2)

2 lbs. or 1 quart steamers (soft-shell clams)
1 cup water
4 TBS butter

Put the water in a pot that can hold the clams, cover tightly, and steam for 5 minutes after the water comes to a boil.

Melt the butter. Strain the broth and put it in a bowl. Now skin the neck of the clam, grasp it by same, dip it in broth, then in butter and eat it. My goodness, but it is good.

FANCY STEAMED CLAMS

(for 2)

2 lbs. or 1 quart steamers
1 cup dry white wine
1/2 medium onion, chopped
1 clove garlic, crushed
1/4 cup celery, chopped
1/3 cup parsley, chopped
4 black peppercorns
4 TBS butter

Put the wine in a pot with a cover that can hold the clams. Add all the ingredients but the clams, bring to a boil and simmer for 5 minutes. Add the clams and simmer for 7 minutes more, 5 minutes if boiling wildly. Drain the clams, melt the butter, strain the broth and go to it. These may even be better than the previous recipe.

You may use these same recipes for preparing small quahogs or mussels. They too will be delicious! You can add a couple of inches of chopped linguica or chourico and a chopped tomato when you simmer the wine and, suddenly, it is Portuguese style. Use your imagination and go for it, but start with the simple recipe.

The leftover broth from these recipes is wonderful for cooking rice, or as the basis of a fish soup.

The Pilgrims brought us periwinkles (Littorina littorea), the most common snail of our coast. They got to our shores clinging to the bottom of the Mayflower or boats like her. Get your kids to collect a mess of these snails and have some fun eating them.

PERIWINKLES IN TOMATO SAUCE

(for 2)

1 quart or 2 lbs. periwinkles in the shell
1 TBS olive oil
1 small onion
1 large clove garlic
1 TBS tomato paste
(1) 14-oz. can crushed tomatoes
A bit of red wine (optional)
A pinch each of thyme, oregano, cumin, basil, in any combination
Tabasco, to taste
Salt and pepper

Sauté the onions and garlic until soft; add all the other ingredients except the snails. Simmer gently for 30 minutes, adding water or red wine if it gets too thick. Add the periwinkles to the sauce, and cook 30 minutes more.

You will need toothpicks or needles to "winkle" out the flesh. Howard Mitcham, of *The Provincetown Seafood Cookbook* fame, advises to "eat them feathers and all."

You will want crusty bread to dip in the sauce, and a little wine. Life is good!

You can make a nice omelet with periwinkle meats. I will save that for another day; meanwhile, cook some periwinkles. You will not be sorry!

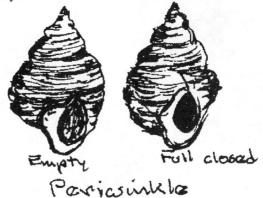

Empty   Full closed

Periwinkle

How To Cook A Hagfish, I Am Asking

In late May my "friend" Steve Boyd, a biologist, called me and asked if I wanted 50 pounds of hagfish. I could have more if I wished, for he had come into several hundred pounds of this potential "delicacy" frozen in 25-pound boxes. How often does one get an offer like that? This was probably a once-in-a-lifetime deal. I said I would accept 25 pounds but no more – not wanting too much of a "good" thing.

What is a hagfish (Myxine glutinosa)? It is a sightless primitive fish with no jaws. It is also known as a slime eel because of its tubular shape and the copious amounts of slime produced by glands on its sides that run the length of its body. The hagfish eats dead, dying and other incapacitated fish (gillnetted, trapped, hooked on longlines) by burrowing through their skins and consuming them from the inside out. I have read of fishermen netting a moving 5-foot-long object, resembling a tuna, which was a tuna skin full of writhing hagfish that had entered the tuna through a wound and consumed its flesh. Despite this seemingly gruesome practice, fish are only part of their diet; marine worms and other invertebrates are their main nourishment.

These fish were long considered a useless bycatch. A market has been found for them in Korea, where they are prized. Steve assures me that charcoal-grilled hagfish, skewered on a wooden rod, are commonly eaten at sporting events in Korea, like hot dogs at our ballparks. It seemed an interesting coincidence that hagfish should show up in my kitchen a day or two before the U.S. was to face Korea in the World Cup soccer competition. I imagine hagfish are present at those games in Korea.

My friend Steve Boyd has been hired by some fishermen who are picking up hagfish as a bycatch (something caught other than what one is mainly fishing for). He needs to help preserve the fish to get them ashore in good condition, as they are worth nearly $2 per pound. Boyd has many more hagfish than he needs for his work. I have at times been called "the man who will eat anything." I would like to amend that by saying that I will eat anything that is enjoyed by other members of my species (Homo sapiens), if properly prepared. I am most omnivorous about seafood, less offended by lobsters than scorpions. I have only found one highly prized fruit inedible in my life – the Durian.

I talked with Mr. K.H. Cho of Ipswich, who invited me to a cookout featuring hagfish. This gracious gentleman I hope will provide me with recipes.

Hagfish skins are used to make fancy leather products. Hagfish have several other interesting qualities. They can both tie themselves into knots and untie themselves. They also can sneeze to clear their nostrils of their own slime. Fascinating!

Now to some more practical considerations – children and fishing. I have taught hundreds of kids how to fish and have yet to find one who was not delighted to catch a fish. I believe we should honor our children by cooking and eating the fish they catch. This is the time of the year when they will present us with their trophies: scup, sea robins, yellow perch, sunfish, snapper blues and, if we are lucky, a black sea bass or a fluke. These are all delicious.

Most children like breaded fried fish, especially boneless pieces. We have fish fingers to thank for this. If your fish are too small to fillet, show the kids how to safely lift the meat off the bones. Many adults frighten kids with their generally unwarranted fear of choking on fish bones. Many more people are choked by steak than by fish bones. A bone is uncomfortable, but rarely fatal.

If you are cooking your kids' fish whole, you must first scale and gut them. This is best done at the shore but can be done with little mess in the kitchen by holding the fish in a plastic bag big enough to accommodate your hands as you scale it. The bag prevents the scales from flying all over the kitchen. With a bit of patience, even small fish can be filleted (look at a canned anchovy); you will find instruction in most fish cookbooks.

FRIED FISH FILLETS
Seasoned flour
Parsley
Oil or butter
Lemon

SEASONED FLOUR
1/2 cup all-purpose flour
1 tsp. salt
1/2 tsp. pepper

You can stop with the above mixture or add any of the following:
1/2 tsp. dried thyme
1/2 tsp. paprika or chili powder
1/8 tsp. cayenne
1 tsp. of a premixed seasoning combination – Creole, adobo, your choice

This much mixture will coat one pound of fillets easily. You can multiply it as many times as necessary. I do not use cayenne when cooking for children unless I know them well.

Melt a combination of butter and oil in a skillet. Heat until the butter foams. Coat the fish with seasoned flour, shake off excess, and put it in the skillet before butter browns. Cook about 2 minutes per side, until golden brown. Drain on brown paper or paper towels, and serve. Kids, and I, like tartar sauce and ketchup with fried fish.

If you want to be a bit fancier, wipe skillet, melt 2 tablespoons butter, add 1 tablespoon lemon juice and 2 tablespoons chopped parsley. Pour over fillets. Serve with additional lemon wedges. You will not be sorry!

For a heavier coating, beat an egg in a cup of milk and dip the fish in this mixture before coating with seasoned flour. You can also add 1/4 cup cornmeal to flour.

FRIED WHOLE FISH OR PAN-DRESSED
(head removed)
Use previous coating or try this:
Seasoned Fish Coating
1/2 cup all-purpose flour
1/4 cup cornmeal
1 tsp. paprika
3/4 tsp. salt
1/2 tsp. black pepper
1/8 tsp. cayenne, optional

Cook like fillets but about twice as long. You may have to lower heat to prevent coating from burning before fish is cooked through.

TARTAR SAUCE FOR KIDS (OR ME)
1 cup mayonnaise
1 TBS chopped onion (scallion better)
2 TBS sweet pickle relish
2 TBS chopped parsley
1 TBS lemon juice (or to taste)

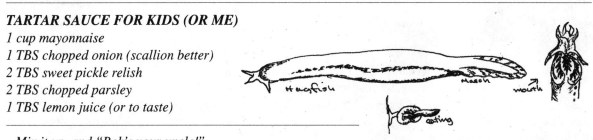

Mix it up, and "Bob's your uncle!"
Your kids will appreciate your efforts, maybe not now, but they will. Keep your kids' fishing simple.

There Is More Than One Way To Poach A Fish

Some Scotch or Irish countrymen I know would agree with that statement without even thinking of poaching as a culinary technique. Snares, nooses, gaffs and weighted treble snagging hooks would come to mind, as well as gill nets and sieves, to be used in the dark of the moon, all illegal, but the only way a working man could get a salmon. Salmon is probably the most frequently poached fish, using either definition of the word. The salmon in the rivers in most of Europe belong to the people holding the fishing rights to the rivers, usually noblemen. This has always been resented by the often-hungry poor of the countryside, so they poached. Taking salmon illegally was once punishable by death, yet poaching continued and still does today. The forbidden fruit is always the sweetest!

I am going to discuss the culinary technique of poaching, far safer than illegal poaching.

Traditionally, fresh salmon is served accompanied by new potatoes and fresh peas on the Fourth of July. This is a noble meal, indeed, simple and lovely.

Two of our more noble sport fish of summer, the striped bass and the battling bluefish, respond well to being treated in this manner. Legal striped bass are usually larger than what most people's poachers will hold, so they must either be halved, or a five-or six-pound section should be cut for poaching. A six-pound blue will fit nicely in most standard poachers. Dividing a whole fish in two, poaching and reassembling the pieces on a platter makes a fine presentation as the surgery scar can be hidden with garniture. The head should be left on for presentation. I will suggest various garnishes later, but first we must poach our fish. Poaching liquids can be as simple as salted water, any fish stock or white wine court bouillon.

WHITE WINE COURT BOUILLON

8 cups water
4 cups white wine
2 celery stalks, chopped
3 onions, chopped
4 TBS chopped parsley (stems are fine)
1/2 tsp. dried thyme
6 cracked peppercorns
1 TBS salt

Bring all ingredients to a boil and simmer gently for 1 hour. Cool and strain.

Salmon Poaching Gear

A SIMPLE COURT BOUILLON

Enough salted water to cover your fish
2 TBS pickling spices (or crab boil)
2 bay leaves
1 sliced lemon
1 TBS fresh ground pepper

Boil everything together for 15 minutes, and you are ready to poach a fish.

If your poacher does not have a removable tray to support your fish so that it will not break when lifted from the liquid, wrap the fish in linen or cheesecloth, leaving pieces long enough at the end for handles. Use these to carefully lift the cooked fish from the poacher. Have someone support the middle of the fish with a spatula as you lift to prevent fish from breaking.

POACHED SALMON, BLUEFISH OR STRIPED BASS
Fish
Poaching liquid

Clean and scale fish, leaving head on if possible. Measure thickness of fish.

Put fish in poaching vessel, and cover with poaching liquid. Bring the liquid to a boil and immediately lower the heat so that the liquid moves but does not boil. Poaching temperature is just below a slowly bubbling simmer. Now poach the fish for 10 minutes for each inch of thickness at its thickest point. Leave the fish to cool in the liquid.

Now carefully remove your fish to a large platter. Realign your pieces if you have cut a fish in two. Remove the top skin carefully; next remove the dark meat that runs down the length of the fish. This meat is edible but strong tasting; removing it makes a more attractive presentation. Next, using needle-nosed pliers or a pair of tweezers, remove any protruding bones; there should be some along the backbone. You are now ready to decorate your fish.

I suggest tucking lettuce leaves of various colors under the fish, interspersed with curly parsley. You can place quartered hard-boiled eggs around the beast; a few nasturtium flowers and leaves are also nice. A small circle of boiled egg white with the sliced end of a black olive makes a fine eye. Sliced half olives can be used to simulate scales as can unpeeled sliced cucumber. Sliced lemons make fine scales as well. Have fun and use your imagination, but do not totally hide the fish. I tend toward overkill in garnishing.

The French sometimes parboil scallions and use the limp greens to draw flower stems or outline a flowerpot and cut flowers out of tomato skins. They fill the pot outline with parboiled carrot shavings. Go for it, I say.

You should serve your beautiful and delicious poached fish with one or more sauces: egg sauce, hollandaise, cucumber, mustard and dill sauces, or a fine rémoulade made with homemade mayonnaise; all are delicious. I suggest the rémoulade. You can use prepared mayonnaise, but you've gone to all this effort, why not go all the way and make your own? Not only will you be entitled to brag, but also your sauce will make you locally famous.

I am going to give you Howard Mitcham's recipe for rémoulade sauce from The Provincetown Seafood Cookbook. If you don't have a copy, buy one.

RÉMOULADE SAUCE
1 quart homemade mayonnaise
2 cloves finely minced garlic
2 TBS chopped onion
2 TBS chopped sour pickle
2 TBS capers
3 chopped hard-cooked eggs
1 tsp. anchovy paste or chopped fillets
2 TBS freshly chopped parsley
1 tsp. paprika

Mix all together and if it is not zingy enough, add more salt and more lemon juice or vinegar to make it sharp as a razor.

MAYONNAISE FOR RÉMOULADE
4 egg yolks
1 quart olive oil
1/4 tsp. Tabasco
1 TBS powdered mustard
1/2 cup lemon juice (or vinegar)
1 tsp. salt
1 tsp. paprika

Beat the egg yolks and the flavoring elements together; continue beating and add the oil a drop at a time at first and then in a slow steady stream while continuing to beat. Do this until all the oil is absorbed. If it curdles or is too thick, it means you added the oil too quickly. Start over again, using a new egg yolk in another mixing bowl, and add the curdled mixture to it slowly while beating. The final mixture should be creamy, smooth and full-bodied.

It sounds like more work than it actually is, and if you do it, you will be proud and deservedly so. You may also be loved. You have prepared a beautiful fish and a marvelous sauce. Go for it!

Striper Days And Lovely Leftovers

I had the pleasure, just the other day, to be taken bass fishing by "Predator Phil" and his sidekick, Gary, the scourges of the striped bass of Woods Hole, top guns!

We were going to troll leadhead jigs dressed with red and white pork rinds; these had to be rigged red side up. When we got to the spindle in the middle of the hole, Phil said, "All right, let them out."

We put out 10 feet of 30-pound-test leader, the jigs attached and 90 feet of wire line, which we would jig forward and back as we trolled along. Both Gary and Phil suggested the best way to jig, I continued as before. Two minutes later, "All right," said Phil, "get ready, we're coming into the zone." Whump! Something struck my jig and hooked up. Phil was gleeful, grinning from ear to ear, proud of his prediction. I reeled in a legal-size bass on our first pass of the morning. I was impressed but not in awe; I was pleased with my fish and pleased about Phil being pleased with himself.

On the next pass Gary and I each picked up another fish. I was still jigging my way, and by noontime I had nine bass.

We went into Little Harbor to raft up with some friends and eat lunch together. Our friends had a guest from Belarus. Once part of the U.S.S.R., Belarus is inland, and here this lovely woman was on a boat for perhaps her first time with bad-smelling but friendly strangers.

After lunch Phil said let's all go for a ride and show our guest how to catch a big bass, so off we went. When we got near the "zone" Phil said, "Let them out." Gary got his line out, but I had a miserable overrun tangle in my reel. Before I could sort it out, Gary yelled, "Fish, and a good one too!" Phil had done it again. There he stood, about to burst with pride, not saying a word.

Gary's fish was almost 40 inches long, the biggest of the day, and the guests were suitably impressed, especially the lovely Russian. It was good that Gary caught the big fish of the day, for my improper jigging technique had him nine fish to one before I got tangled.

We each kept a fish to eat or to give to friends. The bass I kept yielded two 3-pound fillets, a lot of bass for two people.

I cut a 1 ½-pound fillet for my wife and me for dinner, baked it with canned tomatoes with green chili peppers and served it with boiled potatoes and petit pois, nice little frozen peas.

The next day (when bass tastes better than on the day it is caught, in my opinion) I still had 4 ½ pounds of fillet. I decided to cook it all and use it cold and in other dishes.

The easiest way to cook it would have been to poach it for about 20 minutes in simmering water or fish stock, but I wanted to bake it, which is nearly as easy.

BAKED BASS FILLETS WITH GARLIC AND HERBS

4 ½ lbs. fillet (will feed 10)
3 TBS olive oil
6 TBS chopped fresh herbs or 1 TBS dried
 (I have an herb garden so I used thyme, tarragon,
 parsley and basil – plain parsley will do.)
3 cloves garlic, crushed and minced
Salt and freshly ground pepper

Jig and Porkrind   Red side up

Preheat oven to 415 degrees. Put olive oil in a baking pan just big enough to hold the fish. Roll fillets in oil, liberally salting and peppering, sprinkle with herbs, put 1/2 the garlic under the fish, the rest on top, and bake for 10 minutes for each inch of thickness of the fillet, probably about 20 minutes for a fillet from a 16-pound bass.

You can serve this fish right away with lemon and a sauce of your choice, or let it cool and use it in other recipes like fish hash.

STRIPER HASH (for 3)

1 lb. cooked striped bass (or any fish)
1 lb. cooked potatoes, chopped
1 medium onion, minced
2 TBS red or green sweet pepper (optional)
1 TBS parsley, minced
Salt and pepper
1 TBS olive oil or butter

Put all ingredients in a frying pan over medium heat, sauté until a crust begins to form, and turn over or mix crispy bits in. This is good with poached eggs for breakfast. I like it for lunch or dinner served with applesauce.

Old Yankees would render salt pork to get the fat to sauté the potatoes, fish and onion. This makes a kind of dry chowder. Bacon also can be used. Sometimes Yankees would add a grating of nutmeg to this hash. I do, too. I also like to add hot pepper and eat it with catsup. What's right? Ketchup or catsup? Ketchup sounds more nautical.

To use up more of my baked bass, I made striper salad, like tuna salad. Kids will eat this – sometimes.

STRIPER SALAD (for 4)

1 lb. cooked striper
3 TBS or more mayonnaise
2 TBS pickle relish (or capers)
1 stalk chopped celery
1 TBS sweet onion or scallion tops

Mix everything up, taste for seasoning, and serve on soft rolls for kids. You can fancy-up this salad for a more formal lunch.

LUNCHEON COLD STRIPER SALAD (for 6)

One batch of previous recipe
4 slices bacon, fried crisp
2 cups tiny frozen peas
1/2 cup sour cream
1 TBS chopped parsley

Crumble the bacon onto salad, thaw the peas and add along with the sour cream, mix, and sprinkle with parsley before serving.

Serve this on a bed of lettuce or mesclun, garnished with tiny tomato, and you have a simple, unusual and delicious lunch.

If you have more leftover cooked striper, fish cakes are fine, and so are fish tacos.

Even a Man Can Grill

Summer is half gone, but the best is yet to come. The fish are here and will be for a while. It is time for barbecuing, or at least grilling – the only time that many men cook, even happily as they say "throw some big striped bass fillets on the grill" and often destroy them. This does not have to be. Grilling, although not one of my favorites, can be a good way to cook the catch, but it requires care, preparation and often a good sauce to mitigate the effects of overcooking. Preparation for outstanding grilling begins on the boat, especially with bluefish. They must be bled immediately upon coming aboard for the best results. Some meticulous fish lovers also bleed striped bass.

I keep handy a bucket half filled with water when I am into bluefish and bleed each one with an incision just behind the intersection of the gill plates on the ventral side of the fish. I then immediately plunge it headfirst into the bucket where it can drain without covering the boat with blood. I then ice the fish or put it in a wet burlap bag, which keeps the fish cool by evaporation.

If you are going to grill your fish, scale them and leave the skin on the fillets. A whole grilled fish makes a noble dish, the largest you can fit on the grill. Serve this on a huge platter or aluminum-foil-covered plank garnished with cucumbers and greens, along with a couple of sauces, and your fame is guaranteed!

You can even do larger fish on a gas grill by cutting the fish in half crosswise, joining the two halves together on a serving plate and disguising the joint with garnishes. For any fish recipe other than this, I prefer a charcoal grill to a gas grill. If I want to cook over gas, I can do it in the house. The gas grill adds nothing to flavor and charcoal does.

Preheat your grill for several minutes, scrub with a wire brush, and oil with an oil-soaked wad of paper towel held with a pair of tongs.

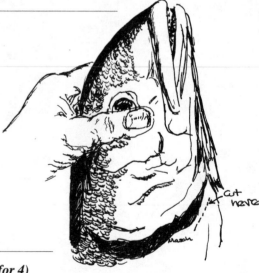

SIMPLEST GRILLED BLUEFISH FILLETS

1/2 lb. bluefish fillet per person (skin on)
Salt and pepper
Enough oil (olive or whatever type you prefer to moisten fish)
Lemon

Salt and pepper fish, brush with oil, and grill skin-side up for 2 or 3 minutes. Carefully turn over and grill second side until, and only until, the fillet is opaque at the center. Serve with lemon or sauce of your choice.

I like to serve each guest's portion on a bed of mixed green salad dressed with vinaigrette. Accompany with potato salad, and "there you are!"

FANCIER CHARCOAL-GRILLED BLUEFISH FILLETS *(for 4)*

4 ½ lbs. fillet of bluefish (I like the skin left on)
1 large clove garlic, minced
1 tsp. Dijon mustard
1/4 cup olive oil
Salt and pepper
1 ½ to 2 TBS lemon juice, to taste

Mix all ingredients except the fish in a small bowl, and whisk thoroughly. Pour over fillets in a flat dish making sure to cover both sides with the mixture. Now refrigerate for half an hour, covered. This can stay in refrigerator for up to 4 hours.

Spread a single layer of charcoal to cover the entire bottom of the grill, and light. All the charcoal should be covered with gray ash before you begin cooking. Put grill rack in place, wire brush it, and cover to preheat, about 5 minutes.

Remove the fish from the marinade and place on grill, skin-side up, and turn carefully after 3 minutes; grill until cooked through, about 3 or 4 minutes. Garnish and serve – proudly!

This rub is based on a recipe in Christopher Kimball's Best Recipe Grilling and Barbeque cookbook. It is especially good on oily fish such as bluefish, salmon and mackerel.

SIMPLE SPICE RUB FOR FISH

1½ TBS fennel seeds
1½ TBS coriander seeds
1½ TBS peppercorns
3 whole cloves garlic
2 whole star anise

Toast all of the above in a skillet over medium heat – we do not want the spices to burn. After 3 to 5 minutes, wisps of smoke will begin to appear. Remove from heat, cool, grind to powder in a coffee mill or with a mortar and pestle.

Rub a thin coating of this mixture on your fillets at least half an hour before grilling. Shake off excess rub, oil fillets, and grill as in previous recipes – the results should surprise and delight you, unusual and delicious.

You can use salmon or striped bass in all of these recipes. It is easier to overcook striped bass than bluefish, so be careful. The secret to grilling fish, and to all cooking, is paying attention.

GRILLED STRIPED BASS (for 4)

2 lbs. bass fillets, about 1 inch thick
2 TBS olive oil
1 clove crushed, minced garlic
 (optional)
Salt and pepper
Lemon wedges

Preheat clean grill, rub fillets with oil and garlic, sprinkle with salt and pepper. Put fillets on grill, slide spatula under pieces every couple of minutes to minimize sticking, turn after 5 minutes and cook about 5 minutes more until opaque in center. Serve as is with lemon wedges, or hot atop a salad. You can coarsely chop the meat and add to a simple tomato sauce and serve over pasta. It is good as is and versatile. It makes a fine fish salad cold, goes well with mayonnaise, aioli, any salsa and oriental dipping sauce.

FAKE AIOLI

1/2 cup decent mayonnaise
2 cloves of garlic
1 tsp. lemon juice or vinegar

Put garlic through press and mix into mayo, add lemon juice, and let sit an hour before eating. If it is too liquid, add a little mashed potato; if too thick, add milk, water or stock. Serve with boiled, small new potatoes, boiled carrots, a few boiled green beans and the grilled fish, and you will be admired; make your own mayonnaise aioli from scratch and you will be loved – but probably not immediately following the meal.

I think you male grillers should present and prepare these meals: "You caught them, you clean them, you cook them." Be a man and step up to the grill.

Chapter Three: Autumn

Autumn – The Rich and Beautiful Times

These are the most beautiful and delightful days of the year here on old Cape Cod. (I wonder why many people call this "old Cape Cod." The glacier formed it only 10,000 or so years ago – "new Cape Cod" would be more accurate!)

The days of September are usually sunny, crystal clear and warm, and they last until late October. The waters teem with fish: Great schools of bait, anchovies, herring young, "peanut bunker" (baby menhaden), sand eels and silversides darken the water and explode with crystalline light into the air when attacked by the schools of migrating false albacore, bonito, bluefish and the grand striped bass. Clams and mussels are full of milt and eggs ready for the last spawn of the year. The ocean's richness is on display, and we can all take part in the show.

I celebrate all the seasons with seafood and overindulge in autumn, knowing the lean months are near.

Today many people freeze fish; in the old days they salted them. I store mine mostly like a bear does, by eating them, and hope to lose the results during the winter.

Autumn is the time for fresh tomatoes, clams and corn, and general gustatory reveling, and the days grow shorter before the next cycle of life begins. Life is good.

Fish Cakes, Croquettes, Conchs, Clams And A Fritter Or Two . . .

I recently received a very pleasant and polite letter from Mr. Al Halfrey of Salem, Massachusetts, who referred to a piece I wrote in On The Water magazine. This story was about a friend of mine who quit fishing for seven years because he would not put a fish in his new car. Then, when the car was old enough, he went back to fishing. This odd fellow would rarely eat a fish unless it was in the form of a fish cake. I had included a recipe for fish cakes in this article. Mr. Halfrey stated, "I have been a fish-cake lover for over fifty years." He goes on to say, "I usually use cod or flounder in my fish cakes, but I am always open to new kinds of fish."

I enjoy hearing from someone with an open mind, and I am happy to tell Mr. Halfrey that he can make a good, even great, fish cake out of just about any edible fish he can get a hold of. Here are some suggestions, starting with a master recipe to which an infinite variety of ingredients might be added.

MASCH'S MASTER RECIPE FOR A MEMORABLE FISH CAKE

1 cup leftover cooked fish
2 cups boiled potato (or leftover mashed)
1 clove minced garlic
2 TBS chopped parsley
1/2 cup chopped onion
1 egg
Salt and pepper, to taste
Seasoned flour mixed with cornmeal to coat the cakes

Mix all ingredients by kneading by hand. (You can use a potato masher if you are squeamish, but this is a bad thing in a cook.) If the mixture seems too dry, add milk, a bit at a time, until you have a workable mess to form into cakes, or patties. Press these in the flour and cornmeal mixture and sauté in olive oil, vegetable oil, butter, whatever, for about 5 minutes on each side. They should be a nice golden brown on both surfaces, sort of retriever-colored. Serve them with a tartar sauce. I like mine with ketchup laced with Tabasco or Thai chili sauce for chicken. This is good food!

To make these cakes Portuguese style, add 1/4 cup of finely chopped or ground linguica, 1/4 cup of chopped green pepper and a couple of minced scallions, green included. I add 1/4 teaspoon cayenne pepper to mine, and I advise you to do the same. Sauté as above.

Spanish style: Use chopped chourico instead of linguica, add a teaspoon of cumin and sauté. Olé! Serve with salsa.

The spicier fish cake mixtures are especially conducive to being made with stronger flavored fish, such as tuna (fresh), mackerel or bluefish. My advice to Mr. Halfrey – go for it! With 50 years of experience, you can't go wrong!

I got a call from my nephew "Little John" (6 feet 7 inches tall, 300 or so pounds) last week who allowed as how the recipes of mine that he has tried are "pretty good." This is praise indeed from a laconic Lutheran from farm country in Michigan. I told him what I was working on, and he urged me to include a recipe for the clam and corn fritters that I made for him once. Corn and clams have almost as great an affinity for each other as I have for each of them.

CLAM AND CORN FRITTERS

2 cups ground or finely chopped clams (quahogs)
1 small onion, minced
1 TBS parsley, minced
2 TBS celery, minced
2 beaten eggs
Milk
1 cup white flour
1 tsp. double-acting baking powder
1/2 tsp. Tabasco sauce
1/3 tsp. salt
Black pepper, to taste
1 cup fresh sweet corn, removed from cob

CONCH FRITTERS

Same as clam fritters but substitute ground conch (whelk) for clams, and seeded and chopped tomatoes for corn. These will surprise you!

Sift the dry ingredients together. Add the beaten eggs and milk to make a thick batter. Mix in all the other ingredients. Drop by tablespoonful into the hot oil, or sauté in olive oil or oil mixed with butter, and brown until golden. Turn once if sautéing. Serve with lemon or anything else you fancy. "Finest kind!" as they say in New England, or "pretty good," as Little John says in Michigan – and he knows a bit about eating well!

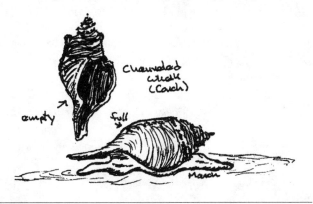

The following recipe will also surprise you, first because you can use canned fish (even I don't catch fish every time I go fishing) and secondly because there is not a better croquette!

LEFTOVER BLUEFISH CROQUETTES

Canned salmon or canned tuna can be used. This stuff is good!
1 lb. cooked bluefish fillet (or 14-ounce can salmon, or 2 small cans tuna)
1/4 cup flour
2/3 cup milk
2 TBS chopped onion
2 TBS chopped parsley
1/4 cup chopped celery
2 tsps. lemon juice
1/4 tsp. salt
Dash pepper (black)
Dash pepper (cayenne)
2/3 cup dry bread crumbs
1 beaten egg
3 TBS butter

Melt butter in a heavy-bottomed pan, add flour and cook gently, stirring the mix for 2 minutes before adding milk. Cook, stirring until bubbling, add all the other ingredients except bread crumbs and eggs, and mix thoroughly. Chill for 3 hours. Wet your hands and shape the mixture into 8 balls or cones or patties or whatever. Roll in bread crumbs, dip in mixture of beaten egg and 2 tablespoons water, roll in crumbs again and either deep-fry at 350 degrees until golden, or sauté in shallow oil on all surfaces until golden. Serve these dressed with peas in cream sauce and you will be loved!

All of these cakes, fritters and croquettes can be kept warm in a 250-degree oven for up to 45 minutes. Keep space between them and they won't lose their crispness.

So quit frittering away your time this summer playing croquet, and start cooking up some conch, clams and fish. It's a piece of cake!

A Short Tall Tale

It is not a good idea to start a story by saying, "You probably are not going to believe this, but..." So, I won't.

I once caught a large quahog (a chowder clam) on a surface plug, a popper, in fact. The clam was four inches across, definitely a keeper. It didn't fight much, but it was persistent. It did not let go. How could this be, you ask?

I was casting for blues using an Atom popper with a single treble hook on its tail. My line got tangled, at least caught, under the spool on my spinning reel. While I was undoing the hang-up, my lure sank to the bottom where one point of the treble hook settled into the gap between the shells of the unlucky clam. The clam, which had been feeding comfortably, secure in its bed, felt the hook and "clammed up," thus grasping the hook. I reeled in my line with my now-functioning reel. I felt the tug of the clam gripping my lure and tugged back. The tug wrenched the clam from the bottom and I reeled it in. I was surprised, puzzled and pleased. I ate the clam, but I saved the shells and the lure for mounting. They sit on my desk, testimony to the veracity of this tale.

No matter how you get your clams, I guarantee you will enjoy them in any of the following recipes!

Just two days ago I was expecting six people for dinner and learned late in the day that there would be nine or ten. I was making white clam sauce for serving over spaghetti. I had used all my clams and felt I didn't have quite enough sauce. To extend the sauce I added an equal volume of chopped mushrooms to the ground clams I had and then finished the sauce. It was a great success.

WHITE CLAM SAUCE WITH MUSHROOMS (for 10)

1 gallon of unshelled clams
3 cups dry white wine
1 large onion, chopped
1/2 stalk celery, chopped
1 carrot, sliced
1/2 cup olive oil
1/4 cup butter
6 cloves garlic
3/4 cup parsley (Italian is best), chopped
1/4 cup basil, chopped (or 2 tsps. dried)
Salt and pepper
Tabasco
10 ounces to 1 pound mushrooms, chopped,
4 TBS flour (optional)

Put the wine, onion, celery, carrot, some peppercorns, a sprig of parsley and a squashed clove of garlic in a covered kettle that is big enough to hold the clams. Bring the wine and vegetables to a boil, then reduce the heat to a simmer to cool gently for 10 minutes. Put the clams into the pot with the simmering sauce, cover, increase the heat and boil until the clams open. Do the clams in batches if you don't have a kettle large enough to cook them all at once. Save the broth between batches to use for cooking the additional clams.

Drain the clams and set them aside to cool. Save the clam broth. I use a food processor to chop the clams, mushrooms and parsley.

Melt the butter in the olive oil in a pot big enough to hold all the sauce ingredients. Lightly brown the chopped garlic in the oil and butter. Now add the chopped mushrooms, chopped parsley and basil, and sauté for a couple of minutes. At this point I stir in the flour and cook it, stirring for at least 2 minutes before adding the clam broth to the pan. This makes a thicker sauce, which I like.

Now add 3 cups of clam broth to the pan and stir. Add the chopped clams, a dash of Tabasco and black pepper. You probably won't need any salt. This is enough sauce for up to 3 pounds of pasta. I use 2 ½ pounds for 10 people.

Serve this with grated Parmesan. A green salad, some crusty bread and a crisp, dry white wine will complete this feast and increase your renown.

The following recipe, based on one by the immortal James Beard, is good. I think many of you will try it and find it good and simple to make. I hope this will inspire you to make the first dish, which is much better.

QUICK CLAM SAUCE

(2) 7-ounce cans clams
3 cloves garlic, chopped
1/3 cup of olive oil
1/2 cup parsley, chopped
Grated Parmesan or Romano cheese

Sauté the garlic gently in 1/4 cup of the olive oil until lightly browned. Add the remaining oil, the clam juice and the parsley, and bring to a boil. Add the clam meats and heat through. Pour this over a pound of cooked pasta and serve with grated cheese. I like crushed red pepper to ignite mine. This is not great, but it sure is good – far better than no clam sauce!

I have always thought it was odd to serve fried clams in a hot-dog roll, but then again, I love a clamburger on a hamburger roll – go figure!

---

1 pint clam meats, ground
1 ½ cups flour
1 tsp. baking powder
1 ½ tsp. salt
2 eggs, beaten
3 TBS melted butter or margarine
Tabasco, to taste
3/4 cup milk

clamburger

Combine the eggs, milk and butter. Add the salt and Tabasco, and finally the clams. Mix this thoroughly to a consistency that allows you to form patties. You may have to add flour or bread crumbs. Fry these patties in oil until brown on both sides and heated through. Serve on buns with tartar sauce. I like Tabasco and ketchup on mine. These are good and allow you to offer an option for vegetarians at cookouts.

Remember to serve a few small clams on the half shell with lemon and freshly ground pepper. You and your guests will agree with me in saying "life is good!"

Codfish Cheeks, Quebec, Culture And County Clare

I have been away, out of the country. Pursuing the Atlantic salmon (Salmo salar), king of the anadromous fish, and culture, I found both but caught none of the former and little of the latter. The salmon were sought on the Gaspé Peninsula of Quebec and in Ireland. The culture was sought in Provence. All three are places of surpassing beauty, a contrast between near wilderness and old, civilized landscapes.

I pursued salmon with flies for the last week of the catch-and-release season in June to no avail, but had a grand time. I tailed two fish for a friend and saw others. One member of our group took a 30-pound fish, the fish of a lifetime. We ate no salmon because of the season. I have caught the salmon bug and will go again next year, "God willing," as the Irish say.

I had an entrée in a Gaspé restaurant that I have not seen on a menu in the U.S. for many years: codfish tongues fried in batter. I ate them a year ago and again this year. One cannot pass up an opportunity to eat something that was once commonplace but has become exotic. In the U.S. cod cheeks were usually sold as tongues and cheeks. They were listed on the menu of Cookies Tap (alas, now gone), a bar and restaurant in Provincetown 30 years ago. They were delicious and still are.

Here is a recipe for preparing them from Mary Luiz Cook's Traditional Portuguese Recipes from Provincetown.

FISH CHEEKS AND TONGUES (for 2)
1 lb. cheeks and tongues (cod, bass, bluefish)
2 eggs, beaten in one cup water
Flour seasoned with salt, pepper and paprika

Place the seasoned flour in a plastic bag. Dip the fish into the egg mixture, then into the bag of flour. Fry the pieces in hot oil and drain them on paper towels.

Luiz Cook writes, and I agree, that small chunks of swordfish cooked this way are especially delicious. You can sometimes find inexpensive swordfish chunks for sale in supermarkets. Get some and fry them up – you will celebrate. I urge you to try this method with other fish (striped bass, cod, haddock) cut into sea-scallop-size chunks and fried.

Only three days after I returned from Quebec, I left for the south of France, Provence and the Luberon Valley, with my wife and a group of painters from Cape Cod. They would spend two weeks and I would spend one in pursuit of culture, before heading for the lakes and rivers of Ireland to visit my friend Barrie Cooke, a noted painter and an avid salmon-fishing nut.

Upon arrival I found that Barrie had caught a 3 3/4-pound brown trout the night before in Lough Arrow, visible from his house, and a fine salmon a couple of days earlier. So even if my salmon curse came with me, we would have plenty of fish to eat during my stay, including wild salmon, the first in many years. We had grilled salmon steaks and the best poached salmon I have ever eaten, from the 4-pound tail section of the grand fish. This recipe will work very well with the tail section of a striped bass. This is a simple preparation.

POACHED (BOILED) SALMON OR STRIPED BASS (for 6 to 8)
Enough water to cover fish piece
3- or 4-pound section of salmon or bass, skin on
1 medium onion, sliced
1 stalk celery, sliced
1 handful of parsley (3 or 4 stalks)
3 TBS salt
4 peppercorns

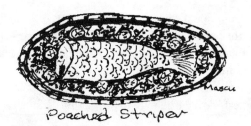

Poached Striper

Bring all the ingredients but the fish to a boil, turn down to a simmer, and cook for 10 minutes. Allow this to cool to room temperature, and add the fish. Bring this to a boil over medium heat, and turn it off. Now ignore the fish until the whole works has returned to room temperature, and put the whole works in the refrigerator until serving time.

Skin the fish and serve the whole chunk on a bed of lettuce or parsley, garnished with cucumber slices, lemon pieces and nasturtium blossoms – beautiful!

Serve with the following simple sauces.

MUSTARD SAUCE

1/2 cup mayonnaise
1/2 cup plain yogurt
1 TBS Colman's dry mustard or
  1/4 cup prepared mustard
1 TBS sugar

Mix all the ingredients and adjust the sugar and mustard amounts to suit your taste.

HORSERADISH SAUCE

1 cup mayonnaise
1 TBS or more of horseradish

Mix and serve – that's it – you will be delighted. Plain mayo is not bad either.

This simple preparation of wild salmon is the best I have ever tasted. Hats off to Barrie Cooke, salmon king!

If I were poaching farm-raised salmon, as almost all available to us is, I would use half white wine and half water in the poaching liquid and possibly strengthen this broth with a cube or two of fish bouillon, available from the Knorr company.

I had smoked salmon in both Quebec and Ireland; in both cases it was made from wild salmon and could not be matched. In France, everything else, culinarily speaking, was superior in Provence to either Quebec or Ireland.

Our smoked, farm-raised salmon is often very good but does not compare with the wild product. I think well-smoked bluefish is as good or better than most domestic smoked salmon and one heck of a lot cheaper, especially if you smoke it yourself. So buy some smoked bluefish and try these recipes; they're easy to make and good!

SMOKED BLUEFISH DIP (for 4 to 6)

1 cup sour cream
1 TBS horseradish
1 minced clove of garlic
1 TBS chili sauce
1 TBS minced parsley
1/2 cup mashed, smoked bluefish
Salt and pepper

Mix it all up, let it sit for an hour, and serve with tortilla chips, potato chips, crackers or whatever. You will not be sorry.

Salmon

SMOKED BLUEFISH PÂTÉ
(for 4 to 6)

1/2 cup cream cheese
1/2 cup smoked bluefish
1 grated medium onion
Salt and pepper

Mash this together and eat it on dry toast or crackers. Wow!

Smoked bluefish, served plainly, garnished with lemon and if you want to get fancy, a few capers, is not to be sneezed at either.

The bluefish and bass are here! Let's eat them!

The Ordinary And The Esoteric Super Sauces!

Here is an update on my adventures with the culinary possibilities for the somewhat repulsive hagfish: Shortly after submitting a column on the subject, I called in my hagfish story to our local National Public Radio listener line, where one can submit stories for possible broadcast on the Cape and Islands NPR stations, WCAI 90.1 and WNAN 91.1, a local service of WGBH Radio. They played my recording on the air where it was heard by Neil Conan and his wife, Liane Hanson, both of whom are hosts on nationwide NPR programs. They were in town for a lecture to help promote our local stations. Neil Conan was interested in trying some hagfish.

I agreed, without any previous experience, to prepare and grill some at a cookout given in their honor. I was a bit daunted by this prospect. I considered the advice I received from Mr. Cho, a Korean exporter of hagfish. The fish had to be skinned and eviscerated, grilled over charcoal and served with a highly flavored sauce. He gave me no details. I searched my cookbooks and found a sauce recommended for grilled fish in the Korean section of The Complete Asian Cookbook, *by Charmaine Solomon. I recommend this sauce for any grilled fish. My wife says you could do shoelaces with it and be successful.*

KOREAN FISH SAUCE *(for 6 – enough for six small whole fish or six 1/3-pound fillets)*

4 tsp. sugar
6 TBS soy sauce
6 TBS toasted, crushed sesame seeds (or tahini)
2 TBS dark sesame oil
2 cloves garlic, crushed or pressed
1 TBS ginger, freshly grated
1 tsp. hot chili sauce, or Tabasco, or crushed red pepper

I toast the sesame seeds for about a minute in a preheated pan or wok, or until a seed pops. I then crush them with a mortar and pestle, along with the garlic and ginger. Add the rest of the ingredients and, presto – you have an unusual and absolutely delicious sauce for fried or grilled fish. Make this as spicy hot as you can enjoy, or serve hot sauce on the side for your meeker guests. This sauce could make you locally famous. Try it; you will not regret it.

Well, I had the sauce, now I had to deal with a 25-pound block of solidly frozen hagfish. This was no small task. I hoped I could break off enough for my needs by bashing the block with a wood-splitting maul. This proved to be unsuccessful. I did not want to thaw the whole works, so I resorted to my 30-inch bow saw that I use to cut fireplace wood and sawed off an 8-pound chunk, which I thawed, hoping to find enough intact fish to meet the needs of the guests. This entire process was a mess, to say the least, but it worked. I finally had a dozen 20-inch, thumb-thick, slippery, eel-like entire fish, which I took to the cookout, where I would demonstrate how to skin and clean them – I hoped.

My skinning technique worked. The process is the same as skinning our local eels: Slice the skin all around behind the head, grasp the skin with a pair of pliers, grasp the head securely and pull off the skin. It turns inside out, leaving a slick length of meat. Scrape off the viscera and you are ready.

I then coated the fish with sauce and put one on the grill, where, like an eel, it writhed, to the consternation of the observers, before cooking quietly. I cut the remaining fish into 2-inch pieces, which eliminated the writhing, and grilled them for several minutes. These fish have no real bones but do have a cartilaginous backbone, which you eat, that takes a while to cook. I served the grilled pieces with additional sauce. Many of the guests sampled the dish; only a few (just 3 of 14) were enthusiastic. My wife said it reminded her of

---

squid in consistency. The sauce was admired by one and all. We also had grilled salmon – good with the sauce, good without it, too.

I somehow doubt that many of you will prepare hagfish, but I hope you will make the sauce and use it with a more familiar fish. You will not be sorry.

My position at the top of our family's epicurean pyramid has been threatened this past year by my number three stepdaughter's delivery of a new life partner into our midst.

This man, Scott Britton, is a very fine cook! I, surprisingly, have found little to criticize in any dish he has prepared that I have tasted. The fact that I cannot find a fault is reason enough to complain, my complaint being that my eminence is being threatened. Scott is particularly good with grilled fish and has given me one very valuable hint to share with you. When you first put an oiled fillet on a preheated grill, do not touch, move or try to turn it for at least 20 seconds. Now, with a modicum of care, it should turn over easily without sticking or pulling apart. This simple trick makes an attractive presentation easy and prevents crumbled fish messes.

I cannot recall a summer during which more striped bass were available than this one. Try this simple and very good bass recipe this autumn. It is good plain, and superb served with Mr. Cho's Korean sauce or Scott's harissa.

MARINATED GRILLED STRIPED BASS *(for 6)*

(1) 3-pound bass fillet
1 bottle Ken's or Wishbone Italian dressing
Salt and pepper
Parsley
Lemon

Marinate the fillets in enough salad dressing to just cover. A heavy plastic bag works very well or a nonreactive dish. Marinate for no more than 2 hours, or the fish will change in texture; even a half-hour is good.

Preheat the grill with charcoal on one side. Put marinated fillets meat-side down on grill, after 30 seconds turn over and grill other side for 30 seconds. Now move fillets to cool side of grill, cover and cook until done, about 10 minutes. It will flake when cooked. Serve on a platter garnished with parsley and lemon slices. Accompany with sauce of your choice or flavored melted butter. Oh my!

SCOTT'S HARISSA

I rinse and drain a jar of roasted red peppers in water (make sure they're in water only, with no vinegar). Fresh roasted peppers would be better but are loads of work to put into a food processor. Grind in a spice grinder or coffee grinder a tablespoon of coriander seeds and a tablespoon of cumin (or use ground). Put in a food processor the peppers, the coriander and cumin, salt (maybe a teaspoon), a clove or two of garlic, and hot chili pepper to taste, but at least a tablespoon or two because it should be quite hot. I've been using the Vietnamese chili sauce from Chinatown and it works fine. Dried peppers could be soaked and used, or any other chili-pepper-based hot sauce. Turn on the processor, and while it's running, drizzle in a 1/4 cup of olive oil. It should turn into a thick, spreadable, spoonable paste. That's it. Keeps well in the refrigerator.

I will try to hold my position on the family pyramid but fear that I will have to share it with the newcomer. Scott also beats me at bocce ball; I hope to threaten him there.

Try these sauces and climb your family's pyramid.

There Are Advantages To Clamming Up

Here on Cape Cod, a clam is usually a soft-shell or steamer (Mya arenaria), and the hard clam (Mercenaria mercenaria) is a quahog. There are many ways to spell quahog; I will use this spelling. Now, to make everything more complicated, a quahog of between 2 and 2 1/4 inches is a littleneck, one of 2 1/4 to 2 1/2 inches is a top neck; one of 2 1/2 to 3 inches is a cherrystone; and all larger quahogs are called chowders. All quahogs are clams, but not all clams are quahogs. Quahogs of less than 3 inches are often served raw and are one of the world's great seafood delicacies. The soft-shell clam is never eaten raw because it is both tough and sandy.

Soft-shell clams can be substituted for quahogs in any recipe, but they are so delicious merely steamed and dipped in butter that it seems almost a waste to eat them any other way. Soft-shells are more expensive than large quahogs, harder to find and dig, so I use quahogs for chowder, sauces and stuffing, and always serve soft-shells fried or steamed.

Here is the simplest steaming recipe I know of and perhaps the best.

SIMPLE STEAMED CLAMS

2 quarts (4 lbs. of soft-shell clams)
1 cup of sea water
1 stick melted butter
1 lemon, quartered

Put the clams and water in a pot that will just hold them, cover, bring to a boil, and steam until clams slip easily from their shells and the black veil slips easily off the neck. This should take about 5 minutes after the pot has filled with steam.

Serve immediately with the melted butter and a bowl of the clam broth to rinse the clams in before dipping them in the butter and eating. Kings and queens do not eat better food than this – the steamer, like the sun and sea, can be relished equally by all. Wonderful!

Steamers, if you dig your own, must be purged of sand. This process can be well begun by putting your clams in a clam basket kept submerged as you dig, or in a bucket of seawater, which you change frequently as you work. A couple of hours in clean water should purge the clams sufficiently. This water should be changed at least twice in two hours. Some people add a handful of cornmeal to the soaking water hoping to aid the purging process. I don't do this because you end up with clams full of soggy cornmeal – not what I am looking for. Another excellent way to purge clams is by suspending them from a dock in an onion bag or in a clam basket hung from a moored boat or a dock.

Many people think they can keep shellfish like clams, crabs and lobsters alive in a bucket of seawater. This is always a mistake if the shellfish are kept for more than an hour or so, for the animals quickly use up the oxygen in the storage water and asphyxiate – dead as mackerels left overnight. Shellfish can live for days in the vegetable drawer of your refrigerator. Clams and oysters survive for a couple of weeks; lobsters, crabs and steamers for two or three days.

Small quahogs and mussels can also be steamed in plain seawater and are delicious. Save the extra broth for a base for fish chowder, a stuffing moisturizer or a delicious liquid to boil rice in.

The following recipe is a Portuguese classic I first prepared in 1975 when it appeared in Howard Mitcham's Provincetown Seafood Cookbook and it was presented again in The Provincetown Portuguese Cookbook by Mary-Jo Avellar in 1997. Don't be put off by the lengthy ingredients list, it is actually quite simple to prepare. You will not be sorry if you go to the trouble (never trouble to me) to prepare this dish, especially if you make *your own tomato sauce. This is a splendid dish. Serve it with rice or crusty bread and a green salad, add a chilled vinho verde and heaven awaits. Here we go.*

AMEIJOAS NA CATAPLANA
(Portuguese Clams)
24 littlenecks in the shell
1/2 stick butter
1/4 cup diced linguica sausage
1/4 cup diced chourico sausage
2 strips crisply fried, crumbled bacon
1/4 cup chopped onion
1/4 cup chopped scallion, green part
1 clove minced garlic
1/4 cup chopped green pepper
2 TBS chopped parsley
1/4 cup sliced fresh mushrooms
1/4 cup chopped fresh tomato
1/2 cup molho tomate (tomato sauce
 – recipe follows)
1/4 cup white wine
2 cups clam or fish bouillon, or broth
 (cut clam broth with half water)
1/4 tsp. black pepper
Dash of Tabasco

Sauté the sausage in melted butter until lightly browned; add onions, scallions, green pepper, parsley, mushrooms, fresh tomato, black pepper and, finally, garlic. Sauté, stirring, until vegetables are soft. Add the white wine, and stir and scrape until all the brown bits clinging to the pan are dissolved. Now add the molho tomate and Tabasco, spread the works over the bottom of pan and top with the clams. Pour in the two cups of broth, cover and cook until clams are open. Discard any clams that do not open for they are either dead or "mudders" and could be dangerous to eat.

Remove the open clams to a bowl, and pour all but 1/2 cup of the sauce over them, discard last bit of sauce for it will hold whatever shell bits and sand may have clung to the clams, and "Bob's your uncle!"

Mitcham says this is one serving, I say it is two when served with rice, salad and bread. He would repeat this dish for each of his guests in turn. I cheat by multiplying the recipe by four and serving eight people at once. Either way this dish is grand!

MOLHO TOMATE (Portuguese tomato sauce)
1 large can pomodori pelati tomatoes
3 medium onions, slivered or chopped
1 green pepper, chopped
2 cloves garlic, finely chopped
1/2 cup parsley, chopped
1/2 cup olive oil (I use Portuguese olive oil)
1 cup red wine
1 cup water
2 TBS vinegar
1 TBS sugar
1/4 to 1/2 tsp. crushed cumin
1 pinch each of dried basil, thyme and red
 pepper flakes
Salt and freshly ground black pepper, to taste

Sauté the onion, green pepper and garlic in olive oil until soft but not brown, add the parsley. Squeeze up the tomatoes as you add them to the sautéed vegetables, add the remaining ingredients, stir and bring to a boil. Now lower the heat as much as possible, and simmer for an hour or two, stirring occasionally to prevent sticking and scorching. A "flame tamer" on your burner is helpful here to maintain a Portuguese simmer, which doesn't even bubble.

This sauce is great to have on hand to serve with fried or broiled fish, or simply over rice or pasta. It makes a great base for a seafood stew.

This whole thing is making my mouth water. Do not delay, give this recipe a try, your life will be better for it!

Cooking The Catch, Or, Scallop This!

We have by now had plenty of bass and bluefish – maybe it is time for a change. Fluke is great, bonito is fine, and false albacore is inedible to some but actually enjoyed by others. Just for variety's sake, maybe it is time for some shellfish, namely littlenecks (quahogs) between 2 and 2 ½ inches, and sea scallops; next month bay scallops, the ultimate scallop, should be available.

I cooked something recently that I want to pass on to you, a pasta dish that grew out of combining a couple of recipes, which produced a dish better than the sum of its parts.

SCALLOP, SHRIMP AND ANCHOVY SAUCE FOR SPAGHETTI *(for 2 or 3)*

1/2 lb. spaghetti or linguine
1/2 lb. sea scallops
1/2 lb. medium shrimp, shelled
3 cloves garlic, chopped
1 can anchovies
2 TBS butter
2 TBS olive oil
1/3 cup parsley (Italian is best), chopped
2 TBS fresh basil, chopped (or 1 tsp. dried)
3/4 cup white wine or chicken broth
1/4 tsp. cayenne pepper (to taste)
Salt and plenty of freshly ground black pepper
1/2 tsp. sugar (optional)

Put water on to boil for pasta. Melt butter in olive oil over medium heat, add scallops and allow one side to caramelize before turning. You can check browning progress by tilting one scallop with a fork. When this one is brown, turn all of them over to brown the second side. When the second side is browned, remove scallops and set aside. Now add shrimp to oil and butter in pan, sauté until just opaque, and remove from pan. Now add anchovies to pan and mash, then add garlic and half of parsley and basil, and sauté until garlic begins to color.

Deglaze the pan with wine, scraping all brown bits off the pan's bottom. Simmer until the alcohol is burned off.

Meanwhile, your pasta should be boiling to al dente point. Drain pasta.

Return scallops and shrimp to pan, add the drained pasta, hot pepper and optional sugar, and stir until everything is hot and pasta is well coated. Garnish with remaining parsley and basil, and serve on a platter or right from the pan.

Even though gourmets and most Italians say "no cheese with seafood," I like good Parmesan (Parmigiano-Reggiano), the real thing, with mine. Remember – it is your dinner and your kitchen.

This recipe grew out of combining white clam sauce and parsley anchovy garlic sauce. These both should be part of every shellfish cook's or seafood cook's repertoire.

Master the basics before you get creative, and then go for it. Remember – cooking is a craft that occasionally becomes an art, and as in all crafts, the basic skills must be mastered before anything good is likely to come of it.

My friend Steve Boyd, who once gave me 25 pounds of hagfish, a gift of dubious worth, is a grill man good with shellfish. He grills squid, marinated in soy sauce, lime juice, hot pepper and olive oil, briefly on both sides for a snack or entrée. He recently brought some delicious littlenecks and scallops and warmed them on a grill at a family picnic.

BOYD'S CLAMS, SCALLOPS AND CHOURICO, GRILLED *(for 3 or 4)*

1 dozen open littlenecks, save top shell
1 dozen scallops (whole bay scallops or cut sea scallops)
Enough chourico to put a slice or 1/2 tsp. ground (ground Portuguese sausage is available in supermarkets)
  on each clam and scallop
Olive oil to moisten bread crumbs
Salt and pepper
1/4 cup bread crumbs
Fresh herbs for sprinkling

Put scallop pieces in each reserved clam shell, put chourico on top, sprinkle with freshly ground pepper, add a dollop of olive-oil-moistened crumbs, and grill over coals until warmed (heated) through, or under oven broiler until brown on top. Eat with lemon or lime or whatever. Delicious, unusual and fairly easy.

Whole quahogs, 2 to 3 inches wide, can be put directly over (or even in) coals to cook. Remove them from heat as soon as they open wide, dip in melted butter, and consume. In the South, oysters are often done this way on top of a sheet of steel with a fire under it. Cold beer goes great with these, as do pork sausages and dark rye or pumpernickel bread.

I would like to try an experiment with you. I want you to take your favorite crab cake recipe and substitute chopped scallops for the crabmeat. If they are half as good as using crabmeat, which costs two to three times as much as scallops, they will be worth making. I know they are!

Here is a recipe for scallop cakes in the Masch Fashion.

MASCH'S SCALLOP CAKES *(for 4)*

1 lb. scallops, chopped finely
1 egg
6 scallions, minced
1/2 red bell pepper, minced
1/4 cup mayonnaise
1 TBS Dijon mustard (or 1 tsp. dry)
Salt and freshly ground black pepper
2 TBS or more white bread crumbs, preferably fresh, but any will do
1 cup seasoned flour for dredging
2 TBS oil and 2 TBS butter for sautéing

Mix all ingredients together except for the flour and oil. If the whole works seems too sticky, add more crumbs until you can form cakes. Cake-forming is much easier if you chill the mixture for an hour.

When you have made the cakes, dip them in seasoned flour, and fry gently in oil and butter over medium heat, about 5 minutes on a side, until nicely browned. Serve with tartar sauce and lemon quarters. Wow!

There is so much to try and so little time. You could use shrimp or leftover fish in this recipe, add a second egg and some parsley, and deep-fry for croquettes. I have had these with chicken gravy in the Bahamas, and they were more than good. Life is good, but far too short to try it all. Never turn down a chance to try something new.

I took a couple of boys, my great nephews Jake and John, fishing yesterday. This was their first time fishing in the ocean; their home is in central Michigan. We tried for scup, and they each caught a couple, one was big enough to keep. The boys were delighted, I was pleased and we all went home happy.

There was a cookout planned at my house for my grandson Sam's twenty-first birthday, so I decided to grill Great Nephew Jacob's scup, amid the sausage and hamburgers. It was a delicious morsel for the young fisherman and his "great" uncle.

JACOB'S GRILLED SCUP

2 scup per person
Salt, pepper
Olive oil for basting
Lemon

Scale and gut the scup, leaving the head on. Slash the scup to the backbone in three vertical cuts on each side. Salt and pepper liberally on both sides, baste with olive oil, and grill over medium coals for about 4 minutes on each side, and there you have it, the simplest and perhaps most delicious scup you will ever taste when drizzled with a bit of lemon juice.

I like to serve a fish prepared in this way on a slice of rustic peasant bread. The bread should be on a plate. The meat will easily lift from the backbone and ribs. When the meat is harvested from the top side, grasp the tail and lift the backbone and ribs from the flesh on the lower side. There will be many tasty bits on the top edge, but be careful of the bones. The head also has fine morsels. Your bread will have absorbed some fine juices by now; put the second fish on the bread, and repeat the demolition process you performed on the first fish – now eat the bread – magnificent!

If you serve this with grilled zucchini and grilled tomatoes that have been bathed in olive oil and liberally salted and peppered, you will more than please your guests and they will applaud you. Do it! Coleslaw and potato chips would go well with this if you had no vegetables. Grilling a bland supermarket tomato will make it not only palatable but also even good.

You could do this same simple grilling with flounder, mackerel, snapper blues or fluke. Some of these would be too big to serve on bread and should be served on a platter rimmed with parsley and garnished with lemon quarters. Beer or cold white wine are called for here, maybe some grilled sweet corn. . . . This is turning into a summer fantasy, time is getting short so get some fish and get them on the grill, and remember, charcoal is much better than gas, no matter what you are grilling.

BAKED OR GRILLED WHOLE SEA BASS OR TAUTOG WITH LEMON
(for 4)

1 whole black sea bass or tautog weighing 4 to 5 lbs.
Salt and pepper
5 bay leaves
1/2 lemon plus juice of two lemons
1/4 cup olive oil
5 cloves garlic, crushed

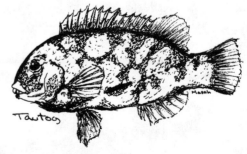

Tautog

Preheat oven to 370 degrees. Score the fish 10 times on each side, salt and pepper generously on both sides, and brush both sides with olive oil. Put lemon slices and bay leaves in alternate slits on top side of fish. Place crushed garlic on top of fish between the lemon and bay leaf slits. Drizzle with lemon juice.

If you are using an oven, place fish on baking dish and put crushed garlic close around it. Put in oven, and baste after 15 minutes, cook 15 minutes more and check for doneness. It will be opaque at the backbone when done. Remove fish from oven, and serve on a platter covered with lettuce leaves, or surround with curly parsley. Garnish with quartered lemons.

If you are using a grill to cook your fish, put charcoal on one side, and after preheating covered grill, put fish on grill on side not directly over the coals, and cook covered, basting every 15 minutes. The fish should be done and delicious after about 45 minutes. You may not believe how good this dish is – do it. What is there to lose?

Here is a recipe and technique new to me that I found in Laurent Tourondel's new cookbook, Go Fish, Fresh Ideas for American Seafood. This is a "slap your grandma"-good dish. You would want to slap her if she tried to take some of yours! Just kidding, all you grandmothers out there!

BROILED STRIPED BASS WITH ROSEMARY PARMESAN CRUST (for 6)
6 skinless striped bass fillets, 6 to 8 ounces each
1/2 cup (1 stick) unsalted butter, room temperature
1 cup bread crumbs (panko is best)
1/2 cup Parmigiano-Reggiano cheese, grated
1/4 cup onion, chopped
2 tsps. fresh rosemary, chopped
Sea salt and freshly ground black pepper
2 TBS olive oil

Preheat broiler. Stir the soft butter, bread crumbs, cheese, onion and rosemary together into a paste in a small bowl.

Heat olive oil in a large sauté pan over medium-high heat until hot but not smoking. Salt and pepper fillets lightly, cook in hot oil, turning once until opaque in center, 3 to 4 minutes a side. Transfer the fish to an oiled baking dish or cookie sheet. Now coat the fish on top side with about 1/4 inch of the bread-crumb butter mixture. This is done easiest by hand.

Put coated fish under the broiler about 4 inches from the flame, and broil until the crust is golden brown; about 3 minutes should do it.

Serve these splendid morsels on a bed of baby spinach dressed with balsamic vinaigrette. This dish could soon be on my all-time short list of great fish dishes. Your life will not be complete without trying striped bass this way, now that you have heard about it. Go for it – increase your fame, become even more lovable – you will not be sorry.

Bass, Blues, Boots, A Fluke And Beatitudes

My now deceased friend, Frank Carey, a formidable man of strong opinions, thought unkind thoughts about the culinary qualities of the heralded striped bass, claiming that they "taste like boots." I do not share this opinion, but I do not think that they are the best of fish when unadorned. I feel that bass needs a sauce or marinade or some other treatment to brighten up its blandness. I also believe that striped bass, like the Dover sole, improves in flavor after 24 to 36 hours of chilling after having been caught and cleaned. Not everyone agrees with me here, but as my friend Ben Oko, another formidable man of strong opinions, says, such controversies are "what make horse races." I do not quite understand the connection between culinary disagreements and horse racing, but I respect Ben's ideas about food, for he is an accomplished cook, particularly on a grill. He has promised to grill fresh striper for me, unadorned, that will knock my socks off. Apparently, I have to provide the bass; he will provide the grill, butter and lemons.

The bass critic Frank has a son, Seth, who has become an admirable fish cook and does not share his father's opinion about the "bootiness" of bass. He has prepared the recipe I am about to present to you on several occasions, using either bass or bluefish. The recipe is a personally altered version that Seth found in the fine book North Atlantic Seafood by Alan Davidson, The Viking Press, New York, 1979. This book should be in every serious seafood cook's library as a source of information about, and recipes for, almost every edible critter in our North Atlantic ocean.

FRESH BLUEFISH OR STRIPED BASS FLAMBÉ WITH GIN

2 pounds fillets
2 ounces butter
3 TBS onion flakes
Salt and pepper
1/2 cup gin

Oil a broiler pan that's just big enough to hold the fish, and put in the fillets. Pour half the melted butter over them, and sprinkle with onion, salt and pepper.

Preheat your oven grill. Put fish 3 inches below heat source, and let them start to brown. Meanwhile, mix gin and remaining melted butter. Remove the pan and browned fillets from the oven. Pour the gin and butter mixture on top, and ignite. You might need to ignite a teaspoon of pure gin (my wife says, "gin is pure") to ignite the gin mixture in the pan. Return the pan to the broiler for another 3 minutes or so, then turn off the broiler. Allow the fish to sit until it flakes all the way through easily. Serve with a parsley garnish and cut lemons. This is more than good!

Seth Carey used a whole stick of butter and about half a cup of chopped raw onions. This is great! Simple, yet splendid! Serve with boiled new potatoes dressed with parsley and butter, and a salad. The glory will be yours.

Seth, like Ben, is a mean hand at the grill, even though his grill is gas-powered. He serves great grilled marinated squid, followed by, or to accompany, spaghetti with grilled vegetables, olive oil, garlic, parsley and basil – with a selection of hot sauces on the side.

MARINATED GRILLED SQUID

1 pound of cleaned squid bodies (tentacles can be included)
Olive oil
Salt and pepper

Marinade

3 cloves garlic (minimum), crushed or finely chopped
1/2 cup (or more) mixed lemon and lime juice (fresh is best, but bottled works)
1/4 tsp. crushed red pepper flakes

Squid + lemon   Masch

Cut squid into strips about 1 inch by 3 inches; these dimensions are not critical. Put strips in a nonreactive bowl; pour lemon and lime juice, pepper and garlic over them. They can be cooked when they become white and opaque; they can sit overnight or an hour.

Get your grill hot, hot! Dip strips in olive oil (after draining off marinade), and flop on the grill. They will be done in 20 seconds or as soon as they are browned by the grate. You can turn them over briefly, but you will risk making them tough. They taste great even if they toughen.

Salt them and eat. Again, simple and splendid. You may need a 12-Step program to get over this experience!

Seth nearly insisted that I include the next recipe. I was reluctant for I have neither tasted it nor cooked it, but out of trust, I will present it – an odd-sounding recipe, indeed! Fluke, pure white, gently delicious, in its pristine form is considered a tabula rasa (blank slate) onto which anything may be applied without fear, anything culinarily worthwhile that is – and Gorgonzola (Italian blue cheese) is certainly worthwhile.

FLUKE AND GORGONZOLA

2 pounds fluke fillets
1/2 pound Gorgonzola (other blue cheeses will
  probably work)
Olive oil or butter to moisten

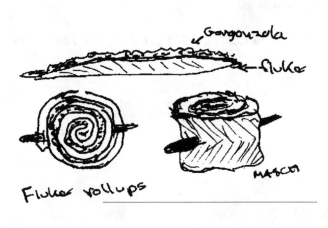

Gorgonzola
fluke

Fluke rollups   MASCH

Spread a thin layer of Gorgonzola on each fillet; roll up with cheese on the inside, and secure with a toothpick.

Now, either grill or pan-fry these rollups until the cheese is bubbly and browning and the fish is cooked through. Seth says this dish is fabulous! I have never heard him use the word before. I am going to try it; so should you.

The goodness of these dishes is guaranteed. Those you serve them to will feel blessed, and so will you for doing so. Your culinary beatitude will not be a fluke.

How Funny Can A Shellfish Be?

October is here, and it is legal to harvest our local culinary treasure, the bay scallop (Aequipecten irradians), tastiest of shellfish.

I have been trying to come up with something amusing to write about bay scallops, to no avail. There is nothing intrinsically funny about a bay scallop's life; it lives for less than two years, spawns once and dies. The fact that it dies after spawning means there is no harm in harvesting the entire post-spawn population.

The bay scallop may not be funny, but it has a couple of interesting, possibly amusing, behaviors that might be of interest to a betting man in the company of self-styled shellfish experts. For example, a bay scallop has a clean side and a dirty side. Algae and tiny creatures grow on this "top," dirty side. If you turn a bay scallop upside down (clean side up) underwater, you can command it to turn over, and it will. It knows which way is up! It may not respond to your command immediately, but it will eventually. Your audience will be impressed by your powers.

The bay scallop is unique among bivalves in that it has eyes and optic nerves that allow it to see light and motion. It is also motile, able to move. It can move voluntarily by compressing its shell, thus forcing water through its lips and scooting about, for fun or safety. But which way does it go? One would guess that if it squeezed water out between its shells that it would move backward in the direction its hinge is pointing. Not so! It moves forward, away from the hinge. It does this by forcing the expelled water out through openings between its hinge and the extremities of its wings. It can also move in the opposite direction, but not nearly so quickly or so well.

Amusing or not, the bay scallop is perhaps the most delicious shellfish when cooked properly, bar none, justly deserving its gustatory fame. The entire meat of a scallop is edible and eaten, but in North America we eat only the adductor muscle. It is delicious raw and should only be cooked briefly. It is ambrosial sautéed in butter with a hint of garlic.

BAY SCALLOPS SAUTÉED WITH BUTTER AND GARLIC (for 4)

1 lb. bay scallops
3 TBS butter
1/2 tsp. salt
1/8 tsp. pepper
1/4 tsp. paprika
1 clove garlic, minced
1 TBS parsley, minced
3 TBS fresh lemon juice

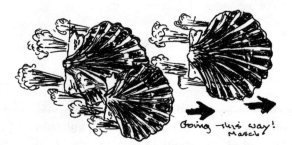

Going this way! Muscle

Melt 2 tablespoons of the butter in a large skillet; add salt, pepper, paprika and garlic. Add the scallops, and sauté over medium-high heat, stirring frequently until scallops just begin to color, about 4 minutes. Remove the scallops to a heated platter. Now melt the remaining butter in the same pan, and add the parsley and lemon juice. Heat through and pour over the scallops. Oh boy!

Serve with plain rice and tiny peas. I cannot tell you how good this is; you must taste it!

This recipe can be made with chives instead of parsley, white wine (dry) instead of lemon juice or with some toasted sesame seeds (1 tablespoon).

SAUTÉED SCALLOPS ORIENTAL
2 TBS peanut oil
1 tsp. garlic, minced
1 to 1 1/2 lbs. bay scallops
1 TBS fresh ginger, minced
3 scallions, chopped
1 TBS dry sherry
1 TBS soy sauce
1 TBS water or stock (chicken, fish or vegetable)
Salt and pepper, to taste

Heat a large skillet or wok over medium-high heat for a couple of minutes; add oil, garlic and ginger. When this becomes aromatic, add the scallops and cook, stirring occasionally for about 4 minutes or until they begin to brown, then add salt and pepper. Remove the scallops from the pan.

Deglaze the pan with sherry, soy sauce and stock or water. Add the scallions, stir, return scallops to the pan, heat while stirring, and serve over white rice. Hah!

BROILED SCALLOPS WITH LEMON
(for 6 to 8)
2 lbs. scallops
Salt and pepper, to taste
6 fresh basil leaves or 1 tsp. dried basil
2 fresh rosemary sprigs and 1/2 tsp. dried rosemary
1 thinly diced lemon
Tabasco
1/4 cup vegetable oil

Mix all the ingredients, add the scallops, and refrigerate for 2 to 6 hours.

Remove the scallops from the marinade, and put them in a dish that can be placed under the oven broiler. Broil about 2 1/2 minutes on each side, about 3 inches from the flame. Do not overcook. Serve with additional lemon, a dusting of paprika and a garnish of parsley. Life is good!

SCALLOP SEVICHE
1 lb. bay scallops (fresh or frozen)
Juice of 1/2 lime
Juice of 1/2 lemon
Juice of 1/2 orange
2 TBS cilantro, minced (parsley may be used)
2 scallions, minced (green and white parts together)
1 tsp. soy sauce (optional)

Marinate the scallops in the fruit juices and scallion mixture for 2 to 6 hours in the refrigerator, stirring occasionally. Sprinkle with cilantro and soy sauce, and serve.

This dish may be extended or beautified by adding any of the following: chopped onion, sliced olives, chopped sweet red or green pepper, or chopped peeled and seeded tomatoes –even avocado. This is a great appetizer served on a bed of lettuce and garnished with quartered limes.

The fruit juices' acidity cooks the meat by chemical action. You can use this recipe with white-fleshed fish, for example, striped bass cut into cubes. You will not regret trying this. It is easy and outstanding!

You may use sea scallops in any of these recipes if you cut them into 1/2-inch pieces.
Scallops may not be very funny, but they are culinarily outstanding, and October is the time to eat them. It is their finest hour.

Fried, Anyone?

I ate delicious fish last week, all simply prepared and all delicious: scup, snapper blues, tinker mackerel, black sea bass fillets and fluke. All were dusted with seasoned flour and pan-fried, served with mashed potatoes and tomato and basil salad. Nothing could be better, a wonderful collection of seasonal treats.

I have to admit, I like breaded, or otherwise coated, pan- or deep-fried fish better than fish cooked any other way. Having said this, I immediately think of the many other methods of preparing fish, all delicious, but less unhealthy. Low class or not, I like my fish fried and that goes for chicken, clams, scallops and shrimp, too. Among the myriad methods for preparing fish, I know that if I had to choose only one to use for the rest of my life, it would be to coat and fry them. I know it is not the healthiest way to go, but you probably won't eat fish every day, and if you fry your fish at the proper temperature and drain them well, you will leave most of the fat in the fryer.

Why am I being defensive about my love for fried seafood? Come on, let's go for it. I am going to suggest several coatings for fine frying, both dry and liquid.

October brings the World Series, so I say "batter up!"

FRYING BATTER
1 cup beer
1 ½ cups flour
1 tsp. baking powder
1/4 tsp. black pepper
1 tsp. salt
2 TBS melted butter
1/8 tsp. cayenne pepper (optional)

Mix thoroughly, but don't overstir. Let sit 1/2 hour before using.

It is best to deep-fry when using batter. Heat frying oil to 375 degrees, dip your favorite shellfish or fish in the batter, and fry.

In Maine clams are usually fried in batter; here on the Cape we usually coat ours with crumbs. Shrimp, scallops, tinker mackerel and small chunks of swordfish are all wonderful done this way. Keep your batches small and your temperature high. Serve with tartar sauce and lemon.

This batter is also good with vegetables: onion rings, zucchini slices, mushrooms and, my favorite, sliced yams. Wow!

A relatively thin coating of seasoned flour is the norm for sautéing, and heavier coatings are more common for deep-frying. There are nearly endless possibilities for coatings: cracker crumbs, matzo meal, cornmeal, cornstarch, rice flour, bread crumbs, oatmeal, corn flakes and even potato chips.

The standard sequence for breading anything is coating with flour (shaking in a bag works), dipping in milk, or milk with an egg beaten into it, and finally into the breading or breading mixture. Thickly breaded items should be allowed to dry for at least 1/2 hour before frying. This helps the breading stick to the fish. Simply dusted items should be sautéed immediately, so the flour doesn't turn to paste.

Fried foods should be served right away or blotted dry and kept warm in a single layer in a warm, not hot, oven (200 degrees is a good bet). Serve within half an hour.

SEASONED FLOUR 1
1 cup flour
1 tsp. salt
1/2 tsp. pepper
1/8 tsp. cayenne pepper (optional)
1/4 tsp. paprika

Mix and use.

SEASONED FLOUR 2
Seasoned Flour 1 plus 1 teaspoon dried herbs: thyme, oregano, rosemary – your choice.

SEASONED FLOUR 3
Seasoned Flour 1 plus 1/2 teaspoon garlic powder and 1/2 teaspoon onion powder.

SEASONED FLOUR 4
Seasoned Flour 1 mixture plus 1 tablespoon adobo seasoning (or any other prepared, dried spice you prefer). I like 1 teaspoon cumin with the adobo.

As you can see, one could come up with an infinite number of variations to the Number 1 recipe. Curry powder is good. Use your imagination and go for it.

To go from seasoned flour to breading, just add your chosen coating to Seasoned Flour recipe 1. A cup of Italian seasoned bread crumbs is good. A half cup of cornmeal will give you a crisp coating; you can even add 1/3 cup grated Parmesan or slivered or crushed nuts. The possibilities are endless. Try some!

ALMOND-FRIED TROUT (OR FLUKE) (for 4)
1/4 cup flour
1/8 tsp. pepper
1/4 tsp. salt
1 egg
3 TBS milk
1 cup cracker crumbs
1/2 cup sliced almonds
1 ½ lbs. trout fillets (or fluke)
1/4 cup vegetable oil
2 TBS butter

Blend the milk and egg. Mix the salt and pepper with the flour. Coat the fish with the flour mixture, dip in the milk-and-egg blend and then in the cracker-crumb-almond mixture.

Heat the oil and batter in a frying pan, or heat the oven to 450 degrees and heat an oiled pan for 5 minutes. Add the coated fish to the oil, either in the oven or in the pan. Cook about 5 minutes per side, turning once. Serve with lemon. Oh my, that is good!

SAUTÉED SCUP (PORGY) (for 2)
2 whole porgies (3/4 to 1 lb.)
1/4 cup milk
1/4 cup cornmeal
1/4 cup flour
2 TBS butter
2 TBS olive oil
2 TBS peeled, seeded and chopped tomato
2 TBS chopped scallions
Lemon wedges

Pat the cleaned fish dry. Dip the fish in the milk, then in the cornmeal and flour. Refrigerate for 30 minutes. Heat the oil and butter over medium heat. Sauté the fish in the heated butter and oil for about 4 minutes per side, or until crispy and golden brown. Serve topped with tomato, scallions and lemon wedges.

This elegant, simple recipe is from Dorothy Batchelder's *The Fishmonger Cookbook.*

FRIED SQUID
(for 4)
2 lbs. large whole squid
3 cups unbleached all-purpose flour
Salt and pepper, to taste
1 TBS baking soda

This recipe is from Gillian Drake's *The Cape Cod Fish and Seafood Cookbook.*

Clean and dry the squid, and cut it into rings. Mix the salt, pepper and baking soda with the flour.

Preheat oil, 2 or 3 inches, in a saucepan to 350 degrees. Toss squid pieces in flour and shake off excess. Test the oil with a piece of bread. It should turn brown quickly but not burn. Fry the squid in hot oil about 2 minutes. Do not overcook. Drain and serve immediately with tartar sauce.

Give these a try, make some of your own mixtures, and have fun!

Simple Delicious Scup Escabeche, Olé!

Fishing has provided me with many of the greatest joys of my life. I have caught some grand, large fish. I have fished with fine, interesting and occasionally amazing people. There have been frightening times, dull periods providing time for meditation and daydreams, and many grand meals. The greatest pleasures for me have come from exposing children to the joys of fishing, the excitement of the bite, the feeling of connection with another life form, and the pleasure and pride in the catch. There's joy in patience rewarded and in the total focus in the present that one has when one feels a fish on the line.

I saw this joy in the eyes of my granddaughter, Mariah Jacobs, this month when she and I finally got out on a scup fishing expedition in Woods Hole. She had been after me to go "scupping" for some time. Last year on one of these jaunts, she and her cousin, Cooper Densmore, caught three large triggerfish, which the Woods Hole Aquarium was happy to accept and display. The kids were very proud. They also caught enough scup for a fine dinner. I think she was hoping for exotic fish on this trip.

We got some squid for bait, rigged our rods for scup fishing and headed out through Woods Hole toward Hadley's Harbor where I knew there were scup – small, but still scup. On the way over we saw the boat that takes families out on educational day trips, introducing people to lobster fishing, plankton towing, bottom sampling and basic marine biology. The captain of the vessel was our friend, Francis Doohan, sea captain, raconteur and entertainer. He also usually knows where the "good" (meaning "big") scup are in local waters. We hailed him and asked his advice.

"There are plenty where you are heading, but they're little. I hear they're little. I hear there have been some good ones between cans number 6 and number 8. You've still got a half-hour of slack tide." We allowed we should "go for them."

We headed back to the Hole and dropped our lines. The tide was slack; it sometimes runs at over 4 knots where we were on the northern edge of the main channel off Penzance Point. My weight had not reached the bottom before an insistent, energetic and surprisingly strong scup inhaled my bait. The fish was 15 inches long and nearly two pounds in weight. I looked up to see Mariah struggling, her rod's butt under her arm, its tip in the water as she tried to reel in her catch. She had a double, two fish, one on each hook and each over 12 inches long and nearly a pound in weight. Captain Doohan was right, once again. During the next half-hour, Mariah landed 12 more large scup, often two at once. Her arms were tired and her cranking hand was cramped. She was relieved when I said we had had enough and that the tide was running hard enough to make it difficult for us to stay out of the channel.

As it was, we were nearly run down by a large powerboat on the wrong side of the buoys. Twice we were nearly swamped by the wakes of large sportfishermen piloted by thoughtless boors with no regard for the effect of wakes on small craft in a hazardous spot like Woods Hole. Mariah was proud and relieved that the fishing was over.

We had a cooler holding ice aboard, so our fish were in good shape when we got home, ready to be cleaned and cooked for dinner. I will get to a couple of simple and delicious recipes but first some advice on scup cleaning. Scup as large as we had on this day can be filleted and skinned.

If you are going to cook them in the round (whole) or pan-dressed (head off), you must first scale them. The sooner you scale them, the easier the scales come off. If they have dried, soak them first and then scale. I find that a clam knife is the best scaling tool. You do not

Fish Scaling Tools

need a sharp knife for scaling.

I now hold the scup upright and cut downward at an angle toward the tail through the backbone. I twist off the head and pull it from the body, thus removing almost all the viscera. I now remove the dorsal and anal fins by making shallow incisions on both sides of them, grasping them with a pair of pliers and pulling them, and the nasty sharp bones that anchor them, from the fish. You now have a pan-ready scup with only a backbone and some easily removed ribs. After these are fried, the fillets can be lifted off easily, leaving the backbone and ribs behind.

BREADED FRIED SCUP *(for 4)*

8 scup (pan-dressed)
1 cup seasoned flour
2 cups bread crumbs
1 cup milk
1 egg
Enough oil to cover pan bottom by 1/8 inch
  (I like peanut oil or olive oil)

Put the seasoned flour in a bag; shake each scup in the bag until well coated with flour. Put floured scup aside, and continue until all are floured.

Beat the egg in the cup of milk. Dip floured scup in egg-milk mixture, and then dip in bread crumbs to coat thoroughly. Preheat oil, brown scup on one side, about 4 minutes, reduce heat and brown second side, about 4 minutes more.

I like this served with sweet corn and sliced tomatoes. Do it now; the sweet summer season is ending!

When I prepare scup in this way, I try to have leftovers to make a fine Spanish dish, escabeche.

ESCABECHE *(for 4)*

Breaded, cooked fish (scup as in previous recipe, snapper
  or blues prepared the same way, or breaded fillets of any
  kind)
Vinaigrette dressing (your own or Wishbone Italian or Ken's
  Italian, both are good for this purpose)
Sliced sweet onion
Sliced green pepper

Cover the bottom of a nonreactive bowl or casserole with a thin coating of salad dressing. Lay fish on this, scatter with onions and peppers, and add enough dressing on top of fish to wet thoroughly. Refrigerate overnight. Turn fish occasionally if you think of it. The fish becomes firm and delicious. It makes a great picnic dish and is good for a couple of days if kept cold.

I urge you to try this simple treatment for leftover fish. You may find yourself frying fish just to make escabeche. Go for it, you will be better for it, and your friends will think you are a gourmet!
  "Scup is a sweet fish to catch!" says Mariah.
  "Scup is a sweet fish to eat!" says Grandpa.

Wonderful Gifts From The Sea

In the modern world with its rapid transportation and good refrigeration, most seafood products are available year-round, but at a price. Neither the quality nor the satisfaction is as good with purchased fish as with those we catch or collect ourselves. It's time to seek out the best of what's available.

In autumn we see the last of the striped bass and bluefish here in New England until next year and the first of the seasonal shellfish, bay scallops and oysters, here on Cape Cod, perhaps the best shellfish in the world. These two paragons of shellfish are in trouble as are many sea creatures, due to ever-expanding demand and pollution around the world, but they are still available here. So let us use what is left wisely, before they are gone or prohibitively expensive for most of us.

My favorite way to eat small quahogs, littlenecks and cherrystones is raw on the half shell with fresh ground pepper and lemon, or cocktail sauce, easily made yourself or purchased. I prefer to make my own so that I can add in zestiness by changing the quantities of horseradish and Tabasco to my own taste. Here is a good basic recipe that you can adjust to your own taste.

COCKTAIL SAUCE
(enough for 3 dozen clams)
1/4 cup ketchup and chili sauce
1 TBS bottled horseradish
1 tsp. lemon juice
1/8 tsp. Tabasco (or other hot sauce)

Mix all together and use immediately, or chill until ready to serve.

Raw, hard clams are wonderful! You will rarely have any opened clams left over, but if you do, there are many, many ways to use them: clam sauce for spaghetti, sautéed in butter and served on buttered toast, or cooked in olive oil until barely firm and served in a chilled salad.

COOKED HARD CLAMS VINAIGRETTE
(for 4)
1 cup cooked, small quahogs, the smaller the better
2 TBS good virgin olive oil
1 1/2 tsp. wine or apple vinegar (or lemon juice)
1/4 tsp. freshly ground pepper
1 TBS chopped sweet red or green pepper
1/8 tsp. Tabasco (or some chopped jalapeño)
1 TBS chopped scallion greens or chives

Mix everything together and chill. Serve as an appetizer, or arrange on a bed of mixed greens or mesclun and serve as a salad.

If your clams seem too large, cut them into quarter-size pieces, and proceed. The big ones make a kind of adult bubble gum without the bubbles.

You may substitute lime juice for the vinegar in the recipe and marinated scallops. This is more than good, it is great!

This same dressing is good on cooked shrimp. Some supermarkets are now selling properly cooked shrimp, not overcooked and dry. If you cook your own shrimp, be careful not to overcook them; when they are pink and opaque they are done. It is not necessary to devein shrimp; after all, we do not devein lobster tails when we eat them and they are much larger.

Another good thing to do with this vinaigrette is to use it as a marinade for large shrimp and then to grill them, ever so briefly, over charcoal until barely cooked through. You may add herbs and spices to the basic marinade and make it your own. I like to add garlic and oregano.

Sea and bay scallops are king and queen of the bivalves in my mind – almost perfect raw from the shell, good sautéed, grilled and stewed. They too should be cooked briefly, but they withstand overcooking better than most shellfish. Here is a simple and delicious recipe. A pound is enough for three diners or two eaters. I am one of the latter.

SAUTÉED SCALLOPS

1 lb. scallops
2 TBS light olive oil
2 TBS butter
1 large garlic clove, crushed
1/4 cup parsley, chopped
1/4 cup dry white wine

Dry the scallops on paper towels; they will caramelize easier if dry.

Light olive oil can stand higher temperatures without burning than virgin oils. Heat olive oil and butter in a skillet, along with the crushed (but not separated) garlic clove until the garlic is lightly browned and the butter begins to color. Remove the garlic and discard. Now add the scallops all at once, shake the pan to distribute them evenly, and do not move them again. Watch to see that the butter does not burn. If it shows signs of burning, lift the pan and lower the heat before returning the pan. When the scallops begin to color on the bottom, give the pan a good shake, and turn the scallops that do not turn on their own. Now cook until they begin to color, raising and lowering the pan as necessary. Now toss in the parsley, and remove the scallops to a warm plate. Add the wine to the hot pan, scrape the bottom and reduce slightly, pour over the scallops, and serve with lemon wedges.

These wonderful sea gifts can be served on a bed of greens or over rice. They are wonderful and will get you praise, if not love.

Most of us are looking for new ways to prepare bluefish by this time. I came up with something last night that was new for me, but given the fact that millions of people have cooked for thousands of years, it is probably not truly unique. The newest "rage" in cooking is "fusion," blending one culture's flavors with another's. Oriental and western cooking combinations are fashionable, so I came up with this.

EAST-WEST PAN-FRIED BLUEFISH

2 ½ lbs. bluefish fillets
2 tsps. hoisin sauce
2 TBS mayonnaise
2 TBS mustard
1 cup sesame seeds
Salt and pepper

Mix hoisin, mustard and mayo. Salt and pepper fillets, and paint with sauce mixture. Roll in sesame seeds, coating completely. Heat oil in skillet, and sauté fillets about 3 minutes on each side, being careful not to burn the seeds. Serve with stir-fried vegetables and rice, and your fame will grow!

Simply Elegant! Or "Ricing" To The Occasion

I recently made a simple, delicious and pretty dinner for my wife and myself: sautéed sea scallops and flavored rice, served with a cucumber salad and a tomato and basil salad. I enjoyed it completely, and I think you would, too.

FLAVORED RICE A LA "POPS" *(that's me)*

1 cup rice (I use jasmine or Uncle Ben's)
2 cups chicken stock or seafood stock
 (this can be made from cubes)
1 medium onion, chopped coarsely
1/4 sweet red or green pepper, diced
1 medium tomato, diced (optional)
2-inch piece of linguica or chourico,
 chopped (optional, but delicious)
Scallion and parsley for garnish
Hot sauce to taste
1 packet Goya Sazon with saffron or annatto
1 TBS olive oil

Sauté onion and pepper (and sausage if used) in the olive oil until onion is transparent. Now add dry rice to pan and sauté, stirring until every grain is coated with oil and somewhat transparent (about 2 minutes). Add two cups of stock and Goya Sazon, and bring to a boil. Reduce heat to very low, cover pot, and cook until rice is tender (about 12 minutes).

CARAMELIZED SCALLOPS
(for 2)

1 lb. sea scallops
2 TBS butter
2 TBS light olive oil
Salt and pepper

Heat butter and oil over medium flame until the butter stops foaming. It is okay if it begins to brown. Use a frying pan large enough to hold all of the scallops without crowding.

Add scallops to hot oil, and spread so they are not touching each other. Free them once, and only once, from the bottom of the pan with a spatula. Now cook about 2 minutes without disturbing them until they caramelize to a rich brown on the bottom, then turn each carefully, and repeat process on the other side.

Deposits of dark, gummy deliciousness will have formed in the pan. You can use these by sprinkling them on the rice for explosions of flavor, or you can deglaze the pan with a glass of white wine and pour the results over the rice.

I would serve the rice on a small, heated platter, surround the rice with browned scallops, anoint the whole works with pan juices, garnish with chopped scallion greens and parsley, possibly a lemon slice or two, and wait for the applause.

MY MOTHER'S SUMMER CUKE SALAD

2 large cucumbers, peeled
2 medium onions, sliced
2 TBS sugar
1 cup water
1/2 cup cider vinegar
Salt and pepper
1/4 to 1 tsp. hot pepper flakes

Bring water, vinegar, sugar and hot pepper to a boil, and pour over the sliced cucumbers and onions. Chill at least 2 hours before serving.

I leave a little green skin on the cukes for color. I also often add some thin slices of sweet red pepper for the same reason. I keep some of this salad in the fridge all summer for snacks or adding to sandwiches. It has been part of my entire life.

I fortunately have a large garden and a surfeit of cucumbers, tomatoes and, always, zucchini.

TOMATO AND BASIL SALAD

Slice ripe tomatoes and arrange on a platter.
Chop a handful of basil and sprinkle on tomatoes.
Add salt and pepper.
Now sprinkle with vinegar (I like balsamic or pear vinegar) and drizzle with virgin olive oil.

The flavored rice, scallops and salad combine for a superb meal.

Please try these simple dishes; you will not be sorry, nor will your dining companion.

SIMPLE BAKED ZUCCHINI

2 medium zucchini, quartered lengthwise
Salt and pepper
Fresh herbs (basil, tarragon, parsley or whatever)
Parmesan cheese (optional)
Olive oil

Here is another simple accompaniment for fish.

Preheat oven to 400 to 415 degrees (a good temperature for baked fish). Arrange zucchini on baking pan, side by side, seeds up. Bathe with oil, sprinkle with herbs, salt and pepper, and optional cheese. Bake about 8 minutes. Zucchini should be cooked but not limp.

I think I should get back to seafood. A simple, great (at least good) idea came to mind – changing the flavored rice recipe to Poor Man's Paella (no lobster).

POOR MAN'S PAELLA *(for 4)*

"Flavored Rice" above, plus:
4 to 8 scallops
4 to 8 shrimp
4 to 8 littlenecks
4 to 8 mussels
4 pork breakfast sausages
1/4 cup white wine
1 cup petite frozen peas

Brown pork sausages, and add to rice. Add wine to broth used in original recipe. Arrange whatever seafood on top of rice and broth, and bake at 350 degrees for about 20 minutes or until clams and mussels are open. If you are using shrimp and scallops, add them during the final 5 minutes, along with frozen peas. You will need a shallow baking pan or casserole with a cover. The pot is covered while baking.

You can use any combination of seafood for this dish. It is good with only fish fillets but gets better and more delicious with each variety – squid is good, a slipper shell or two, whatever you have. Fresh herbs, especially tarragon, enhance this mélange. Go for it, have some fun! Serve hot sauce on the side. Increase or decrease the amount of rice, always using twice as much broth as rice. You cannot fail.

Add crusty bread, cold white wine or beer and a green salad, and reap the rewards.

"Oh! What A Dinner!"

- -

Last night I had the pleasure of sharing a splendid paella prepared by my good friend Ben Oko, gardener, birder, grouch, psychiatrist, critic and fine cook. The dish was based on Howard Mitcham's recipe in his classic Provincetown Seafood Cookbook.

I am going to list the ingredients as Mitcham presented them and provide my own instructions for putting them all together. Don't be put off by the number of ingredients, all are readily available. You do not have to have every variety of seafood listed, but the more the merrier. Scallops could be added or used as a substitute for the lobster; cod or striped bass could be used instead of haddock. You could, in fact, make this dish without any seafood, using chicken stock, and have a fine arroz con pollo (rice and chicken casserole), but you would not have paella. The former is a good dish, the latter is splendid! Go for it, you will not be sorry!

PROVINCETOWN PAELLA (for 10)
2 doz. littleneck quahogs (in their shells)
2 doz. mussels (in their shells)
(2) 2-pound live lobsters
1/2 doz. squid
1 lb. haddock fillet
1 lb. shrimp
1/2 lb. smoked ham, cut in strips
(1) 3-pound frying chicken, cut into 10 pieces
1/2 chourico sausage (Spanish) or chourico or linguica
1 ½ cups olive oil
6 cloves garlic
3 medium onions, chopped
(1) 16-oz. can plum tomatoes
(1) 8-oz. can tomato sauce
1 green pepper, chopped
1 pkg. frozen defrosted peas (I like the tiny ones)
1 small jar pimientos, cut in strips
1/2 tsp. Tabasco
1 cup fresh mushrooms, sliced
2 lbs. (4 cups) rice (Uncle Ben's for me)
Fish stock
Salt and pepper, to taste

Fish Stock Ingredients:
4 lbs. fish heads, bones, racks, tails, trimmings
4 quarts water
4 cloves garlic, minced
3 onions, chopped
1 cup parsley, chopped
1 lemon, sliced
1/2 tsp. cumin powder
1 pint dry white wine
1/2 tsp. powdered saffron or 1 tsp. stringy saffron (if you have no saffron, use 1 TBS turmeric for color)
1/2 tsp. each basil and thyme
4 tsps. salt
1/2 tsp. pepper

Don't be afraid, you are on your way to renown. I will present Mitcham's directions and my variations.

Preheat oven to 350 degrees. Put all the stock ingredients in a large pot, and bring to a boil, simmer with liquid bubbling for a 1/2 hour. You will cook the crustaceans and shellfish in the stock, adding their glorious flavors. Drop lobsters in, raise heat, and cook for 20 minutes; scrub the clams and mussels, put them in a cheesecloth bag, and cook in stock for about 10 minutes or until they are open. I use a stainless colander, suspending the shellfish in the stock until they open. Put shrimp in a cheesecloth bag, and cook for 5 minutes. I add them to my colander of shellfish for the last 5 minutes of cooking. I sometimes skip the colander and bags altogether and throw the shellfish and crustaceans in the liquid and pick them out after straining the stock through a colander at the end of the 30 minutes. Taste the strained stock, and add more salt and pepper if desired.

Take the lobsters and break off their tails, claws and knuckles (the best bits to me). Crack the claws and knuckles with a hammer or nutcracker, cut the tails in 3/4-inch sections with a heavy knife or cleaver, and set aside. Open lobster bodies, and scrape out white fat, tomalley (the icky green stuff) and roe, if you're lucky; put in a bowl, cream with the back of a spoon (mush it up), and stir into the stock. Discard lobster bodies (my wife always saves them and picks out the bits of meat therein).

Clean and dice the squid bodies, cut off the tentacles just in front of the eyes and keep them whole.

Cut the chicken up into 10 pieces. Heat 1/2 cup olive oil in a large frying pan, and fry for about 15 minutes, turning once or twice. Mitcham says to remove the chicken and then sauté the ham, sausage slices and squid meat. I add the whole works about 5 minutes before the chicken is done and sauté until it all begins to brown, stirring frequently. Set the whole works aside with the shellfish and crustaceans.

We're getting there, by now your cooking area will be a mess and your kitchen will smell heavenly, and soon will smell even better.

Now to make sofrito, the base of many Puerto Rican dishes and a flavorful addition. Heat 1/2 cup olive oil in a skillet, in it sauté the onions, garlic and green pepper until soft and transparent, add the parsley. Add the tomatoes squeezed through your fingers to break them up, the tomato sauce, mushrooms, pimientos, Tabasco sauce and lemon slices. Mitcham puts the peas in at this point, I do not. I put them in at the very end to preserve their color and glorify the presentation. Mix this well, and cook over low heat for 20 minutes. If it seems too dry, add some stock.

Now add and heat the final 1/2 cup of olive oil in a skillet (I use the large casserole I will finish the dish in). Stir the rice in the oil until it begins to turn golden yellow.

Now mix everything but the stock gently into the rice so things remain identifiable, also add the fish fillets which you have cut into 1-inch cubes. Now Mitcham says to pour in enough stock to just cover everything; I cover mine by about 1/4 inch. Bring to a boil, cover, and bake for 20 minutes, uncover, add the peas, and bake for 10 minutes more – and Bob's your uncle! You have created a marvel!

I like to serve this with a tomato and basil salad, both red and chilled white wine, beer, corn on the cob, and hot sauce on the side.

Paella Pan

This is a grand dish to serve at the end of summer, which does not end here on Cape Cod until October. Mitcham concludes his instructions with "Oh! What a dinner!" He makes an understatement. It is a great dinner, a celebration of life. Do it!

What? Eat Menhaden? Eat Raw Fish?

Some years ago my good friend Frank Carey and I decided to see if we could find some way to make menhaden (pogies) palatable or even edible. We baked, broiled, sautéed, fried, boiled and grilled them. We marinated them in various potions, basted them and doused them with hot pepper; we anointed them with soy sauce, drenched them with lemon juice, coated them with barbecue sauce and smoked them. We tried eating them while drunk; we tried eating them sober – we could not eat them.

Recently my wife and I dropped in on one of our kids who lives on the shore in Woods Hole. On the way there, I noticed flocks of birds swimming, diving, wading and generally carrying on along the beach.

My grandson and cohort, Cooper, ran up to me to announce a mass of fish along the beach. These fish proved to be an almost unimaginably large number of 3-inch menhaden, pressed by their own numbers against the beach so that some were forced out of the water onto the sand where they lay gasping, feebly flapping and dying. Thousands of others were going belly-up in the wash from lack of oxygen. This tremendous horde of fish extended as far as we could see in either direction down the shore in a dense band about 50 feet wide. The outer, offshore edge of this horde of fish was boiling with ravenous bluefish, savaging these helpless menhaden that they had trapped against the beach. It was a wild scene of carnage, awakening some atavistic need in us to take part in the harvest. We wanted to join the melee.

We caught seven 6-pound bluefish as fast as we could get a lure to them beyond the menhaden. By the time we landed the last blue, all four available rods were out of commission, snarled, broken or lureless. We had enough fish. The bluefish continued the slaughter until after sunset. This was truly awesome! Whew!

More and more schools of 3-inch menhaden are gathering all along the Cape's southern and western shores – more than I have ever seen before. You can sometimes gather them with your bare hands, as on the night of the massacre of menhaden in Woods Hole. I cannot help, after experiencing this abundance, but to offer a recipe for preparing small menhaden.

FRIED MENHADEN FRY
2 lbs. 3-inch menhaden
1/2 lb. bacon
1 cup milk
1 egg
2 cups flour
1 cup cornmeal
Salt, pepper, paprika, etc. to season flour

Fry the bacon until crisp, saving the fat in the pan. Drain bacon on a brown paper bag and save.

Beat the egg in the milk. Combine cornmeal, flour, salt, pepper and your favorite seasonings.

Dip the menhaden in the egg and milk, then in the seasoned flour. Fry them in bacon fat until crisp and nicely browned on each side, drain on brown paper and throw them away.

Put your drained bacon on a slice of your favorite bread, spread with mayonnaise, top with a thick slice of vine-ripened tomato and lettuce, and you will have a fine sandwich – a BLT-M. You will not regret throwing away the menhaden. I promise!

Now that we have dealt with the menhaden question, I am sure you are ready for another culinary adventure – raw (or nearly raw) fish.

The following recipe uses the bluefish the menhaden brought us, instead of salmon, in a classic Scandinavian preparation called gravlax. The salmon is salt-and-sugar cured, flavored with dill and served uncooked with a sweet, mustard-flavored vinaigrette.

GRAVLAX

2 lbs. center cut bluefish fillet (skin on)
1/2 cup salt
1/2 cup sugar
1 tsp. allspice (optional)
1 bunch fresh dill, coarsely chopped
2 tsps. peppercorns, crushed

Mix salt, sugar and optional allspice, and rub some on the fillets. Sprinkle some of the mixture on the bottom of a nonreactive vessel. Put a fillet, skin-side down, on top of flavorings. Spread this with dill, pepper, salt and sugar mixture, and cover with second fillet (skin-side up). Sprinkle remaining mixture on top, cover with foil, and put a weight on the fillets (a 2-pound can, full, will do). Chill the whole works for 4 or 5 hours, and drain the accumulated liquid. Return to the fridge for at least 48 hours, turning at least twice each day. It can stay for four days, even longer, before being eaten. Cut this in slices a 1/2 inch thick, and serve on crackers or dark pumpernickel bread, accompanied with the following sauce.

GRAVLAX SAUCE

1 TBS sugar
3 TBS oil
1 TBS red wine vinegar
1/3 tsp. salt
1/4 tsp. pepper
2 to 3 TBS prepared mustard
3 TBS minced fresh dill

Mix thoroughly and serve. Fame is yours.

Now that we have had some semi-raw fish, it is time for raw fish. Striped bass, especially now that the water is getting cooler, makes fine sashimi (Japanese for raw fish). You must try this; it is surprisingly good, in fact delicious, and easy.

STRIPER SASHIMI

Cut a couple of fairly uniformly thick, rectangular pieces out of a striper fillet. Trim them neatly, and chill for at least 4 hours or overnight. Slice these thinly, and serve with the following dipping sauce.

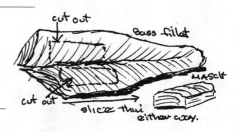

SASHIMI DIPPING SAUCE

Soy sauce
Wasabi

Wasabi is a pale green horseradish-flavored root, ground into a potent powder in Japan. Most supermarkets now carry it in either a powder or paste form.

Start by mixing 1 teaspoon of wasabi with 3 tablespoons of soy sauce, and try it with the fish. Now alter the ratio of soy sauce to wasabi to your own taste, or better still, let your guests mix their own. This will prevent possible lawsuits.

Try these recipes, and convince others to try them. You will thank me, they will thank you, joy will spread and it will be a better world!

The Sacred Cod – Is It Really A Turkey?

The noble fish after which our peninsula is named is the cod (Gadus morhua), often referred to as Cape Cod turkey because it was eaten by locals who could neither afford nor find a turkey of the feathered variety. Currently the feathered variety is more readily available and far less expensive than the scaled variety on Cape Cod. There are more wild turkeys around every year – one has even become a volunteer fireman in Woods Hole. (You can often see it hanging around the fire station on Woods Hole Road.) There are now thriving turkey farms on the Cape.

Cape Cod Turkey?

We have never lacked for that variety of turkey that has neither feathers nor scales here on the Cape; I am referring to man (Homo sapiens), the only featherless biped. As we feather- and scale-less turkeys grow in numbers, cod are declining drastically; some men even fear for its survival. Conservation practices show signs of success. The cod is available and still as delicious as it ever was. So let's cook it right!

You could do a lot worse than dining on baked stuffed cod for Thanksgiving dinner; add extra seafood to the stuffing (my family called it dressing), and you will have something grand! The following recipe for stuffing can be used with either fish or fowl. Whichever variety you choose will leave your guests talking turkey, happy to be your friends.

CAPE COD STUFFED TURKEY (Or Codfish)
(1) 8-lb. codfish (or 12-lb. turkey)
3 cups of mixed seafood, chopped (shrimp, scallops, crabmeat, squid, lobster, quahogs and oysters in any combination)
1 sweet pepper, diced
1 large onion, diced
1/2 cup celery, diced
4 strips bacon
1 tsp. powdered mustard (optional)
1 tsp. Worcestershire sauce
2 dashes or more of Tabasco
1/2 tsp. thyme
3 TBS parsley, chopped
4 eggs
1 loaf Portuguese bread
1 cup white wine
1/2 cup sherry
1 stick butter
Salt and pepper

If you are using a fish, you will also need the following ingredients:
1 cup olive oil
2 large tomatoes
1/2 lb. mushrooms, sliced
2 TBS flour

Remove the backbone from a whole codfish, or have your fishmonger do it for you. Leave the head on.

Sauté the celery, onion, garlic and green pepper in the butter until soft and lightly colored. Add the mixed seafood, Tabasco, white wine, thyme, parsley, and a little salt and pepper. Sauté, gently stirring, for 5 minutes.

Tear the bread into small pieces, and moisten it with broth. Beat the eggs, add them to the moistened bread, and mix thoroughly. Cook the bacon until brown, then crumble it into the bread mixture. Add the bread mixture to the sautéed seafood and vegetables, and mix, adding more broth if necessary. Add the sherry to the paste. It is now ready to put into the cod or turkey.

If you are using a bird, roast it in the usual manner. I recommend 15 minutes per pound (stuffed weight) at 350 degrees. Cover the bird with foil for all but the last 1/2 hour of cooking. Most turkeys are cooked too long. Follow these directions, and you will be delighted and so will your guests.

To do a genuine Cape Cod turkey, a cod, sew the stuffing into the partially boned fish. Pour a cup of olive oil into a roasting pan, and add 1½ cups of fish or chicken broth to the oil. Lay the cod in the stock. Slice up a couple of onions and tomatoes and lay some on top of the fish; spread the remainder in the pan. Cover the pan with a tent of aluminum foil, and roast in a 450-degree oven for 1 hour. Baste every 15 minutes. Forty-five minutes into the cooking, uncover the fish, and sprinkle 2 tablespoons of flour into the broth and the sliced mushrooms. Finish cooking uncovered.

Lift the fish onto a serving platter. Spoon the cooked vegetables and broth over the fish. Garnish with parsley and lemon slices. Serve with mashed potatoes or rice, or both. My, my! This is an unforgettable dish. This recipe is based on a creation of Howard Mitcham, fish cook extraordinaire and author of *The Provincetown Seafood Cookbook*.

I have been asking around and reading to learn of additional Thanksgiving seafood traditions and learned little. It seems that seafood is not common at Thanksgiving feasts. This is not true at my house. We often have clams and/or oysters on the half shell. We usually have spicy stir-fried shrimp for an appetizer. Sometimes we have smoked bluefish, either straight or in a savory pâté. There would be no end of bellyaching if scalloped oysters were not served! But, so far, the feathered turkey has remained the star. Sometimes whole oysters appear in the stuffing, to the chagrin of some of the young and ignorant.

SCALLOPED OYSTERS (for 12)

6 cups of oysters, shucked (3 pints)
1 ½ sticks of butter
1 large onion or 6 whole scallions
4 ½ cups of fine bread crumbs mixed with cracker crumbs (or use all cracker crumbs)
Salt and pepper
Paprika (optional)
1/2 cup parsley, chopped
1 ½ cups heavy cream

Melt the butter, and lightly sauté the onions or scallions. Blend in the crumbs. Add salt, pepper and paprika (about a teaspoon of each). Mix 3/4 of the crumbs and onions with the oysters, and put the mixture into a buttered casserole. Cover with the remaining crumbs, dot with butter, and pour on the cream. Bake in a 375-degree oven for 25 minutes or until brown and bubbly. Wow! This is terrific! I love a little cranberry sauce with mine.

You will not be sorry if you follow these recipes, whichever Cape Cod turkey you choose! If you choose neither, I hope you will include some seafood in your feast.

Learning From The Locals

November again – another fishing season over – time for Thanksgiving, my favorite holiday. I have been reading through several records and books about life on the Plymouth Plantation and in early seventeenth-century New England. The Pilgrims lost half of their population during their first year on North American soil preceding the first Thanksgiving, yet they offered thanks for what they had and for what they could hope for. So should we!

I was searching in my readings for information about and recipes for seafoods likely to have been used at a Pilgrim celebration. The first food references I found were in The Times of Their Lives: Life, Love, and Death in Plymouth Colony by James and Patricia Scott Dietz, published in 2000. This is a fine book about the everyday, sometimes-seamy side of life in the colony. Early in the book they write, "[Of] foods that probably were present, we can include various kinds of fish, eels, and shellfish, including lobster. Lobster, if taken with venison, would constitute the first surf and turf served on American soil."

The Pilgrims were aided and instructed by the English-speaking Native American, Squanto, who had learned English after being captured by Captain Thomas Hunt. He managed to escape and find his way back to New England, where he met the Pilgrims and enriched their lives while trying to enrich his own. He served both as an interpreter and agricultural and fishing advisor. He taught the Pilgrims how to fertilize their corn, beans and squash hills with buried herring, and how to obtain, prepare and preserve other fish and shellfish for food.

Ed Zern, renowned outdoor writer, wrote that "Fishermen are born honest, but they grow out of it."

Squanto was a fisherman, as I am, and thus not completely honest. I promise 80 percent honesty personally; I will let you decide for yourself about Squanto.

In Mount's Relation, A Journal of the Pilgrims at Plymouth, the author relates this tale: "Squanto went at noon to fish for eels; at night he came home with as many as he could well lift in one hand, which our people were glad of. They were fat and sweet; he trod them out with his feet, and so caught them with his hands without any other instrument."

What do you think? Squanto must have had some scary hands! I would like to know how he caught them, but however he did it, some got to the Pilgrims' table.

Squanto's seemingly harmless duplicity finally got him in trouble with his own people. William Bradford relates, in the classic Of Plymouth Plantation 1620-1647, a record of the colony, that "Squanto sought his own ends and played his own game, by putting the Indians in fear and drawing gifts from them to enrich himself, making them believe he could stir up war against whom he would, and make peace for whom he would. Yea, he made them believe they [the Pilgrims] kept the plague buried in the ground, and could send it amongst whom they would, which did much terrify the Indians and made them depend more on him, and to seek more to him than to Massasoit. Which procured him envy and had like to cost him his life; for after the discovery of his practices, Massasoit sought it both privately and openly, which caused him to stick close to the English, and never durst go from them till he died."

Squanto should have stuck to interpreting and teaching. The Pilgrims used what they were taught and "exercised in fishing, about cod and bass and other fish, of which they took good store, of which every family had their portion," according to Governor Bradford.

While buying my copy of Mount's Relation in Mashpee, I noticed a new cookbook, The Cape Cod Wampanoag Cookbook, by a Native American of that community, Earl Mills Sr., written in collaboration with Betty Breen. The author and his family have been involved in the Native American cultural presentation at the Plimouth Plantation, a living museum of Pilgrim life in Plymouth, Massachusetts. This fine book seems the perfect place to start finding Native American recipes for autumn feasts.

On page 60 the authors relate how 90 Wampanoags attended the first Thanksgiving and were directly or indirectly responsible for most of the victuals.

This first Thanksgiving would not have been possible without the Wampanoags, for the seeds brought over the Atlantic did not grow well in the New World, and the Pilgrims were actually in danger of starvation.

Instead, the large outdoor tables were filled with turkey, as well as venison, duck, goose, clams, eel and other fish, wild plums, leeks, watercress and corn bread.

Author Mills reports on how his father brought home eels, skinned them and prepared them in this way:

EELS *(for 4)*

4 lbs. eel (2 or 3), skinned
1/4 cup cornmeal for coating eels
1/4 cup flour for coating eels
1 tsp. salt for coating eels

Make a gash with a sharp knife across the length of the eel every inch or so. After three gashes, cut the eel all the way through to create a serving piece. Then gash the other side. Gashing allows the eel to heat through and become crisp.

Make a mixture of cornmeal, flour and salt, and roll the pieces in the mixture to coat. Using the black spider frying pan, add a little bacon fat – not too much, because the eels are oily – and let the black spider do its work.

Turn often, and continue to cook until the eels are well browned.

Serve with tartar sauce and lemon.

GRILLED EEL *(for 2)*

2 lbs. eel
2 tsps. thyme
Pepper and salt
1/4 cup olive oil

Mix eel, cut in 2-inch pieces, with salt, pepper and thyme. Allow to marinate while grill heats. Grill for about 10 minutes, basting with the olive oil. Serve with crusty bread and salad. This is hard to beat.

The Pilgrims would have used this method with bacon fat for basting.

Eels were also stewed. If you do not try these recipes, you will be poorer for it.

BAKED SCROD *(for 6)*

6 TBS butter or oil
1 cup cracker or bread crumbs
(6) 6- to 8-ounce scrod fillets
Salt
1/2 cup water
Lemon juice
Newburg sauce

This recipe is also from *The Cape Cod Wampanoag Cookbook.*

Preheat oven to 450 degrees.

Melt the butter in a baking pan. Place the crumbs on waxed paper. Coat each fish fillet on the top side with melted butter or oil. Then dredge in crumbs, adding a couple of shakes of salt over each fillet.

Put a small amount of water in the baking pan – about 1/2 cup, just enough to lightly film the bottom of the pan – to keep the fish moist and prevent it from sticking to the pan. Gently place the fish in the pan, separating the pieces so they don't touch. Don't get water on the crumbs.

Bake for 7 to 8 minutes. As soon as the crumbs begin to brown, squeeze a little lemon juice on each piece. Fish should be flaky and firm. Gently lift the edge of the fish with a wide spatula to test for doneness. If the fish is sticking to the dish, add a little bit of water to the dish, not to the fish. Scrod may be placed under the broiler if it is not brown enough. Do not turn the fish!

This can be served as is, with additional lemon, but becomes magical if dressed with Newburg sauce.

NEWBURG SAUCE

1 lb. lobster meat
2 TBS butter
1/2 cup dry sherry
3 cups cream sauce

Sauté lobster meat in butter until the color begins to come off and the meat is coated. Add half the dry sherry, and simmer for 10 to 15 seconds, coating the meat with the sherry. Add the necessary cream sauce to complement the lobster meat. Bring to a simmer for 30 seconds. Add the remaining sherry to thin the sauce or add flavor if desired.

This sauce is terrific for Newburg lovers. You can make it more economical by substituting shrimp for the lobster meat, or even fake crabmeat. Serve with baked fish or crab cakes or on toast. Wow!

Buy this cookbook and enjoy it. We, like the Pilgrims, still have much to learn from our Native American neighbors!

The Turkey Or The Stuffing, Which Came First?

Every year at this time I try to remember or find traditional recipes for seafood dishes that one serves on the holidays: Thanksgiving, Christmas and New Year's. Particularly, I want dishes that use our locally available seafood. However, by Thanksgiving almost all the inshore fish available to anglers are gone, so we must use fish from offshore sources – cod, haddock, yellowtail, halibut or whiting, if you are lucky enough to find it, and ocean catfish or wolffish if you are even luckier. Wolffish are perhaps my personal favorite.

We can, however, get shellfish year-round. Lobster, with its bright color, always seems festive, particularly appropriate at Christmas, surrounded by a wreath of parsley. Clams, mussels, oysters and quohaugs are always available to buy or to dig oneself. I am tempted to spell the word "quohaug" differently every time I use it. My edition of The Shorter Oxford English Dictionary spells it "quahog," and says that "quahaug" is also acceptable, but that "cohog" is rare (I guess it is rare, I have never heard of such a spelling). Then there is my spelling of the moment, quohaug. I say it is as good as any; after all, what do the Brits know about clams anyway?

In some quarters, the usually overcooked turkey is seen as mostly a carrier for the more succulent stuffing. No matter how you spell it, quohaug stuffing is grand in the Thanksgiving turkey and is nearly as good without the turkey. Just put the stuffing back in its shells, and you have stuffed quohaugs.

There are nearly limitless possibilities for variations on this dish. I will provide a master recipe that will be good, but you can modify it in many ways. I will suggest some variations.

MASTER RECIPE, QUOHAUG STUFFING

(for turkey or clam shells)

1 quart quohaug meat (Grind or prepare in a food processor. Do not purée; leave chunks. For some reason unknown to me, ground or processed clam meat is more flavorful than the same meat chopped by hand.)

1 loaf dry bread or unseasoned stuffing bread (about 2 quarts)

2 cups onion, chopped

1 green pepper, chopped

1 rib celery, chopped

4 cloves garlic (amount optional)

4 TBS parsley, chopped

1 ½ sticks butter or margarine

1/2 to 1 cup white wine (or a combination of clam broth, wine and water; be careful of the saltiness of the clam broth)

Salt and pepper

1/4 tsp. Tabasco (optional)

Be sure to buy chowder (big) clams for your stuffing. They cost only one tenth of what littlenecks or cherrystones cost.

Put about an inch of water in a pot big enough to hold your clams (about 5-dozen chowders should do it), add the clams and steam until they open. You may do this in batches. Now process or grind the clam meats coarsely, do not purée.

Melt the butter or margarine in a saucepan or skillet large enough to hold the whole works. Sauté the chopped vegetables gently until translucent, adding the garlic last so it does not burn and become bitter. Add the ground clams, cubed bread and parsley to the pan. Moisten the whole works with the wine, water and clam juice until it is as moist as you want it to be. Taste for seasoning; you will want some black pepper.

I always add a little Tabasco and sometimes lemon juice, depending on how tart the wine is. I always add lemon juice (about 1/4 cup) if I use only diluted clam juice to moisten the stuffing.

This recipe will provide enough (you can use even more bread than I have recommended if you are a Yankee) to stuff a large turkey and have some left over to return to their shells, freeze, and serve on New Year's Eve as stuffed quohaugs.

I like to add a teaspoon of thyme to my stuffing; sage is also a good addition, especially for turkey stuffing.

For a Portuguese variation, sauté 1/4 pound of chopped chourico or linguica along with the vegetables in the master recipe. A Yankee might sauté 1/4 pound cubed salt pork with the veggies and add 2 tablespoons or so of sherry to the mix. A half pound of crumbled pork sausage would also be good. You can add favorite flavorings of your own, but do not overwhelm the flavor of the quohaug.

I always add hot pepper in some form to my clams for stuffing. You can serve crushed pepper flakes, Tabasco or any pepper sauce on the side.

Remember, a quohaug by any other spelling tastes just as sweet! Stuff that turkey with clams, and rejoice!

You can make the stuffing a day in advance, but be sure to bring it to room temperature before refrigerating overnight. Stuff the turkey in the morning just before putting it in the oven. Try not to overcook the turkey. I know it is the American way, but it is not virtuous, even if you got up at 6 a.m. to do it.

Now here is an easy, guaranteed delicious recipe for cherrystones or littlenecks.

BAKED OR BROILED QUOHAUGS WITH BACON (for 4 or 5)
2 dozen littlenecks or (I prefer) cherrystones
6 slices bacon

Open clams, place 1/4 slice of bacon on each clam, and bake in a preheated 450-degree oven, or broil in oven until the bacon is crisp. Serve with a bit of Tabasco (optional) and lemon quarters.

This is, perhaps, the best-tasting clam recipe for the effort it takes to prepare it that you will ever taste. I will bet my reputation on it.

You could do the same with oysters. You could use oysters instead of clams in the stuffing. Why not try oysters before dinner and clams in the stuffing? You will not be sorry; you may even become famous!

Turkey stuffed Clam

Turkey stuffed with clams

Fried Minnows and Post-Thanksgiving Paella!

The last of the bass and bluefish are rapidly disappearing from our waters here in Southern New England, and until ice fishing begins, we anglers will be relatively fishless, but shellfish, at least bivalves, will be available in many places, so all is not lost. There will be quahogs and oysters available for holiday dinners. I'll bet the Pilgrims included shellfish in meals at holidays as I do. Scalloped oysters and oyster, clam or oyster-and-clam stuffing are always part of holiday dining at my house, as are the same shellfish served raw, perhaps the best presentation of all.

I am going to suggest preparation of a fried fish appetizer. Why not? Fried calamari has become ubiquitous on local menus; ten years ago I was lamenting the fact that one could not find squid on local menus at all. I am also going to make a suggestion for leftovers from Thanksgiving dinner that I enjoy as much as or more than the main event itself.

In autumn the sandy shallows off our coast are often teeming with silversides (Menidia menidia), a small fish that resembles a smelt (Osmerus mordax) and is equally delicious floured and fried. The British consider these and similar small fish floured and fried great delicacies, as I do. In England, fish prepared this way are called white bait and demand a high price when available. In France, small fish prepared in the same manner are called goujon and are also highly prized. When you cut small pieces of fish fillet to minnow-size pieces and flour and fry them, you have goujonettes, delicious morsels of fish, a grand appetizer! I first ate these at a wild-game dinner provided by my friend Phil Stanton, a grand storyteller, writer, fisherman and confused friend of wildlife on Naushon Island. He called them fried fish bits – every bit as good as goujonettes.

FRIED FISH BITS – GOUJONETTES

1 1/2 lbs. white-fleshed fish fillets
1 cup white flour
1 tsp. salt
1/2 tsp. pepper
4 cups vegetable oil (peanut is best) for deep-frying

Cod or haddock is fine, fluke and black sea bass are better, striper is fine, and though not white, bluefish will work if very fresh.

Cutting the fish into strips about 4 inches long and 1/3 inch on a side is easiest if done with chilled or partially frozen fish. Slice the fillets on the diagonal into 4-inch slices, now slice these pieces into 1/3-inch-wide strips. Refrigerate, covered, until ready to flour and fry. If you flour them ahead of time, they will stick together in the fryer.

Heat the oil in a heavy pot, no more than half full, over medium heat until it reaches 370 degrees.

Put the flour, salt and pepper into a bag, toss in small handfuls of fish strips, and shake to coat with seasoned flour. Remove strips to a wire strainer, and shake off excess flour over a bowl. Fry immediately for about 15 seconds until barely golden, and drain on paper towels. Put excess flour back in bag and continue until all the fish strips are cooked. Garnish with fried curly parsley, and serve with lemon slices and tartar sauce. I like ketchup laced with Tabasco with mine. These fish bits are great! I promise you! Swordfish is grand this way, so are squid rings and tentacles.

To fry parsley, merely take small sprigs of curly parsley that are totally dry and drop into 370-degree oil. It will sputter. Remove after 5 seconds, and drain on paper towel. A grand tasty garnish sure to add to your fame.

After picking at the carcass of the Thanksgiving bird for a day, I am ready to use it and some shellfish to make a post-Thanksgiving paella, at least as good as turkey tetrazzini and more unexpected. I always buy a bird large enough to provide plenty of leftovers for grazing and cooking.

POST-THANKSGIVING PAELLA (for 8)

24 small quahogs (littlenecks)
24 mussels
1 lb. shrimp, shelled
3 cups rice (Uncle Ben's is good)
Leftover turkey
2 medium onions, chopped
2 cloves garlic, minced
1/2 cup parsley, chopped
1 chourico or linguica, minced
1/2 cup olive oil
1/2 stick butter
2 packets Goya Sazon seasoning with annatto or saffron (optional but delicious)
1/2 cup white wine (optional)

Remove meat from turkey carcass, and set aside. Put oil and butter in a large (at least 3-quart), heavy-bottomed pan with cover, and heat over medium heat, add chopped onion and sauté until translucent, about 7 minutes. Add minced sausage, garlic and parsley. After 3 or 4 minutes, add the 3 cups of rice, and stir while sautéing for about 5 minutes until rice is translucent and just beginning to color slightly. Now add 6 cups of turkey stock (made from carcass) and optional Sazon, and bring to a boil. Turn heat down, add saved turkey, and simmer covered for 1/2 hour on top of stove or in a 325-degree oven. After 1/2 hour, rice should be almost tender; push the clams and mussels down into rice, cover, and continue cooking. If the rice seems too dry to provide enough steam to cook the shellfish, add up to a cup of stock or white wine at this time. Shellfish should be open after 20 minutes, now add shrimp, cook for 5 minutes more or until shrimp are pink and translucent. Taste for salt and pepper, stir, garnish with parsley, wait 5 minutes, and serve. Your guests will be properly thankful. I like to serve several kinds of hot sauce with this for my guests to choose from; sometimes I make a mild Creole sauce to serve alongside. Good stuff, indeed.

To make turkey stock for this dish, break up turkey carcass to fit in a pot, cover with water, add 1 teaspoon salt, 8 peppercorns, a carrot, a medium onion (you don't need to peel it) cut in half, a stick of celery, some parsley stems and a teaspoon of dried thyme. Bring to a boil, reduce heat, simmer for 2 hours, and strain. Taste for seasoning – do not add much salt, for the clams and mussels will add salt when they open.

These recipes will easily serve eight. I would add a green salad and have pears and cheese for dessert. I can hardly wait. In the meantime, I am going out to seek the lingering fishes of summer.

Fame And Love Are Available!

The bass and bluefish are either gone or soon to go, so most of us saltwater fishermen who haven't loaded the freezer will be heading for the fish market when the hunger for fish strikes. I usually buy fish that I do not catch in summer. Flounder and swordfish are autumn and winter favorites.

I had one very good fish dinner last week and one superb one. I cooked the very good one, and my new son-in-law, Scott Britton, prepared the one that was superb.

My dinner was a sort of Portuguese oven-braised swordfish steak served with mashed potatoes and a mesclun, tomato, basil and arugula salad and homemade bread, with tart tatin and ice cream for dessert. This is an easy and delicious meal, even if cooked for a crowd.

PORTUGUESE BRAISED SWORDFISH (for 4)

2 lbs. swordfish steak
2 cans Del Monte diced tomatoes with zesty jalapeño (14 1/2-oz. cans)
1 can Del Monte stewed tomatoes (14 1/2 oz.)
1/4 cup diced celery
1/4 cup diced sweet green or red pepper
2 cloves chopped garlic
1/2 cup green or black olives
1/2 cup diced chourico or linguica (optional)
2 tsps. ground cumin
1 tsp. ground coriander
1/4 cup white wine (red can be used)
3 TBS olive oil

Swordfish & clams

Preheat oven to 415 degrees.

Put olive oil in a casserole that can be put on direct flame.

Put vegetables (except garlic) and optional sausage into pan, and sauté over medium heat until soft. Add garlic for the last minute or so of sautéing so it does not burn.

Salt and pepper swordfish liberally, and add to pan. Turn over so both sides are lubricated. Now pour in tomatoes around swordfish without submerging it. Crush the stewed tomatoes in your fist as you add them, add olives, spices and wine. Put the whole works in the preheated oven, and cook for 15 minutes or until the fish barely flakes.

To make garlic mashed potatoes, boil potatoes with a few cloves of peeled garlic. Mash with garlic and butter or olive oil or cream or whatever addition suits your fancy.

Serve the fish in the casserole, garnished with parsley and lemon quarters.

Some chilled white wine, crusty bread and salad make a memorable meal.

You will not be sorry if you serve this meal. I would serve it confidently to anyone on earth. How's that?

You can use shark instead of swordfish, or halibut, or big bass steaks. You will not go wrong.

The menu for Scott's superb dinner started with a cold shrimp appetizer – four steamed shrimp, each with homemade cocktail sauce.

The main dish was sole meuniere (probably grey sole or maybe yellowtail flounder, which are both sold as sole in this country since there is no true sole caught in North American waters), accompanied by orzo dressed with a fine basil pesto made by my stepdaughter Lis, and baked tomato slices sautéed in olive oil and topped with seasoned bread crumbs that were basted with the oil.

An apple tart with vanilla ice cream was served for dessert.

This was one of the best meals I have ever eaten and certainly the best fish meal I have ever had in an amateur kitchen. I am not kidding or exaggerating, even if my memory is becoming suspect with age.

SOLE MEUNIERE (for 4)

2 lbs. sole (flounder) fillets
Salt and pepper
1/4 cup flour
4 TBS butter
2 TBS olive oil (virgin)
1 lemon
1 shallot sliced thin or
  2 sliced scallions
1 TBS parsley, chopped
2 TBS capers

Lightly coat the fillets with flour seasoned with salt and pepper.

Melt 3 tablespoons butter and 1 tablespoon olive oil in a skillet large enough to handle fish in two batches. When the butter stops frothing, lightly brown sole fillets on both sides about 1 minute a side. When lightly browned, remove to platter and put in a 250-degree oven while you do the second batch and make the sauce.

After the second batch is browned, return skillet to stove over medium heat. Put a tablespoon of olive oil and remaining butter in skillet; cook shallots or green onions briefly. Pour in 1/4 cup white wine to deglaze the pan, and add the juice of the lemon, 1 teaspoon grated lemon zest and the rinsed capers, and heat thoroughly. Another tablespoon of butter can be stirred in just before serving.

Plate the fish, and pour 1/4 of the delicious sauce on each serving.

Sole
Dover Sole   Winter
                                     Flounder

This, as I have said, was superb! Try it, it is not difficult, and it will increase your renown, which should be growing if you are serving my recipes. How's that for modesty?

Thanksgiving is this month, and I think clams or oysters, or both, should be part of a New England Thanksgiving. Clams and oysters raw are a perfect appetizer on the great day, and oyster stuffing can make a turkey a marvel.

OYSTER STUFFING (enough for a 12- to 16-lb. bird)

1 pint oysters and liquid
1/2 lb. unsalted butter
1 cup chopped onion
1 cup chopped celery
8 cups cubed day-old bread
2 beaten eggs
1/2 tsp. ground sage, thyme, marjoram
  and rosemary
Salt and pepper

Coarsely chop oysters, save liquid. Melt butter in a skillet, save 1/2 cup. Sauté onion and celery in remaining butter until soft, add oyster liquid, and simmer 5 minutes. Mix this into bread cubes and cool slightly. Add eggs and herbs, gradually add reserved butter. While tossing with a fork, add oysters, and salt and pepper to taste – and stuff your bird.

The first oyster stuffing I ever had was on Thanksgiving in Truro, Massachusetts, in 1960. It was so good that I have never forgotten it. You, too, can be remembered.

Can You Imagine, Lobster With Vanilla?

Last week my son-in-law, Scott Britton, did it again! He created a seafood meal that was as good as, and probably better than, any I have cooked. The first time he did it, it was flounder, this time it was lobster, and it was splendid.

I am writing this in mid-September, but I think the meal I will describe will be more than suitable for the holiday season. The day Scott invited me to dinner, I was making stuffed tomatoes Provencal because the tomatoes were finally ripe in abundance in my garden. I asked if I could bring them.

Scott said, "Yeah, they will probably go." I took that to mean they wouldn't conflict with what he was making but asked anyway. Scott knows I am somewhat conservative about some foods, like chowder, and strongly opinionated.

"You may not like it," said Scott. "It is lobster, roast lobster with vanilla sauce."

"Hmm. . . ." I answered. "We'll see."

It sounded very odd to me, but it piqued my interest – it was also free lobster.

Eating lobster is usually a messy business involving squirting juice, spilled butter, and loud cracking and slurping sounds. Lobster is rarely served in the shell at even a semi-formal dinner. The following dish could well be served at a polite dinner. It would make a perfect meal for a dinner party around the holidays, the colors even add to holiday ambience.

ROAST LOBSTER WITH VANILLA SAUCE
2 lobsters, 1 ¼ to 1 ½ pounds each
1 TBS good olive oil
7 TBS plus 2 tsps. unsalted butter
3 shallots, peeled and finely chopped
1/2 cup dry white wine
1 ½ TBS white wine vinegar
1/2 vanilla bean, split lengthwise
1/2 tsp. kosher salt
Freshly ground black pepper
1/2 lb. baby spinach
1 lb. watercress, stemmed

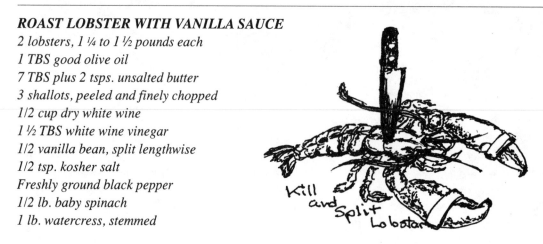

Kill and Split Lobster

Heat a roasting pan, big enough to hold the lobster, in a 450-degree oven. With a sharp knife, pierce the lobster between the eyes or at the cross on its thorax to sever the spinal cord. Crack the claws with a hammer (or if you are going to serve out of the shell, crack shells after cooking). Drizzle lobsters with oil, place in the preheated pan, and roast until red, at least 15 minutes. Remove and set aside.

Melt two teaspoons butter, add finely chopped shallots, and sauté over low heat until soft and transparent. Add wine and vinegar, raise heat and boil moderately, reducing to 1 tablespoon. Remove from heat and whisk in 6 tablespoons of butter, about one at a time, until all the butter is used. Scrape the seeds from the vanilla bean into the sauce, stir to combine, and strain into a clean saucepan. Season with salt and pepper to taste. If you used salted butter, skip the salt.

When the lobsters are cool enough to handle, remove the meat from the claws. Break off the tails, cut the shell on the underside lengthwise with scissors, remove the meat and slice lengthwise in 1/4-inch slices. Cover the meat with foil, and keep warm in a 180-degree oven.

Melt 1 tablespoon butter in a large pot, and add spinach and watercress (if you cannot get watercress, use only spinach). Stir until greens are wilted, stir and cook gently for about 5 minutes or until greens are tender. Salt and pepper to taste.

Reheat sauce over low heat until warm, whisking constantly (we do not want this to separate). Put a bed of greens on each plate, arrange lobster meat on greens, and spoon the sauce over the lobster, saving some for those who might want more. This recipe is supposedly for two, but easily feeds three or even four if you serve a starch or stuffed tomatoes.

I was prepared to dislike this dish, but it was nearly marvelous, splendid at the very least! Scott had done it again! I might be better at bulk foods like chowder for 50, but maybe not. I will hold onto this possible illusion.

Lobster served on bright green spinach and watercress has a very Christmasy look. The recipe is actually easy despite the long instructions. It will probably be new to your guests – and it is terrific – you will not be soon forgotten! That's what we all want, isn't it?

I mentioned tomatoes Provencal earlier – what does this have to do with seafood? Well, they can accompany the lobster dish or anything else, or they can have quahogs added to them and become a main course or a fine luncheon dish.

ROAST STUFFED TOMATOES PROVENCAL (for 4)

4 medium tomatoes (even winter tomatoes)
1 small onion
1/4 medium green pepper
1 small clove garlic
1/4 cup chopped parsley
1/2 tsp. dried thyme
1 scallion chopped
1/2 to 1 cup bread crumbs
1/4 cup Parmigiano-Reggiano (or any inferior Parmesan cheese)
3 TBS olive oil
Salt and pepper

Put 2 tablespoons olive oil in saucepan, and gently sauté onion, green pepper, garlic, scallion and chopped parsley until translucent and soft.

Slice tomatoes in half horizontally, and cut out centers and seed with a spoon, making 8 small red bowls. Remove seed from tomato pulp. Chop the pulp to a near purée and add to sautéed vegetables. Add 1/2 cup of bread crumbs, the thyme, and salt and pepper. Mix in enough crumbs to have a moist, moldable mixture of vegetables and crumbs to mound into your tomato cups. After filling cups, dust each with Parmesan, drizzle with oil, and bake in a 350-degree oven for about 15 minutes, and there you have it.

To convert this to a main dish, combine equal amounts of stuffing and ground or chopped quahogs, and you have quahog-stuffed tomatoes, or tomato-stuffed quahogs, if you put them in shells. You could add about 2 inches of linguica chopped fine and have Portuguese Stuffed Tomatoes or Quahogs. The possibilities are dizzying. I am getting too wound up for an older gentleman.

Go for it, make this stuff, serve your friends and family! Life is good!

Cooking The Catch

Chapter Four: Winter

C'mon Winter

Today is gray and chilly, 5 to 10 inches of snow are predicted for tonight. Last week a friend caught a 33-inch striped bass on a fly. This morning I brought in my eight fishing rods that have been leaning on a boxwood in my front yard for six months when they were not out fishing with me. Another fishing season is over for me – no more fresh fish until spring, unless my ice-fishing friends come through with charitable contributions – but I will not despair. There is salt cod to soak, canned fish to open, and shellfish for the brave – maybe even a frozen swordfish steak or two at rock-bottom prices. I may even try crab cakes made from the 1-pound cans available now in some markets. I will be doing these things and so should you. The worst that can happen is that you will never have to try them again if you are disappointed, but you may find something you love. Make the best of the situation, I say.

This is the season for clam and fish chowders, oyster and lobster stew and many other warming dishes, welcome anytime, but especially in winter. The best heater of all is a fine Portuguese squid stew laced with piri-piri pepper sauce. I can feel my spirits rising as I write. Bring on the snow and cold, I have antidotes in mind and bowls at the ready!

Christmas Customs

Every December my father would come home with a small wooden barrel containing salted herring. I do not know where, or if, these kegs of herring are available today. I grew up in Michigan, almost as far from the sea as one can get in North America. This was the only saltwater fish I ever saw as a child. I still remember their briny smell.

My father would soak most of the salt out of the herring, and then he would marinate them in vinegar with lots of sliced onion, black pepper and commercial pickling spices. He added sugar to his taste. He would eat these on crackers during the Christmas holiday season. These fish were an absolute must on New Year's Eve. Herring is considered essential to a successful holiday season in all of northern Europe; my family originates from Germany.

At midnight, the men, i.e. my father and his brothers, would fire shotguns in the air. Before coming back in the house, they would hide small change (pennies and nickels) outside. If the money was still there in the morning, it was a sign that you would have enough money throughout the year. Upon returning indoors, they would, along with their wives and children, have a midnight meal of homemade bread and butter, onions, Limburger cheese and the essential herring. This was always washed down with a copious amount of beer.

Some years, raw oysters were added to our repast. They were also purchased from huge barrels (at least they seemed huge when I was a child) that had been shipped from the East Coast to Detroit's wholesale market. Oysters were not as critical to the feast as were the herring, but when available, they were a most welcomed addition to some, disgusting to others. I remember their smell – the wild sea odor.

The custom of making loud noises, the gunfire, was probably pagan in origin. One made noise to frighten away the evil spirits that were weakening the sun. You checked your hidden money the next morning, and if it was still there, the demons were gone and the sunlight would strengthen, crops would grow and you would survive another year.

The traditional meal of fish and bread was most certainly Christian in origin, connected with the miracle of the loaves and fishes. I have no clue how the Limburger cheese got in there except to once again ward off evil spirits with its pungent aroma.

In southern Europe, traditional holiday meals have a more obvious connection to Christian religion. Christmas Eve is a fast day for most Catholics, so only seafood was served, and the more variety the better. Fried eels, stuffed clams, squid, steamed mussels and salted cod in spaghetti sauce over linguine, with a side of grilled octopus – all might adorn a Christmas Eve table. A cornucopia of fish to welcome the Christ child – what could be nicer?

The northern European holiday seafood dishes are fine, but given a choice, I would choose a southern Italian Christmas Eve every time!

QUICK MUSSELS MARINARA

4 quarts cleaned mussels
Olive oil to cover cooking-pot bottom
2 cloves garlic, chopped
1/4 tsp. red pepper flakes
2 TBS parsley, chopped
1/4 tsp. dried oregano
1 TBS dried basil (1/4 cup if fresh)
1/4 tsp. tarragon, chopped
1 cup dry white wine
(1) 14-ounce can chopped tomatoes

Scrub mussels. Throw out the clunkers; you will know them when you hear them. Sauté the garlic, parsley and all the herbs and spices gently in the olive oil for about 3 minutes. Be careful not to burn the garlic. Add tomatoes and some salt and pepper, and simmer for about 15 minutes. Add the wine and mussels, cover and steam for 6 to 7 more minutes. Eat with crusty bread or over linguine, or both!

FRIED SMALL EELS

3 pounds fresh small eels (the size you use for bass bait)
1 cup flour
Salt and pepper
1 cup olive oil
1 lemon for garnish

Skin and behead the eels, and cut them into 2-inch pieces or your kids will have nightmares. Place flour, salt and pepper in a paper bag. Shake a few pieces in the bag, and fry them in oil over medium heat for about 8 minutes or until quite crisp.

Drain, sprinkle with salt and pepper, and serve with lemon. You may never waste an eel on bait again!

FRIED (YES, FRIED) SWORDFISH PIECES

2 pounds swordfish steaks or kabobs (3/4-inch thick)
Salt and pepper
2 eggs
1/2 cup olive oil
3 TBS chopped parsley
1/4 cup lemon juice
Enough vegetable oil to be 1/4-inch deep in your frying pan
Lemon wedges

Mix olive oil with salt and pepper, parsley and lemon juice. Place swordfish pieces in mixture, and stir around. Marinate for 1 hour but no more than 2. Dry pieces.

Dip pieces in beaten eggs, dredge in flour, and fry on both sides until nicely golden. Sprinkle with salt and serve. You will not believe it – this may be the best swordfish you ever tasted!

I'm getting carried away. Please try these recipes for the good of your soul; they are guaranteed to bring back the light and will strengthen you. Merry Christmas, and mangia!

Christmas Fish – Why Not?

• •

This year's fishing ended for me last month, just before Thanksgiving, and I must admit, I was almost relieved. It happened just before Christmas fantasies about next season began and I started hoping for some fishing paraphernalia to appear under the Christmas tree. The evergreen tree is a pagan symbol for life continuing through winter; it stands at the center of the most important Christian holiday. It assures Christians that light and life will return in springtime, bringing back the fish and birds of summer.

The fish itself is an old symbol of Christianity. Christ himself was a fisherman, not one to sneer at a great haul. He also promoted fish as food, choosing it as the main course in the story of the loaves and the fishes. I wonder how it was cooked.

In early Christian art, a fish was the symbol of Christ because he was the fisher of souls and because the Greek word for fish (ichthos) formed an acrostic for Jesus Christ, the Son of God, the Savior. Christians were spoken of as fish in the sea of baptism. There are many more biblical associations between fish and Christian beliefs, so it is no surprise that seafood is part of many Christmas celebratory meals. In many Catholic countries, Christmas Eve is a fast day, so seafood is the center of pre-holiday festivities.

Here are two glorious swordfish recipes to celebrate the passing of the solstice and Christmas. These recipes require some preparation that can be done well ahead of the final cooking. The first is a classic Portuguese recipe, the second a grand, more modern, preparation.

SWORDFISH AND CLAMS, PORTUGUESE STYLE

2 to 3 lbs. swordfish, cut into 18 pieces about 1/4-inch thick
6 TBS. olive oil
2 lbs. onion, finely chopped
24 littleneck clams or 2 lbs. mussels, or a combination
1/2 cup dry white wine
2 large cloves garlic, chopped and mashed
2 cups canned tomatoes, crushed up
1/2 cup of the juice from the canned tomatoes
1 bay leaf
2 tsps. mild paprika
Dash of cayenne
Coarse salt
Black pepper
Flour for dredging
1 TBS parsley, chopped

Advance work: Heat 4 tablespoons olive oil in a heavy skillet; add the onions and stir. Cover the pan and cook over low heat for 15 minutes, stirring once or twice. Uncover the pan, raise the heat, and reduce the liquid produced by the onions. Lower the heat, return the cover, and cook another 15 minutes. Repeat this process until the onions are a light caramel color. Four 15-minute periods should do it. Do not scorch.

While the onions are reducing, steam the shellfish open, and reserve it in the shells. Reserve the broth, about 1 cup.

Cook the garlic briefly in the reduced onions. Add the rest of the ingredients, except the parsley, flour and swordfish. Cover and simmer for 15 minutes, then uncover and reduce to a thick sauce. The recipe may be prepared in advance to this point.

At dinnertime, heat the sauce and shellfish together. Lightly flour the swordfish slices, and brown them briefly in olive oil on both sides. Put the fish pieces on a serving platter, top them with the sauce and shellfish, and serve sprinkled with parsley. This is magnificent and well worth the effort. I would serve this with rice barely warmed and tiny frozen peas. Have some crusty bread on hand and a couple of bottles of vinho verde, Portuguese wine, and you will be revered! This recipe serves six highly fortunate people.

This next recipe will serve twelve. With a little advance work preparing the herb rub, it is easy to prepare.

ROAST SWORDFISH
5 to 5 ½ lbs. swordfish, single fillet or big steak (If a fillet is used, it should be 3 inches at its thickest point.)
1 recipe herb rub
1/2 cup water for deglazing
3/4 cup Nicoise olives, optional

Cut the garlic into slivers. Make small holes in the fish flesh (not through the skin). Insert the garlic slivers in the holes.

Place the fish in a roasting pan that just accommodates it, with the skin side facing to the side. Rub the exposed meat with the herb rub, then turn and rub the other side.

Preheat the oven to 500 degrees. Place the oven rack in the center of the oven. Roast for 37 minutes or 10 minutes for each inch of thickness. If you are using a steak, it will be thinner and cook more quickly. You may have to tent your fish with aluminum foil during the final 10 minutes of cooking.

Remove the fish to a platter, deglaze the pan with water on top of the stove, add the juice accumulated in the fish platter to the pan along with the olives, and warm. Serve this as a sauce with the fish.

HERB RUB
12 cloves garlic
1 TBS oregano, dried
1/4 tsp. rosemary, dried
1 TBS thyme, dried
2 TBS kosher or sea salt
2 tsps. black pepper
1/4 cup olive oil

Purée all this stuff in a blender or coffee grinder, and you are all set. I would serve mashed potatoes with this, and cherry tomatoes roasted in the oven with the fish and flavored with basil. To do this, put 1 ½ pounds of cherry tomatoes, dressed with 1 ½ tablespoons olive oil, in a pan that will just hold them. Roast them for 25 minutes, rolling them around once or twice. Dress with 2 tablespoons chopped basil.

This is splendid stuff. A little wine, a simple vegetable or salad on the side, and you have a festival, indeed!

Try some plain boiled shrimp, a raw littleneck and a couple of oysters before the main meal, and you will have a Merry Christmas.

More Christmas Fish

This time of the winter solstice, the celebration of the birth of Christ and the beginning of a new year is a reflective time, a time of resolution and hope, both sorely needed by all of us.

I am resolved to appreciate the joys and pleasures of life and work more than I have in the past, and hope to continue doing so for years to come. I hope these blessings will be present for you as well. One of the things I will appreciate is seafood, its capture, its preparation and its consumption.

In my childhood, far from the sea, my father always had herring and sometimes oysters at Christmas. He would buy salt herring and pickle them himself. I learned to love them but not until I was an adult. Children don't always share their parents' taste.

About 30 years ago when my daughter Amanda was five, I read The Night Before Christmas to her. When I was finished, I said, "Well, Amanda, what did you think of that?"

"I like the part where he got sick!" she said.

"Got sick?" I responded, puzzled. "When did he get sick?"

"You know," she said. "When he ran to the windows and threw up the hash!"

A few days earlier I had made a kind of "red-flannel" hash out of leftovers – fish, potatoes, onions and beets. It tasted good to me, but she was not about to eat any and now she was vindicated by the classic Christmas tale. I still like fish hash, though I make a better one now than I did then.

At my house we have fish and shellfish on Christmas Eve, and almost always have scalloped oysters with Christmas dinner.

The shellfish are raw on Christmas Eve, quahogs and oysters on the half shell, with lemon and ground pepper, or cocktail sauce and sometimes even mignonette sauce. We sometimes add a few steamed shrimp to this mélange. The sauces can be applied to each; you could even add a few fried squid rings! Oh boy!

The following sauce is for the snobs I was referring to. However, I like it, too, and so will you.

SIMPLE MIGNONETTE SAUCE

1/4 cup finely minced shallots (or green onions)
1 cup balsamic vinegar
2 tsps. ground pepper (Snobs like white.)

Mix and serve.

LESS-SIMPLE MIGNONETTE SAUCE

1/4 cup finely minced shallots (Green onions will do.)
1/2 cup dry white wine
1/2 cup tarragon vinegar
2 TBS chopped chives
2 tsps. pepper

Mix and serve.

These sauces may be made up to a day in advance. They will improve with an overnight stay in the fridge. For the main dish on Christmas Eve, we often have baked fish fillets, Portuguese style.

BAKED FILLETS PORTUGUESE (for 8)

4 lbs. fish fillet (cod, haddock, salmon)
1 green pepper, chopped coarsely
1 medium onion, chopped coarsely
2 cloves garlic, minced
3 TBS celery, minced
(1) 2-lb. can whole or chopped tomatoes (crushed up if canned whole — that means squeezed through your fingers)
1 tsp. thyme

---

2 tsps. cumin
1/4 tsp. Tabasco
Salt and pepper
Parsley, for garnish
1/2 cup bread crumbs (optional)
4 TBS olive oil

Put 2 tablespoons olive oil in a saucepan over medium heat. Sauté onions, peppers and celery gently, adding garlic halfway through the cooking time, until the onions are transparent. Add tomato, cumin, thyme and salt and pepper. Simmer for 10 minutes. Preheat oven to 400.

While tomatoes simmer, put 2 tablespoons olive oil in a baking pan large enough to hold the fillets and sauce without submerging the fillets; their thickest parts should stick up like islands in the middle of the sauce when it is added to the pan.

Pour the sauce (tomato mixture) around the fillets. You may sprinkle bread crumbs over the exposed fish and drizzle it with olive oil. Bake this for about 10 minutes per inch of thickness of the fillets, or until it flakes.

Garnish with parsley leaves, and serve. The red sauce, snowy fish and parsley look very Christmasy!

I like plain boiled or mashed potatoes with this and tiny frozen peas, barely cooked after defrosting.

This is a fine meal, indeed. You may use fish steaks instead of fillets if you wish; swordfish, even tuna, would be outstanding.

I always try to have leftover cooked fish so I can make fish cakes or hash on Christmas morning, whether my daughter likes it or not.

FISH HASH *(for 2)*
1 cup cooked fish
1 ½ cups cubed, cooked potato
1/2 cup chopped onion
2 TBS butter or oil
Pinch of nutmeg
1 tsp. chopped parsley

Melt the butter or heat the oil over medium heat. Add the rest of the ingredients, and sauté until a crust begins to form on the bottom. Stir crust into the unbrowned portion, and allow a second crust to form. Invert to serve. This is good with a poached egg or two and some of the leftover cocktail sauce from the night before.

My daughter does not like this, but I love her anyway!

Holiday Greats

The Christmas holidays are my favorites. I especially enjoy the food, and as I get older I find the anticipation of eating more exciting than the anticipation of the gifts I coveted in my younger years.

I have adopted an Italian tradition at my house of serving only seafood on Christmas evening. Christmas Eve was a fast day in the Roman Catholic community for centuries. Many Italians, and I, carry on this tradition by serving a variety of seafood on Christmas Eve. A wreath of cold shrimp surrounded by parsley, with a bowl of cocktail sauce in the center, is delicious and beautiful. A platter of raw oysters on the half shell, another of littlenecks, and some smoked bluefish pâté and crackers will get us off to a good start.

SMOKED BLUEFISH PÂTÉ

1/2 lb. smoked bluefish
1 medium onion (grated or puréed in your food processor)
1/2 lb. cream cheese
1/2 tsp. Worcestershire sauce
Juice of one lemon
Whiskey or Cognac (to taste) up to 2 TBS (optional)
Dash of Tabasco
1 or 2 TBS horseradish sauce or 1 TBS prepared horseradish

You can process all the ingredients together until very smooth, or mix by hand in a large mortar and pestle. I like the lumpy texture, which occurs if you mix by hand. Serve with crackers or chips, along with the shrimp, clams and oysters.

I like to cook the shrimp myself because I can avoid overcooking them, which supermarkets often used to do. I have found that supermarkets seem to have learned to avoid ruining shrimp in this way. So if you do not have time to cook your own, take a chance with the market-cooked shrimp. At best they will be moist and succulent, at worst, edible. If you should end up with dull shrimp, add more Tabasco and horseradish to your sauce, and most will not notice.

It is best to buy shrimp frozen (fresh shrimp are not usually available in New England) and defrost them in your refrigerator. There is no way of knowing how long the shrimp have been thawed in the supermarket case.

BOILING SHRIMP *(for 8)*

2 lbs. large shrimp
Salt
Water to cover

Put shrimp in salted water to cover. Put over high heat, and bring to a boil. Reduce heat to low immediately, and simmer for 3 to 5 minutes (I recommend 3) until shrimp are pink. Drain and cover with, or rinse in, cold water to immediately stop cooking. Peel the shrimp (I do not bother deveining them), and serve with a cocktail sauce.

MARK BITTMAN'S COCKTAIL SAUCE

1/2 cup ketchup
1 tsp. chili powder
3 TBS freshly squeezed lemon juice
Salt and pepper, to taste
1 TBS Worcestershire sauce, or to taste
Several drops Tabasco or other hot sauce
1 TBS prepared horseradish, or to taste
1 TBS finely minced onion (optional)
Iceberg lettuce (optional)

This is better than any you can buy, and you can adjust the ingredients to your taste. I use chili sauce rather than ketchup.

Ketchup, chili sauce and iceberg lettuce are often scorned by "gourmets" but are grand here! Serve the shrimp on leaves of lettuce, and dip these leaves in the sauce after the shrimp are gone. You will not be sorry! Happy New Year!

Serve this sauce with the raw oysters and littlenecks, along with lemon wedges and freshly ground black pepper.

My imaginative stepdaughter Elisabeth came up with the idea of putting a dab of sour cream and a dollop of caviar on top of a raw oyster. It sounded like gilding the lily to me, but it proved to be marvelous, especially with a little spritz of lemon juice. You do not need the best caviar for this; lumpfish caviar is fine. Try it! Oh my! Lis is good at unpretentious extravagance.

I sometimes break the meatless vow and serve browned pork breakfast sausages along with the raw oysters and clams. I cut them each in quarters and encourage my guests to pop a bit in their mouths along with the clam or oyster. I learned this from an early James Beard cookbook. Try it; you will be a changed person, having had a gustatory epiphany!

Now we will prepare a fish main dish using the red, white and green colors of the Christmas season. It will be both pretty and delicious.

BAKED FISH AND TOMATO (for 8)

4 lbs. white fish fillets or steaks (haddock, cod, striped bass, halibut or swordfish)
3 cans, 14.5-oz. diced tomatoes, flavored with Italian herbs
Olive oil
Salt and pepper
Bread crumbs

Lightly oil the fish with olive oil, and season with salt and pepper. Put the fish in the center of a large casserole. I choose a round one as I prefer to make the presentation wreathlike. Pour the diced tomatoes around, not on, the fish. Cover the fish with bread crumbs. Sprinkle olive oil on the crumbs. Now bake in a preheated (400-degree) oven for approximately 10 minutes for each inch of thickness of the fish. You should be safe at 15 to 20 minutes. The fish will not dry out as easily in this liquid medium, and it can be kept warm in a 200-degree oven.

I like to jazz up the tomatoes with some hot pepper (cayenne, flakes or Tabasco), one tablespoon of sugar and additional (1 ½ teaspoons) oregano.

I like to serve this dish with boiled or mashed potatoes with parsley, barely cooked tiny frozen peas and a green salad. Pasta also works!

I urge you to try this menu. It is actually quite easy to prepare and serve. I recommend a sit-down serving of the appetizers while the fish is in the oven. You should sit down for two reasons: one is comfort, the other, safety. These dishes are so good that people have been "floored" by the experience of eating them!

I could not come up with a seafood dessert; maybe you could serve "Phish" ice cream – don't Ben & Jerry make something like that?

Holiday "Devils" and "Beans"

Each year at this time as I prepare for the holiday season, I ask my friends and acquaintances for information about seafood that is traditional in their holiday feasts. Every culture has celebrations around the time of the winter solstice. This is true from the most primitive society to the modern world. We celebrate the return of the sun and the warmth and light it affords us, making all life possible. I have also searched my library and found little that I have not already written about, so let us start a tradition.

My friend Cam Gifford – biologist, gardener, apple-pie baker, shellfish culturer and librarian at the Massachusetts Maritime Academy (he is pretty good at all of those things, though I would take a run at his apple pie) – said his family on the western shore of Buzzards Bay, Padanaram I think, used to traditionally serve split grilled or fried eel with Boston-style baked beans at this time of year. This is delicious, and I will tell you how to prepare it, though I probably will not convince many of you to try it, but you should, you will be better for it. The last sentence makes me sound just like my mother.

If you do not attempt the split eel, you must attempt all, or at least some, of the fancy, hot hors d' oeuvres platter that I am going to present.

I have decided to attempt beginning a tradition by first advocating "Many Devils on Horseback." Scallops wrapped in bacon, baked or broiled until crisp, were the first "Devils on Horseback," the only ones in fact, I had ever heard of, and they are delicious! They are often served at catered events and disappear as fast as they come out of the kitchen, yet somehow are considered "de classé." You do not find recipes for this marvelous treat in many cookbooks. By adding several more "devils" to the hors d' oeuvre tray, I egomaniacally hope to launch a new tradition. I have prepared and served each of these "devils" individually, but I have never presented them all at once in this festive and, I hope, soon-to-be traditional manner. How quickly can a tradition be established? This may be our only chance to find out, by preparing a platter or several platters of "Many Sorts of Devils on Horseback."

GRILLED OR BAKED SEAFOOD AND BACON – "MANY DEVILS ON HORSEBACK"

Scallops
Cherrystones (2 for each guest, at least)
Shrimp
Oysters
Swordfish in 1-inch cubes (salmon or tuna will work, too)
2 pounds or more of bacon (not maple flavored)

Shell the shellfish, peel the shrimp, cut swordfish cubes. These will all be wrapped in partially cooked bacon and finished on a grill, or more easily, in a 425-degree oven.

Use ordinary sliced bacon (not thick sliced). Preheat oven to 325 degrees. Separate bacon slices, arrange on oven tray or trays, and put in oven. Bake until half done, most fat rendered but still flexible, not yet browned. One slice of bacon should wrap two pieces of seafood. Now wrap each piece of seafood with bacon, and secure with a

toothpick. One toothpick will work for most, but oysters and clams may require two. Arrange on the tray that the bacon was cooked on, and bake in oven heated to 425 degrees, or grill (much more trouble), and serve.

I would serve these on platters with a rim of parsley (or English holly – poisonous, but who would eat it?), decorated with grape tomatoes or cranberries so the tray looks like a wreath. You may not believe how good these tidbits are even as you eat them. Your guests will be so impressed that you will never be forgotten. You cannot go wrong unless you burn these beauties to ashes. This must become a tradition.

This already is a tradition.

CAM'S SPLIT EEL AND BAKED BEANS (for 4)

2 split, 1-pound eels
1 quart baked beans (homemade, I hope)
Salt and pepper
Cornmeal
All-purpose flour

Skin and split your eel. Carefully cut down each side of backbone and remove it. You will now have a lovely length of delicious, boneless fish.

Mix 1/2 cup cornmeal with 1/2 cup all-purpose flour, season with salt and pepper. Dampen eel with milk, or if you want a heavier breading, dip eel in egg and milk mixture before rolling in seasoned flour and meal. Put coated eel pieces (about 4 inches long) aside to dry for an hour or so, or longer in refrigerator, until ready to pan-fry.

At dinnertime fry in 1/8 inch of oil over medium heat for about 20 minutes, lowering heat if eel coating is getting too brown. Serve with beans, coleslaw and beer.

You probably will not try this, though you should, but you must try the "Devils on Horseback"!

BOSTON BAKED BEANS

(from *Cooks Illustrated*)
These are fine baked beans and should be part of everyone's repertoire.
4 ozs. salt pork, cut into 1/2-inch cubes
2 slices bacon, cut into 1/4-inch pieces
1 medium onion
1/2 cup plus 1 TBS mild molasses
1 ½ TBS brown mustard
1 lb. small white beans (Navy or Great Northern)
1 tsp. vinegar
Black pepper

Heat oven to 300 degrees with the rack in low-middle position. Put salt pork and bacon in an 8-quart Dutch oven (or other covered baking dish that can go on direct flame), cook over low to medium flame until fat is rendered and browning begins, about 7 minutes. Add onion and cook, stirring occasionally, until soft. Add 1/2 cup molasses, mustard, beans, 1 1/4 teaspoon salt and 9 cups water; bring to boil. Cover pot and put in 300-degree oven. Bake until beans are tender, about 4 hours, stir well after 2 hours. After 4 hours, remove lid and cook uncovered until syrupy consistency is reached, about an hour longer. Remove from oven, and stir in 1 tablespoon molasses, vinegar, and salt and pepper to taste. These are outstanding beans, I promise. You could substitute knockwurst for the eel and still have a fine holiday supper. Sometimes simple is super.

A Christmas Wish – Fish!

I have found that fish and shellfish make fine Christmas gifts. Who wouldn't enjoy receiving a side of smoked salmon or a couple dozen oysters, or a 4- or 5-pound lobster as a holiday gift?

I have requested and received jumbo shrimp, $12 a pound, on holidays. Many fish markets provide gift certificates. Many fish that were once considered poor man's food have now become luxury fare. No one would have paid $15 a pound for swordfish 20 years ago, or $8 a pound for salt cod. Who would have imagined?

By the way, a whole salt cod, split and dried, makes a very amusing gift. A split cod, stiff as a board, gift-wrapped and laid under the tree, would be loved by any serious fish cook. These "Portuguese tennis rackets" can be found in ethnic grocery stores in New Bedford and Fall River. Even Yankees love salt cod but prefer to get theirs in little wooden boxes.

Oysters or littleneck clams are good gift choices. They will keep for many days in the vegetable drawer of your refrigerator, ready to be served as a treat for holiday guests.

A big jar of pickled herring is not a bad idea, nor is a small jar, or even high-quality sardines. These are good gifts for children to give adults as they are cheap and something they might not buy for themselves. I hope my grandchildren read this. If you guys do remember, jarred caviar is not really very expensive – lumpfish is especially good.

Things can get pretty hectic for cooks during the holidays. There are the traditional feasts on top of the everyday meals that must be prepared. I will give you some quick and easy seafood dishes to serve this joyous season.

Split Salt Cod

SALMON IN GIN (for 6)

3 lbs. salmon (fillet or 6 steaks)
1/4 lb. butter
6 tsps. onion flakes
1 ½ TBS Jane's Krazy Mixed-Up Salt (or table salt)
3 ozs. of gin

Put the fish in a broiler-proof dish. Melt the butter, and pour one half over the fish, coating both sides. Sprinkle with Krazy Salt (or another flavored salt, maybe a little cayenne added) and the onion flakes. Broil until onion flakes begin to brown. Meanwhile, add gin to remaining butter, warm it, ignite the gin, and allow it to go out, then pour over the fish. Put the fish back under the broiler to brown a bit. It should broil for about 10 minutes, start to finish.

I would garnish this dish with parsley and lemon quarters; serve it with mashed potatoes, tiny peas and a green salad. Remember to pour any remaining butter from the pan over the fish before serving. This is easy and fine!

Gin, Salmon, onion

Here is a very quick recipe for shrimp or scallops using the stir-fry technique.

STIR-FRIED SHRIMP OR SCALLOPS IN GARLIC SAUCE
2 TBS vegetable oil (peanut is best)
2 TBS minced garlic
2 quarter-size pieces of ginger (optional)
1 ½ lbs. scallops or medium shrimp (or some of each)
1 bunch scallions, cut in 1-inch lengths
3 TBS soy sauce
2 dried chilies

Put a wok or a nonstick skillet over your hottest burner. About a minute later add oil. (Peanut oil has a very high smoking temperature, which is why I prefer it for any frying.) Put ginger, garlic and chilies in oil, and stir until garlic begins to color. Add shrimp or scallops, and cook about 2 minutes, stirring once or twice until browning begins. Now stir in the white part of scallions and cook, stirring, 1 more minute. Stir in the green parts of scallions and soy sauce, cook 30 seconds longer. Serve at once over white rice.

Peapods go well with this and look very pretty if you stir-fry them with sweet red pepper strips.

This dish is quick, simple and delicious. Try it, please.

SEARED SCALLOPS WITH SPINACH OR SALAD (for 2)
1 lb. scallops
Salt and pepper
2 TBS olive oil (light oil is best here)
2 TBS butter
A mesclun salad for two or a package of creamed spinach

Prepare spinach or salad vinaigrette.

Melt butter in oil, and heat to nearly smoking; be careful not to burn butter.

Sear scallops until caramelized on both sides, about 4 minutes, and serve over salad or spinach.

The scallops can be kept warm in a 200-degree oven.

I would serve this with small boiled potatoes dressed with parsley and butter, or with olive oil and salt and pepper. Now *that* is an elegant and easy dinner of which you will be rightfully proud!

Ask a Bivalve to Dinner

It is holiday time, the fishing season is over for most of us and the long winter is beginning – at least three months will pass before the first herring is reported in one of our ever-dwindling runs. Time to light a fire, read a few fishing books and go over last summer's successes and failures, and plan next year's assault on our finny friends.

I'm writing this in late October, some bass and blues are still here, but things are definitely winding down. One bright spot is that bay scallops are in season, one of Nature's most delicious gifts to mankind.

Two days ago "Predator Phil" and his henchman Jules came up with a few for an appetizer for the dinner I was told I was going to cook for him, Julie, Gary, myself and my "lunatic" Irish friend, Barrie, and maybe even my wife. I got this news shouted to me from his boat to mine in one of the gutters of Hadley's Harbor, where Phil had told me to take my Irish friend to catch stripers on a fly. He and Julie came to see how we were doing (not well) and to show us how or, more likely, up. Well, he hooked three on five casts and landed two. He said I should cook an already marinated leg of venison that was at his house, scallops, preferably broiled, for an appetizer, and anything else I wanted that night. He would bring wine and beer, and his other henchman, Gary, would show up on his own. He and Julie went off to kill a few scallops while we continued casting.

PHIL'S EASY GRILLED SCALLOPS
1 pint shucked bay scallops
2 TBS melted butter or virgin olive oil
Salt and pepper

Coat scallops with oil or butter, place them on a baking sheet, and broil about four inches below heat source in oven. Turn once, broiling about 2 minutes on each side.

Bay scallops can only be ruined by cooking them to oblivion. There are many more elaborate things to do with one simple and delicious addition – cream. Either make a white sauce with a roux from cream, or merely boil down some heavy cream. Put the sautéed or grilled scallops on toast, and pour the cream or sauce over them. You can add petit pois or cut asparagus to this combination and have a grand luncheon dish. These are too good to miss, as good as a sunrise – I am serious**!**

Dinner with "Predator Phil" and his cohorts was marvelous and will be long remembered. Now back to shellfish for the holidays. Raw littlenecks or local oysters are always a grand opener to a holiday meal. Some benighted souls do not eat raw shellfish, so here are a few recipes for pleasing those shy diners (I am being nice).

ANGELS ON HORSEBACK? *(4 tiny servings)*
(I guess the bacon resembles a saddler?)
1 dozen shucked oysters
1/2 cup dry white wine
1 clove garlic, crushed
Salt and freshly ground pepper, to taste
6 slices good-quality bacon (no maple flavored)

Marinate the oysters in wine, garlic, salt and pepper for 15 minutes, no more than half an hour. Preheat broiler or grill. Wrap each oyster with 1/2 slice bacon, secure with a toothpick, and grill or broil about 4 to 6 inches from the heat source. Turn once, and grill until bacon is crisp.

You can substitute halved sea scallops for the oysters, with grand results. I think bay scallops are too good on their own to bother with much tarting up.

Avoid the tiny scallops in seafood cases of supermarkets that cost less than $10 a pound, sold as bay scallops. They are edible but nearly tasteless, having been frozen and possibly refrozen on their journey from the Far East.

Mark Bittman, great cookbook writer, says he eats as many angels on horseback as he can get his hands on at wedding receptions because they will probably be the best thing served. I "borrowed" my recipe from him.

CLAMS CASINO (for 6)
36 small clams on the half shell
1/4 lb. butter
1/3 cup chopped scallions or shallots
1/4 cup chopped parsley
1/4 cup chopped green pepper
Lemon juice
9 slices bacon, partially (about half) cooked

Melt the butter, mix in the chopped vegetables, and spoon a bit on each clam, add a dash of lemon juice, and top with partially cooked bacon. Bake in a preheated 425-degree oven until bacon is crisp. Boy, oh boy, that's good.

You can substitute oysters for the clams in this recipe without harming your culinary reputation in the least.

Invite some shellfish to your holiday feasts, you can even use the shells for decorations!

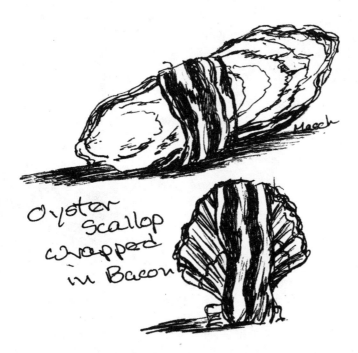

Oyster
Scallop
wrapped
in Bacon

A Fine Kettle of Fish

"A fine kettle of fish." This phrase has come to mean a confused mess of unpleasant circumstances. I tried to find the origin of this phrase and its uncomfortable implications, without success. To me, "a fine kettle of fish" is just that – a soup. There are few meals better for dinner on a cold winter night than a hot fish soup. Serve the soup with warm crusty bread, butter and a glass of white wine. Follow this with a tossed salad, fruit and cheese, and I promise you will be loved.

Every coastal culture has its own version of fish soup or stew. There is chowder in New England and cioppino in San Francisco, the famous zuppa di pesce in Italy and the classic bouillabaisse of Provence, France.

Most of these dishes grew out of the need to find a use for the extra fishes in a commercial catch (now known as the bycatch) that were not the primary target but were too good to throw away. Many of the signature dishes of an area grow out of the savory peasant fare of the community. The wealthy got the fillets of the fish; the peasants kept the racks, or skeletons and heads, for making fine stocks and the fish chowder of New England. The assorted small fish, the odd crabs, the lone lobster, a few oversized clams and a handful of mussels are all great for the soup kettle. Add some aromatic vegetables, herbs and a little wine or vinegar, and you are on your way. Now make some garlicky mayonnaise, aioli or rouille (see below) to add to your soup, and culinary joy will be at hand. This is ambrosia, food for the gods, but is more often fed to humble fishermen.

The soul of all fine soups is in the stock. Good stock is the foundation of the final product. Here is the essence of quality stock.

FISH STOCK

(makes three quarts)
5 pounds white-fish racks (cod, haddock, flounder)
1 large onion, chopped
1 large carrot, sliced
2 ribs celery, chopped
1 bay leaf
1 tsp. dried thyme
1 cup white wine (optional) or 1 TBS vinegar

Make sure the gills are removed from the fish. Put the racks in a large kettle, and add other ingredients and water to cover. Bring to a boil, and reduce to a simmer.

Cook 25 minutes, strain, cool, and refrigerate. When you use the stock, leave the sediment behind in the container. Clam juice can be used instead of or in addition to the fish stock.

CAPE COD FISH CHOWDER

2 lbs. cod, tautog, haddock or striper fillets OR 6 lbs. racks of assorted fish OR 5 lbs. cod heads
Water to make 4 cups of stock OR 2 cups clam juice and 2 cups water
Salt and pepper, to taste
2 pounds potatoes, peeled and diced
2 medium onions, peeled and diced
2 cups milk or half-and-half, or 1 cup milk and 1 can evaporated milk
1/2 tsp. thyme
2 TBS butter
1/4 pound salt pork

Cook the fish slowly in your stock until it flakes easily. Strain the stock, and return it to the kettle, adding the diced potatoes. Slowly boil until the spuds are cooked. Meanwhile, dice the salt pork, and gently fry it with the onions until the onions are transparent. If you like thicker chowder, add extra flour now to the onions and salt pork. Continue to sauté for 2 more minutes to form a flour, onion and salt pork roux. Add the roux to the stock and potatoes, and watch the chowder thicken. Now add your salt, pepper, thyme and milk or half-and-half. Drop the temperature because you don't want the soup to boil after you add the milk. Serves 6 hungry fishermen.

ZUPPA DI PESCE
(Italian fish soup)

2 quarts fish stock
3 lbs. mixed fish fillets
3 TBS olive oil
1 cup onions, chopped
3 TBS garlic, chopped
2 TBS celery, chopped
2 TBS fresh parsley, chopped
2 cups tomatoes, chopped or crushed (canned or fresh)
1/2 cup white wine
Salt and pepper, to taste
Cayenne or Tabasco, to taste
Squid, small clams, mussels, shrimp and/or lobster (Any or all of these may be added to the basic soup. Use what you have or can easily find.)

Sauté the onion until soft, but not brown, in the olive oil in a large kettle. Add the garlic, parsley and celery, and sauté for 3 minutes. Add the tomatoes, and simmer for 5 more minutes. Now add the stock, wine and seasonings. Bring to a boil. Add the fish and shellfish, and cook 10 to 12 minutes or until the clams are open and fish is done. Correct the seasoning, and serve with rouille.

ROUILLE

5 cloves garlic
1/4 cup fish soup liquid
1 egg
1/2 tsp. cayenne pepper
1/2 cup olive oil

Process the first four ingredients in a food processor. Add the oil slowly to make a fine mayonnaise. Use this on your crusty French bread, and try pouring the soup over the mayonnaise bread.

A SIMPLE FISH SOUP

3 to 5 lbs. cod racks
2 to 3 TBS olive oil
10 cups water
1 cup onion, sliced
1 cup celery, sliced
1 cup scallions, diced
1/2 cup fresh parsley
2 ½ cups fresh or canned tomatoes
1/2 tsp. anise seed
1 tsp. turmeric
1/2 tsp. tarragon
1/2 tsp. rosemary
1/2 tsp. thyme leaves
1/2 tsp. black pepper
2 ½ tsps. salt

Remove gills from heads. Place oil in a large heavy kettle big enough for all the ingredients. Sauté the heads and bones over high heat for 2 to 3 minutes, stirring so as not to burn them. Add the water and boil the heads and bones for 15 minutes. Skim off the scum. Strain this stock, and put it back in the kettle. Add the rest of the ingredients, except for the fish, and gently boil for 30 minutes. Strain the liquids from the solids, and purée the solids in a processor. Stir the purée back into the liquid. Add the fish pieces carefully picked from the racks, and heat thoroughly. Add some rouille just before serving. This is good stuff.

Try these soups and you will not be sorry; you may even be famous, at least locally. I have gotten myself into many "fine kettles of fish" in my lifetime, and I can safely say that I prefer the culinary variety to the social variety every time.

Y2Fish?

If we cannot wait for fish that we catch, we can eat canned fish.

Is this the first month of the millennium or is it next January? Are we in a crisis? I am, but then I am every winter at this time, for the fish are gone until spring – shellfishing requires bravery and since the decline in the commercial fishery, I have to buy fish! I do not like it! Or I can use some of the canned fish I always keep on hand and seldom use, except for tuna in universally popular tunafish sandwiches. (Try adding a tablespoon or two of pickle relish to your usual mixture.)

I think I unconsciously augmented my usual store of canned fish in preparation for a possible Y2K food distribution crisis. Well, if we're in a crisis, we might as well use our stock of "tinned" fish as deliciously as possible. So here goes.

We will start with "the classic" from my boyhood.

TUNA, NOODLE AND MUSHROOM SOUP CASSEROLE
(for 4)

2 cups uncooked noodles (I like elbows)
(1) 6-oz. can (or more) tuna
(1) 10 ½-oz. can condensed mushroom soup

Tuna, Noodle, Mushroom

Cook the noodles, then open the can and drain the tuna. Put a layer of noodles on the bottom of a greased (use butter, margarine, oil) casserole dish. Sprinkle (arrange) flaked tuna on the noodles. Layer the tuna and noodles, ending with a noodle layer on top. Pour mushroom soup on top. Cover the top with buttered corn flakes or cracker crumbs. Bake in preheated, 450-degree oven until the top is brown.

If you want to be fancy, you can add your choice of flavoring to the mushroom soup (Worcestershire sauce, A-1, sherry, curry powder). Some philistines even top this casserole with potato chips.

This stuff is good, worth reviving. I like cranberry sauce with mine, also straight from the can.

QUICK SALMON (OR TUNA) LOAF

1 lb. cooked or canned salmon (or tuna)
3/4 cup soft bread crumbs
1 egg
1/4 cup evaporated milk
1/4 tsp. paprika
2 tsps. lemon juice
1/2 tsp. salt
1 TBS melted butter
2 TBS chopped celery, green onion, olives or peppers
3 TBS chopped fresh parsley or 1 TBS dried parsley

Preheat oven to 400 degrees. Mix all ingredients thoroughly, and add flaked fish. Put the works in a buttered bread pan or casserole, and bake for 30 minutes. This can be eaten hot with a sauce of tomato, cream, cheese or whatever, or cold with mayonnaise. Try it.

Now we will get a little fancier. The next two are based on recipes from Jacques Pepin's The Shortcut Cook.

SALMON CROQUETTES WITH CUCUMBER RELISH

1 cup fresh bread crumbs
1 can (7 1/2-oz.) salmon in water
1/2 cup minced scallion
1/2 tsp. dried tarragon
1 TBS hot salsa
3 TBS mayonnaise
2 TBS oil

Mix together all the ingredients, and form into 8 patties. Heat 2 TBS oil in a skillet, and carefully brown the patties for about 2½ minutes on each side. Keep them warm in a 200-degree oven.

HOT CUCUMBER RELISH

1 large cucumber (the burpless, hothouse or
  English cucumber is best)
1 tsp. salt
2 TBS sugar
1 tsp. crushed red pepper flakes
  (I think a half tsp. is hot enough)
1/2 cup white or cider vinegar
1 cup boiling water

Peel and slice the cucumber. Pour the other ingredients over the cucumber slices, and refrigerate for at least 2 hours before using.

Chop 1/2 cup of these marinated cucumbers finely, add about 1/4 cup marinade to the chopped cucumbers, and serve over or under the still-warm croquettes.

This cucumber relish is worth keeping on hand. I love it!

SARDINES IN TOMATO SAUCE SALAD
(for 2 to 4)

2 or 3 cups salad greens (I like romaine lettuce here)
1 large (16-oz.) can or two small cans of sardines
  in tomato sauce
1 medium red onion, sliced
1 TBS olive oil
1 TBS red wine vinegar
1/4 cup parsley, chopped
2 ripe tomatoes, quartered

Put the greens on a platter, and place the sardines on top. Arrange the tomatoes around the edge of the platter, and put the onions on top of the fish. Sprinkle the whole works with oil, vinegar, salt and pepper. I like to add a couple of quartered boiled eggs to this and accompany it with crusty bread.

This one is very good, and no cooking! The next recipe may be the best of all!

SUPERB CRAB CAKES

3 cans crabmeat (about 1 lb.)
1 cup crushed soda crackers
1/2 tsp. dry mustard
1 tsp. Worcestershire sauce
1 medium onion, chopped
1 small green pepper, chopped
1 egg, beaten
2 TBS parsley, chopped
Salt and pepper
4 TBS oil

Sauté the peppers and onions, then mix all the ingredients together. Shape into patties, dip in bread crumbs or corn flour, and sauté in about 4 tablespoons oil until nicely browned on both sides. Serve with tartar sauce and lemon wedges. Oh boy!

This recipe makes me want to join the stripers in Chesapeake Bay where it comes from.

There Is Something Fishy About This!

I should hope so! I get irritated when people, ignorant people, say that they do not like fish because of their fishy flavor. What on earth do they expect – chocolate, peach, pork? I may be being a little unfair, for most people who speak of fishy flavors have never had good, fresh, well-prepared fish. Someone may have tried to feed them one of the bloody-eyed mackerel you frequently see in supermarket fish displays. These disgraceful mackerel are sometimes so soft that you can squeeze the flesh out of them like toothpaste from a tube. They have nothing in common with a broiled fresh mackerel fillet or a tinker mackerel (a mackerel shorter than nine inches), breaded or floured and fried crisp while almost twitching with life – two of life's great culinary treats.

They may have been given a bluefish that lay two hours on a hot deck and then two hours in the trunk of a car, unbled and ungutted, its own gastric juices breaking down its tissue from the inside out. Fishermen and fishmongers who perpetrate such crimes have a special place in hell reserved for them.

Maybe it is good to give eating fish a bad name. Maybe there will be more around for those of us who like to catch, cook and eat them. Maybe I am cutting my own throat by teaching people how to cook fish right, but I am not going to quit!

I agree with A. J. Liebling, longtime writer for The New Yorker, who wrote in an essay reproduced in The Best of A. J. Liebling, Simon and Schuster, 1963:

"Personally I like tastes that know their own minds. The reason that people who detest fish often tolerate sole is that sole doesn't taste very much like fish, and even this degree of resemblance disappears when it is submerged in the kind of sauce that patrons of Piedmontese restaurants in London and New York think of as characteristically French. People with the same apathy toward decided flavor relish "South African lobster" tails – frozen as long as the Siberian mammoth – because they don't taste lobstery. (South African lobsters are a kind of sea crayfish or langouste, but that would be nothing against them if they were fresh.) They prefer processed cheese because it isn't cheesy, and synthetic vanilla extract because it isn't vanillary. They have made a triumph of the Delicious apple because it doesn't taste like an apple, and of the Gold Delicious because it doesn't taste like anything."

I would like to enlighten these lost souls by introducing them to some fish that tastes like fish and will not scare them off but will open their worlds to new, almost limitless, pleasurable culinary possibilities.

The first requirement is fresh fish that have been handled well. The second requirement is not to overcook the fish. The rule of thumb to remember is 10 minutes of cooking for every inch of thickness of the fish you are cooking; so you would pan-fry a thick fillet for five minutes on each side, or broil it for 10 minutes, or sauté it for 10 minutes at 400 degrees. No matter what method you choose (even poaching in a simmering sauce), it will take about 10 minutes for each inch of thickness to cook your fish.

Here we will stick to simply prepared fish, all available in fish markets (alas, it is winter and we cannot easily catch our own), served in their almost unadorned beauty.

OVEN-FRIED FILLETS

1 ½ to 2 lbs. white fish fillets (cod, haddock, catfish, sole...)
1 ½ cups milk
Salt and pepper
Bread crumbs
Butter or oil
Lemon

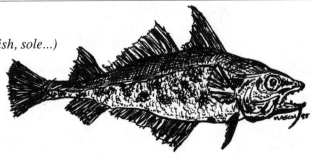

Heat the oven to 500 degrees. Soak the fillets in milk – 5 minutes is long enough. Season the bread crumbs with salt and pepper. Dredge the wet fillets in bread crumbs, patting in the crumbs to make sure they stick. Melt some butter. Butter a 9x13-inch baking pan (nonstick is good). Lay the breaded fillets in the pan. Drizzle the melted butter or oil on top of the fillets, and bake for 7 or 8 minutes in the upper third of the oven. The higher temperature and shorter cooking time bends the "400 degrees/10 minutes per inch" rule but assures a crispy result. Serve with lemon wedges and tartar sauce. Nice!

BROILED FLATFISH FILLETS

2 lbs. flatfish fillet (flounder, fluke, sole)
2 TBS melted butter or olive oil
Salt and pepper
Lemon

Preheat the broiler oven shelf on the highest level. Oil the baking sheet or broiler pan. Put the fillets on the sheet or pan, oil or butter the upper side, and sprinkle with salt and pepper. Broil for 3 to 4 minutes, until browning begins. Remove fillets from the oven, and serve immediately, drizzled with lemon juice. What could be quicker or simpler?

You can enhance (if you love garlic) this dish with garlic and parsley by combining 1/3 cup of olive oil, 1/2 cup of chopped parsley, 1/4 cup of lemon juice, 1 teaspoon of minced garlic, and a little salt and pepper. Spoon half of this mixture over the fillets before broiling. Serve the remainder as a sauce.

If the broiler scares you, you may bake the fillets following the "10 minutes per inch of thickness" rule at 400 or 450 degrees.

SAUTÉED COD STEAKS

4 small cod steaks, 3/4- or 1-inch thick
Lemon and parsley (for garnish)
4 TBS olive oil
1/4 to 1/2 tsp. cayenne pepper
1 cup flour, for dredging steaks
Salt and black pepper

Heat a big skillet for a couple of minutes. Heat the oil briefly in the hot pan. Mix the flour with salt, cayenne and plenty of black pepper. Dredge the steaks in this mixture, and put them into the pan with the hot oil. Lower the flame to medium, and sauté for 4 to 5 minutes on each side or until the translucence is gone from their centers. Serve garnished with lemon wedges and and chopped parsley.

I like to serve mashed potatoes and tiny peas with sautéed or broiled fish. Maybe I should say I like to eat mashed potatoes and tiny peas with fish. If you eat what I have cooked, that is probably what you will get. A good variation on this menu is pasta (linguine) rather than potatoes. Add a tablespoon of chopped garlic to the sauté pan about a minute before the steaks are done. Boil the pasta, dress with a little butter and Parmesan, pour the oil and juices from the pan on the pasta, and toss with chopped parsley. I would still have the tiny peas – some people would like a green salad with this. This is good.

These three simple recipes may convince those benighted souls who find something "fishy" about fish. I certainly hope so!

Try Something New For New Years

My young (I say "young" though he is nearing 40) friend Seth Carey of West Falmouth, Massachusetts, is the most accomplished and adventurous amateur fish cook I know. He has also become just about the best fish, poultry and pork smoker around. He has recently built a smoker that does both hot and cold smoking. Seth says, "It's big enough to smoke a grown goat." He hasn't done this yet, but I wouldn't put it past him.

I have sampled his smoked striped bass, bluefish, bonito and snapper blues, all caught locally by him, and farm-raised salmon that he purchased. They were all good, and some were excellent! Striped bass is my favorite; bonito is Seth's, and everybody likes smoked bluefish (an otherwise often unappreciated fish). My wife, who doesn't like smoked turkey, thought the smoked chicken Seth gave us was delicious and proved it by eating it down to a skeleton a taxidermist would love.

I am not going to give smoking instructions here but will suggest a couple of ways to present smoked fish and give you Seth's brining technique.

SETH'S DRY BRINE

(1) 3-lb. box of kosher salt
3 lbs. brown sugar
A handful (as Seth puts it) of chili powder: 3 TBS
2 TBS ground cumin
1/2 tsp. hot pepper flakes
Garlic powder, optional

Seth uses a cooler for brining, putting a 1/4-inch layer of brine mixture on the bottom, then a layer of fillets, skin-side down, another layer of mixture, then fillets, until all the fish is covered.

Seth allows this to steep for an hour to an hour and a half – no longer or your product will be too salty. Remember, we are preparing fish to eat now, not for preservation, so they do not have to be as heavily salted or smoked as dry as if we were preparing them for preservation.

Try this method of brining, and proceed with your smoking technique. You will not be sorry!

SMOKED BLUEFISH PÂTÉ

1/2 lb. smoked bluefish
1/2 lb. cream cheese
1 medium onion
Juice of one lemon
1 TBS horseradish

Mix the whole works in a blender until smooth, or grate the onion and mash the rest into a homogenous paste. You can add whatever touches you might wish to this basic pâté, perhaps Worcestershire or chili sauce, even cognac or hot sauce.

When served as an appetizer, plain smoked bluefish on a plate with crackers, sliced cucumbers, sliced sweet onion and lemon quarters will disappear about as quickly as reading this paragraph. Stand back if your guests already know how good this is!

CREAMED SMOKED FISH

(for 4)

2 lbs. smoked fish, cubed
1/2 stick butter
2 TBS flour
1 cup milk
1 cup light cream
Salt and pepper
Pinch of cayenne
Pinch of nutmeg

Pour boiling water over the smoked fish, then drain after 5 minutes.

Melt the butter and the flour, and cook, stirring over medium heat for 2 minutes. Remove from heat, and add milk and cream, 1/2 teaspoon salt, pepper, nutmeg and cayenne (or hot sauce). Put back on the heat and stir until thickened; add the fish and heat thoroughly. Serve on toast. Oh boy! I like a boiled egg or two, cut in quarters, added to mine!

You could vary this to suit yourself by sautéing onions in the butter before adding the flour or celery. You could garnish with mint or parsley; some people even add capers.

Seth is impresario and head cook at sushi banquets at his home that are certainly unequaled on Cape Cod and probably not equaled in Massachusetts or even New England. To be invited is to be blessed.

Raw-fish eating is relatively new in New England, though we have consumed the more immediately repugnant raw oyster for many years and swallowed the slippery littleneck gleefully with equal zeal.

These Japanese feasts convince most of the skeptical very quickly that raw fish can be wonderful and surprise almost everyone with how quickly they become accepting of the concept. Here is another idea: pizza without tomato sauce or cheese, made with quahogs, clams or oysters.

Seth introduced me to oyster pizza just last week, two days after Thanksgiving. Pepe's Restaurant in New Haven had introduced me to clam pizza. This stuff is so good as to be addictive. Try it at your own risk. It may change your life.

Last week Seth's oyster pizza wiped out my memory of a Thanksgiving feast prepared by me two days earlier. It had to be good.

SETH'S OYSTER OR CLAM PIZZA

1 Boboli pizza bread (Or make your own crust, or buy a prepared crust. Seth swears by Boboli.)
Rub the bread with olive oil (1/4 cup).
Sprinkle on way too much chopped garlic, says Seth (3 TBS, I say).
Add too many clams or oysters (1/2 to 1 pint, I say). The clams should be chopped, the oysters whole.
8 slices of half-cooked bacon, chopped and sprinkled over the shellfish and garlic

Bake this beauty at 400 degrees for about 15 minutes, and serve. Words fail me!

Seth says adding tomato sauce or cheese to this is bastardization.

If you insist on cheese and tomato as the basis for your pizza but still want a bit of seafood other than anchovies, put a pound of cleaned medium shrimp on your standard cheese pizza for the last 5 minutes of cooking. It is critical not to overcook the shrimp for they will lose their joy!

Oyster Pizza

To Market, To Market, To Buy A Fat?

Winter again, the slowest time of the year. For most fishermen, it is a time to work on gear (though I usually put this off until it becomes urgent in the spring), eat some smoked fish, use up the stuff in the freezer and even buy fish from the supermarket, some of which can be very good; salmon, farm-raised catfish and shrimp are the most dependable for good quality. It is interesting that these three are usually products of aquaculture. If one is fortunate enough to live near a source of fish from "day boats" (ones that go out in the morning and come home at night) catching cod on hook and line, you can get the best cod there is without catching them yourself.

My friend Seth Carey got a mess of fresh mackerel from Mike Ryan of Woods Hole. He had some fresh and wanted to smoke the rest. He asked me to help split and salt them in preparation for putting them in the smoker, which I did. I am now anxiously waiting to sample the finished product. Ryan caught these mackerel during lulls in the codfish jigging action off of Plymouth. There is no fish better than a fresh mackerel (the day it is caught) and few fish worse than the kind you often see in the fish cases of supermarkets, so soft that an impression is left when you push your finger into its side, eyes opaque and bloody-looking, flesh beginning to liquefy. This is one of my pet peeves. The supermarkets turn people away from fish by selling these things, giving all fish a bad name. Perhaps this is a conservation measure on their part, but I doubt it.

I went to Seth's and picked up some freshly smoked mackerel. They were delicious – my dogs liked the skins as much as I liked the meat.

Seth lays split mackerel, skin-side down, on a quarter-inch layer of kosher salt, covers them with more salt, and puts down another layer of mackerel, covers that layer with salt and continues until all the mackerel is buried in salt. After one hour the fish are removed from the salt, rinsed and placed on smoking racks, or laid on racks to air dry until it is time to smoke them: overnight at 40 degrees is long enough for drying.

Seth then fires up his smoker that can both slow smoke (low temperature) or hot smoke (high temperature) the product. He usually uses fruit wood prunings from his orchard for the smoker fuel. Seth smokes the mackerel at about 75 degrees (cold smoking) for six hours or so, depending on instinct. He then heats the smoked raw fish in the oven to a bacteria-killing 160 degrees. He then vacuum-seals the split, smoked, super savory fish. His smoked bluefish done this way is outstanding and his striped bass better than I expected – kind of like Finnan Haddie. He is going to do more mackerel next week. I will be there to help with the extras.

A PERFECT WINTER BREAKFAST
(for 4)

4 bagels or 8 slices homemade bread, toasted
Butter
Homemade strawberry jam
Cream cheese
1/2 cup chopped scallions or chives
1 lb. smoked local fish (fancy salmon is good, too)
Sliced sweet onion
6 eggs (to scramble)
Orange juice
Plenty of hot dark-roast or chicory-flavored coffee

Toast the split bagels and bread, butter them lightly, and serve along with the cream cheese, all the other condiments and most of the smoked fish. Each guest will make his or her own open-faced sandwich.

Beat the eggs, along with 1/2 teaspoon salt, 1/4 teaspoon pepper, 1/3 cup chopped smoked fish (trimmed from original piece), 1 dash Tabasco and 1 tablespoon chopped chives or scallions. Melt 1 tablespoon butter in a heavy-bottomed skillet or in a double boiler; when the butter is melted, add the egg mixture and stir it constantly over as low a heat as your patience will tolerate until creamy and smooth, and serve. You will have taken another step toward beatification in the eyes of your guests. Do it! You will not be sorry.

Farm-raised catfish is perhaps the best newly available fish in our supermarkets. I think it is far tastier than tilapia. Give it a try. Allow at least 1/2 pound of fish for each diner.

BREADED FARM-RAISED CATFISH (for 4)

2 or 2 ½ lbs. catfish fillets (cut in 4 pieces)
1/2 cup flour seasoned with 1/2 tsp. salt, 1/2 tsp. black pepper,
  1/4 tsp. cayenne pepper or some prepared seasoning
  mixture you like for fish
1/2 cup milk
1 egg, beaten
2 cups (or more) fine bread crumbs
1/2 cup corn flour (not meal)
Peanut oil

Bullhead Catfish

Shake the fillets in a bag containing the seasoned flour until thoroughly coated. Dip each one in the milk and egg mixture and then in the corn flour and crumbs mixture. Pat the crumbs on, and put fillets on a plate. They should sit at least 15 minutes, but they can stay all day in the refrigerator.

Heat about 1/8 inch of peanut oil in a skillet large enough to hold your fillets, or cook them in batches (keeping cooked ones warm and crisp in a 200-degree oven until serving time). Fry the breaded fillets for about 5 minutes on each side, turning once. Be careful not to burn coating.

Serve with coleslaw and french fries, lemon wedges and tartar sauce. I like some Tabasco-laced ketchup as well.

THE EASIEST BAKED SALMON

1/2 lb. fillet of salmon for each guest (can be one piece)
1 TBS prepared seasoning (Emeril's Essence, Prudhomme's Blackened Redfish Seasoning)
Olive oil
Salt and pepper
Bread crumbs

Preheat oven to 425. Put salmon fillets in an oiled baking pan, sprinkle (cover) fish with prepared seasoning and salt, pepper and bread crumbs. Drizzle olive oil over crumbs and put in hot oven. Bake 10 minutes for each inch of thickness. At 10 minutes, begin checking fish for doneness. The moment it flakes through at its thickest point, remove from oven. It will be, it must be, moist inside. Delicious.

Serve with mashed potatoes and tiny frozen peas. Garnish with lemon and parsley. What a treat! – and quick!

Shellfish and bivalves are also good (if tightly closed) from supermarket cases. So is frozen swordfish.
In this book, I have included a recipe for stuffed quahogs that could also be used, and should be, for turkey stuffing, so I meant the recipe to be larger than necessary for stuffing a single bird, but I did go overboard suggesting that you use five dozen chowder clams.
An old friend, and shipmate of 40 years ago, Sam Vincent called me. I had not heard from him for some time. Sam pointed out you could probably stuff an ostrich with five dozen chowder clams. The idea that some "chowders" might go to waste disturbed his penurious "Yankee soul" enough to inspire a phone call.
Sam's instincts are right: We must not waste our precious fish and shellfish while we still have them. So let us cook them right! Forget the ostrich, stuff some quahog shells, and celebrate a New Year.

Coldwater Cod And "Flying Mackerel"

Two of my favorite people are important in the following recipes. Phil, the conservationist assassin, and my son-in-law to be, bocce impresario and gourmet cook, Scott.

There is something effete and precious about the word "gourmet" to most people. To me a gourmet is a person who respects and treats food with respect, from the humble turnip to the exalted truffle, and enjoys eating them. The gourmet cook is one willing to spend the time and energy and attention to bring out the best in all foods, a noble goal, in preparing everything from fried haddock to Coquilles St. Jacque.

Phil, a lover of ducks alive and dead, sometimes fishes and hunts simultaneously, jigging for a cod with one hand while scanning the sky for sea ducks and holding a shotgun in the other. He told me that once late in the fall – late for summer fish, early for sea ducks – he hooked a large bluefish just as the first common eiders came within range. You can imagine the pandemonium that followed. He put his foot on the butt of his wildly bucking rod, raised the gun and killed an eider. He landed a 10-pound bluefish and complained that he missed with the second barrel. It is rare that anyone scores a double of a big blue and common eider, but Phil is the man! He has had cod and duck doubles many times, but they are not nearly as exciting.

Years ago, when new to the Cape, I asked a couple of "old timers" if sea ducks were good eating. I got the same answer from Coot Hall, Cuttyhunk striper fishing guide, and Oatie Hathon, maker of black-powder shotguns.

"Yeah, they're alright if you like mackerel. They taste like flying mackerel."

Oatie would hunt with black powder. I remember watching his boat among a flock of eider off Nobska Point early in the morning and seeing a great puff of black smoke followed seconds later by a loud boom as an eider, sometimes two, fell out of the sky. Often when I examined the birds, I could find no wounds on them, no apparent cause of death. Oatie claimed that the smoke and noise scared them to death and the ones that died mysteriously made for the best eating.

I was recently given several pounds of sea duck breasts and several pounds of cod after Phil had a day of successful "multi-tasking" off Marshfield. Coldwater cod eaten the day it is caught is one of the finest gifts from the sea. Phil, who does not cook much, gave me his recipe for fresh cod, which results in a dish reminiscent of baked stuffed lobster.

A Double

FISH FILLETS A LA BETTY (PHIL'S MOM)
(for 2)

2 ½ lbs. fillets of white fish (cod, haddock)

1/2 stick butter

Mayonnaise

1/2 sleeve Ritz crackers

Salt and pepper

Lightly butter a baking pan (Pyrex is good). Lay fillets in pan. Season lightly with salt and pepper. Coat with a thin layer of mayonnaise for the buttered crumbs to stick to. Melt butter in pan; stir finely crumbled cracker meal into melted butter until crumbly. Spread this evenly on each fillet.

Bake this for 10 minutes per inch of thickness in a 375-degree oven or until nicely browned, not blackened, on top. Garnish with parsley, and serve. You will be loved, as is Phil's mother. A fine lady, indeed!

I had people invited for dinner on the day Phil gave me the cod. I had planned to serve pasta with a plain marinara or simple tomato sauce, with cooked shrimp and scallops on the side for the guests to add to their pasta or their salad, whichever they preferred.

SIMPLE QUICK TOMATO SAUCE

(1) 28-ounce can diced or whole tomatoes (packed in juice, not packed in purée or sauce)

2 cloves garlic, minced

3 TBS extra-virgin olive oil

3 TBS chopped fresh basil leaves (about 8 leaves or TBS dried)

1/2 tsp. sugar

Salt and pepper

Codfish

Drain canned tomatoes, saving juice. Chop into 1/4 pieces if whole. Measure 2 2/3 cups; add juice if necessary to get this amount.

Put garlic through press, or chop very fine, add 1 teaspoon of water. Heat 2 tablespoons oil and garlic in sauté or saucepan over medium heat or until fragrant – do not brown garlic. Stir in tomatoes, and simmer about 10 minutes over medium heat until slightly thickened. Stir in basil, sugar and salt.

Meanwhile, bring 4 quarts salted (1 tablespoon) water to a rolling boil, add pasta, and cook until al dente, drain, reserving 1 cup pasta water. Return pasta to pot and add reserved water, sauce and last 1 tablespoon of olive oil. Heat, stirring for one minute, and serve.

You may skip the final step. Put pasta on platter, pour sauce on top and serve.

I served this with baked cod, boiled shrimp and pan-seared scallops on the side for guests to add to their pasta, along with a green salad, crusty bread and cheap wine, and it was a grand success. It looked like I went to a lot of trouble – always good when serving guests even if that isn't the case. Go for it.

My son-in-law to be, Scott, agreed to do some experimental cooking to see if we could make sea duck not only edible but also good. We were both successful. Scott's were probably better than mine, hard for me to admit but true. My testosterone level must be going down, but alas that always comes with age, occasionally accompanied by wisdom.

SCOTT'S SEA DUCK BREASTS
Rub the breasts on both sides with a marinade consisting of:
2 tsps. coarse salt
2 TBS shallots, minced
Handful of fresh parsley, finely chopped
2 bay leaves, crumbled
About 2 dozen peppercorns, crushed
2 cloves garlic, minced
Just enough olive oil to moisten it, maybe a tablespoon

Common Eiders

I let the breasts marinate in a Ziploc baggie two or three days, once or twice a day moving them around and flipping them. To cook, pull them out an hour before to warm to room temperature. Scrape off the marinade, and put it into a small saucepan with a cup of duck stock and 1/2 cup port (I like Fonseca Bin 27; it's about $11 and very good to drink on its own). Boil it down to maybe a half or quarter cup total. I thickened that one with a butter/flour roux, but I don't think it's necessary.

Heat a cast-iron skillet on high until it's very hot. Put the breasts on it, and don't touch them for a minute or two, at which point they will not be stuck on the bottom. Flip them over and sear the other side. I like them rare, a couple of minutes on each side does it, until a finger pressed on the meat just begins to give a little resistance. Let them rest a couple of minutes, then slice thinly across the grain, and serve with the tomato sauce.

An alternative marinade:
2 TBS juniper berries, ground in a coffee grinder
2 dozen peppercorns, crushed
1-inch cinnamon stick, ground
2 cloves, ground
1 tsp. coarse salt
1 TBS or so calvados (or Armagnac or brandy) to moisten
Using this marinade I advise letting the duck sit for four or five days. Same basic deal, but for the sauce I used duck stock, calvados (only 1 or 2 tablespoons), 1 tablespoon red wine vinegar, and a quarter or half cup of dry white wine. I also served it with that mango and cranberry salsa I think goes well with it (cut up some mango, cook cranberries in simple syrup until they pop, and then cool, minced fresh ginger, lime juice).

"Memorable Medleys"

• •

Here we are, another year, the dead of winter, a good time to stay inside and cook some fish and shellfish in ways we may not have tried before. Most of our fish will come from the market in winter and seem much more costly than the "free" seafood of summer. It will take me three limits of "free" quahogs to pay for a new clam rake. I don't even want to think about the actual cost of "free" fish in fuel, tackle, gear and time, but for me the process is what I love and the quality of the product is what I appreciate. So let's be careful to buy good fish and to keep the fish dealers on their toes, especially the supermarkets whose fish sometimes lacks in quality. If you ever doubt the quality of fish you are buying, ask to smell it; if it smells at all bad to you, do not buy it, and tell the fishmonger why you are rejecting it. Demand quality for your money, especially now that fish is a luxury product.

I want to get you to try squid stew, but you probably won't. It may be an acquired taste, but like many such tastes, it can become addictive. I am victim to it. I think it made the Portuguese brave enough to sail around the African continent. So I will start with my version of Portuguese paella of seafood, a kind of fake Jagacita.

POPS' "PORTUGUESE" PAELLA
(for 8)

4 TBS olive oil
2 cups white rice
1 lb. linguica, chopped in 1/4-inch cubes
1 lb. small shrimp
1 lb. white fish fillet (cod, tautog, wolffish, etc.)
1/2 lb. sea scallops, cut in fours (optional)
8 or 16 mussels
8 or 16 littlenecks
1 ½ medium onions (about a cup), chopped
3 cloves garlic, chopped
1 red sweet pepper, chopped
1/4 tsp. cayenne or Tabasco, to taste
1 tsp. cumin, ground (optional)
2 packets Goya Sazon with Saffron
4 cups chicken or fish broth
1 pkg. frozen petit pois (tiny peas)
Parsley for garnish

Heat 4 tablespoons oil in a pot big enough to hold all ingredients (at least 4 quarts). Sauté chopped linguica until slightly browned. Remove sausage from pan, leaving as much oil behind as possible.

Sauté peppers, onions and garlic until opaque and soft; add rice to pan and sauté until all grains are coated with oil and turning opaque. Return sausage to pan and add 4 cups of broth. Add hot pepper or Tabasco to broth, the optional cumin and the two packets of Sazon with Saffron.

Put covered pot in oven and bake for 1/2 hour, then add shellfish, cover and return to oven for 15 minutes. Add fish, shrimp, optional scallops, and peas, cover and return to oven until rice is tender and all shellfish open, about 15 minutes more. Remove from oven carefully, mix and fluff up, garnish with chopped parsley, and serve to acclaim.

Some crusty bread, a chilled dry white wine and a tossed salad will get compliments and maybe even love. Paellas have strange powers.

The next dish is perfect for you and a few friends on a cold winter night. It contains enough garlic to prevent closeness unless shared by all present.

Two days ago my friend and mentor, "Predator Phil," brought me about four pounds of fish fillets from four species. I had some oysters and a fennel bulb so I thought it would be the perfect time to make a bourride, or French seafood soup. It was delicious, and I will pass the recipe on to you. Do not be dismayed by the long list of ingredients, it is not hard to make.

For the fish stock, if you don't make your own, use fish bouillon from cubes or bottled clam juice.

BOURRIDE (FISH SOUP) (for 8)

(based on Shirley King's recipe in her book
Fish, The Basics)
1/2 cup olive oil
2 celery stalks, finely chopped (3/4 cup)
1 medium onion, finely chopped (3/4 cup)
1 small fennel bulb, finely chopped (3/4 cup)
1 medium leek, chopped
1 medium carrot, grated coarsely (1/2 cup)
3 garlic cloves, 2 minced, one cut in half
*4 medium tomatoes, peeled, seeded and chopped (I
 used a 14½-oz. can of stewed tomatoes)*
1/2 tsp. dried thyme
Salt and pepper, to taste
Pinch cayenne pepper

1/2 lb. cubed potatoes (red-skinned look nice)
Wide, 4-inch strip of orange zest
Wide, 4-inch strip of lemon zest
1 loaf French bread
8 littlenecks
2 lbs. fish of at least two varieties
1 lb. mussels
1/2 lb. shrimp
1/2 lb. scallops
1/2 lb. squid
1½ cups aioli (recipe below)
1/4 cup dry vermouth or 1/2 cup dry white wine
1 scallion, thinly sliced
2 TBS parsley, chopped

You do not have to have all of the shellfish. I made my soup with only fish and six oysters, but the greater variety, the better and more impressive.

Heat oil over medium heat in a large saucepan. Add the chopped vegetables, and sauté until onions are transparent.

Add the stock, tomatoes, thyme, cayenne, citrus zests, and salt and pepper. Go easy on salt if you are using clams, they are salty. Add potatoes and wine, and simmer until potatoes are nearly done.

Fish Soup

Now add shellfish and simmer until they begin to open, and then add fish. When fish is barely done, stir in 3/4 cup aioli, garnish with parsley and scallions and, "Bob's your uncle," beautiful bourride! Serve over garlic toast with toast on the side to spread with aioli to eat along with soup.

EASY AIOLI

1 ½ cups mayonnaise
3 cloves garlic, crushed, pressed or made into paste with mortar and pestle
2 TBS white wine
1/2 tsp. salt
1/2 tsp. saffron dissolved or softened in wine for 10 minutes, or 1/2 tsp. turmeric powder for color

Beat all ingredients into mayonnaise, and you've got it.

Serve the soup with a piece of dry, garlic-rubbed toast in each bowl, and more toast on the side to slather with aioli and eat along with soup.

Slice French bread about 1/4 inch thick and toast, then rub each toast with cut clove of garlic. This is a great dish!

You can vary your shellfish if you cannot get or do not want to use them all. The more you use, the more delicious and interesting the soup will be. You should end up with about equal amounts of broth and solids. If you think your soup is too thick, add more stock or white wine.

If you present this to guests, you will be remembered and spoken of favorably – raved about in fact. Fame, even local, is fine! Go for it!

Cod And Man In New England

I thought twice before including these cod recipes as some believe it is wrong to recommend eating fish that are believed to be in danger. (Swordfish are depleted; eels may soon be as well.) I decided that if we are going to eat the last member of any species, we should be damn sure to cook it right!

Giovanni da Verrazano, an Italian explorer looking for a route to China in 1594, sailed north up the Atlantic coast from Cape Fear. He found New York's Hudson River (where a great bridge now bears his name), Narragansett Bay and a hook of land that he called Pallavisino, but nobody cared much.

Bartholomew Gosnold, a British explorer looking for sassafras (which was believed to be a cure for syphilis), found Pallavisino in 1602 and named it Cape Cod because of the great abundance of codfish in the surrounding sea. The magic word "cod" brought fishermen from all over Europe to the Cape, starting a fishing effort that carried on and grew for 350 years until it had to be curtailed in the 1990s because the stock was dangerously depleted.

Mark Kurlansky, in his first and fine book, Cod, A Biography Of The Fish That Changed The World, relates that Basques were fishing cod off Newfoundland, drying them ashore and transporting them to Europe for many years before Columbus discovered America, but being fishermen, the Basques never revealed their "hot spot." I can hear the conversation now: "Hey Vernaro, where did you get all the fish?" asks the buyer. "Oh, you know, the West and . . . ." answers Vernaro, motioning toward the North Atlantic.

Explorers bragged about what they found, but fishermen caught the fish, salted and dried them, and sold them without ever revealing their source. The cod was only known as a salted product in southern Europe. Kurlansky tells us that there is no word for fresh codfish in Portuguese, Italian or Spanish, but one word for salt cod is shared by all three and is spelled bacalhav, baccala and bacalao, respectively. One must say "fresh salt cod" to get an unsalted piece.

The salted product can be prepared in many ways; most recipes begin with soaking the dried fish. Cover your dried fish with fresh, cold water and soak it at least overnight, changing the water at least three times. Twenty-four hours is not too long a soak. Now separate the bones, skin the meat, and proceed with your recipe.

CODFISH BALLS (for 4)

A frugal Yankee classic that's often eaten with baked beans.

1 cup shredded salt cod (desalted)
2 cups mashed potatoes
1 egg (beaten)
1 TBS butter
Salt and pepper, to taste

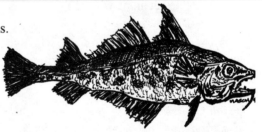

   Mash all the ingredients together, form golf-size balls, and fry them in hot oil or lard until golden brown. Drain on paper towels and eat.

COD AND SCRAPS

I once sailed with a skipper who had to have this dish once a day, no matter what else was on the menu. This is not health food, but it will keep out the North Atlantic chill and damp – and it's surprisingly delicious!

1 pound salt cod
1 ½ pounds boiling potatoes
1 large onion, chopped
1/4 pound salt pork, diced
1 tsp. black pepper

Render the salt pork until crisp, add the onions, and sauté until clear but not browned. Add codfish and heat through thoroughly. Add the pepper, and pour the whole works over the hot, boiled potatoes. Delicious!

I served the next two dishes at a Christmas party. The cassoulet was acclaimed; the brandude was enjoyed. Both recipes are from Gillian Drake's fine new cookbook, The Cape Cod Fish and Seafood Cookbook, published by Shank Painter Publishing Company.

CASSOULET OF SALT COD (for 6)

1/2 pound white beans, soaked overnight
1 pound salt cod, also soaked overnight, changing the water 3 times
4 ounces salt pork, diced
1 onion, diced
1 large carrot, diced
6 cloves garlic, crushed
1/2 cup olive oil
1 pound tomatoes, skinned, de-seeded and sieved OR 2 cups tomato purée plus 1 TBS tomato paste
1 tsp. sugar
1 bay leaf
2 sprigs fresh thyme or 1/2 tsp dried thyme
A pinch of saffron threads (optional)
2 TBS parsley, chopped
1 cup dry white wine
Salt and pepper
2 ounces dried bread crumbs

Boil the beans until tender; save the water. Drain and de-bone the cod; cut cod into 1-inch pieces. Fry salt pork, onions and carrot in olive oil until they begin to brown. Reduce heat and add garlic. Continue sautéing while adding tomatoes, sugar, bay leaf, thyme, saffron and half the parsley. Cook 3 to 4 minutes longer, stirring occasionally. Now add 1 pint of bean water, wine, beans and pepper, and bring to a boil. Simmer gently for 40 minutes. Crush some of the beans to thicken the sauce. Add the salt cod and simmer for 10 minutes. Check the spices, being careful about adding salt.

Transfer to a casserole; spread bread crumbs, mixed with remaining parsley, over the surface. Drizzle with some olive oil, and bake for 30 minutes at 375 degrees or until golden brown. Serve with a big salad and bread.

I added a 1/4 pound of linguica to mine. It didn't hurt. My friend Bill Banks, a fine cook, said this dish adds a whole new dimension to baked beans.

BRANDADE DE MORUE

1 ½ pounds salted cod, soaked 24 hours with 3 water changes
1 cup extra-virgin olive oil
4 cloves garlic, crushed
A few dashes of Tabasco
A dash of nutmeg
Freshly ground black pepper
1 cup heavy cream
Juice of 1 lemon
1 cup mashed potatoes

Ptown Laundry 1963

Boil salt cod gently for 1 ½ hours. Drain and remove the skin and bones, then flake. Put olive oil and garlic in a blender or food processor and mix well. Add the cod, Tabasco, nutmeg and black pepper, and purée. Add the cream, a little at a time, and also the lemon juice, blending slowly and tasting to correct spices.

Place mixture in a mixing bowl, and add mashed potatoes until correct consistency. Check your spices one final time. Serve hot or at room temperature with crackers or toast. Great for a cocktail party!

Try one or more of these and your life will be better for it. Remember, there are hundreds more ways to prepare the sacred salted cod!

Partake In Some Steaks!

Here we are, hopefully happy in a new millennium, but we must not forget the old axiom – do not overcook fish! It is a truism that most fish is overcooked much of the time in most restaurants and almost all of the time in most homes. Remember this general guideline: cook any cut of fish (or whole fish) for 10 minutes for each inch of thickness at a fairly high temperature (400-degree oven). This rule applies to most methods of fish cookery such as sautéing, braising, baking, grilling, boiling and steaming. Deep-frying takes less time.

This rule of thumb is not absolute but very reliable. After cooking for 10 minutes (5 minutes on each side if sautéing), test the fish for doneness by seeing if the muscle segments will flake apart easily when tested with a fork. If they do part easily, stop the cooking process by removing the fish pan or dish from the oven. The fish will cook a bit more after removal and should be served immediately if possible, though it can and may be kept warm in a 200-degree oven for up to 20 minutes.

In February there are few fish to be caught locally, so I do much of my fishing by trolling the fish markets, casting my eye over their often dismal offerings. Although the quality of fish in supermarkets has improved greatly, it still often leaves something to be desired. (I wouldn't buy and eat a mackerel from a chain store on a bet.)

This is a good time of the year to buy fish steaks, either nice big slabs of mako, tuna or swordfish, or smaller halibut and salmon steaks. Salmon steaks are now easily gotten and often inexpensive because of aquaculture and are quite good.

Remember, you don't have to fire up the outdoor grill to cook fish, you can use your oven broiler or cook in your fireplace. Kids, and I, love fireplace cookery.

SIMPLE MARINATED MAKO
(for 4)

2 lbs. mako steak, 1 inch thick
1 cup highly flavored vinaigrette (commercially made Robusto is good)

Soak steaks in marinade for 4 to 8 hours. Grill over medium coals (about 4 inches from a charcoal surface or 4 inches below an oven broiler flame) for 5 minutes on each side. Test for doneness and serve.

SIMPLE DELICIOUS SWORDFISH WITH GREEN SAUCE
(for 4)

2 lbs. swordfish steak (in 4 pieces)

Grill 5 minutes on each side. (Dot with butter or rub with olive oil before grilling.)

Green Sauce
4 anchovy fillets
1/4 cup minced scallions
1/4 cup watercress leaves
3/4 cup fresh parsley
1/4 cup drained capers
1 clove pressed garlic
3/4 cup olive oil
1/4 cup sour cream

Put all of the ingredients, except the oil and sour cream, in a food processor or blender, and chop for 20 seconds. Now add the oil slowly while the machine is running. Pour the sauce into a glass bowl, and whisk in the sour cream.

If you lack one of the greens, use more of another; only the garlic, anchovies and capers are critical. This sauce is good with any white fish. It is also grand as a dip for raw vegetables or cooked beef. It's a good sauce to know. Put a dollop of sauce on each steak, add a slice of lemon, and go to it! Very nice!

GRILLED MARINATED TUNA
(for 4)
2 lbs. tuna steak, cut 1 inch thick

Ginger-Soy Marinade
1/4 cup water
1/4 cup soy sauce
1/3 cup honey (or syrup, maple or sugar)
1/3 cup dry sherry (or 1/2 cup white vermouth)
1 clove garlic, minced or pressed
1 TBS ginger root, minced

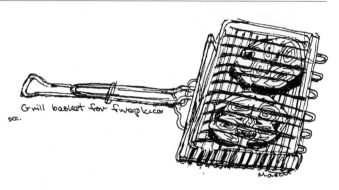
Grill basket for fireplace

Put the tuna in a glass or ceramic vessel. Combine all the marinade ingredients in a stainless or ceramic saucepan, and bring to a boil. Reduce heat and simmer for 5 minutes. Cool and add to the tuna steaks.

Grill tuna over hot coals or under the broiler for 3 minutes per side, basting a couple of times with the marinade.

The tuna should be pink in the center when you serve it, with additional marinade on the side. Oh boy!

SIMPLE GRILLED SALMON
(for 2)
Two 1/4-inch-thick salmon steaks
1 TBS olive oil

Preheat grill, oil fish, and grill for 5 minutes per side. Serve with lemon. Simple!

You could try this method from Rima and Richard Collins' *The Pleasures of Seafood*. "Preheat the grill for at least 25 minutes. Place the salmon steaks at a distance of 6 inches from the coals and grill for 15 minutes on each side. If there is no way you can set up your grill for a 6-inch distance, you can manage and reduce the grilling time to the following ratios: 13 minutes per side for a 5-inch distance, 12 minutes per side at a 4-inch distance, 11 minutes per side at a 3-inch distance. To serve, sprinkle with salt and pepper, and garnish with lemon."

This sounds well worth a try. I would serve this with plain, boiled potatoes, peas and melted butter flavored with dill.

Beware! Steaks are the easiest fish cut to dry out by overcooking, especially on the grill. Remember to baste and to heed the recommended times. The goodness of the steak is at stake here, and these can be high stakes indeed if you are grilling swordfish!

Give the fireplace a try for grilling. It is great fun!

Beyond Tuna Casserole

Years ago, while pursuing some secrets of the sea on an oceanographic cruise out of Woods Hole, we came upon a set of Japanese longlining gear that extended over the horizon. There was no boat in sight. These sets of gear were sometimes 40 miles long, carrying as many as 4,000 hooks, suspended in the water column, held up by the macramé-bound glass floats one often sees in the decor of seafood emporiums. We hauled in the terminal buoy and tied a three-pound can of tuna to the final hook and relaunched it. We then delighted in imagining their reaction to this unlikely catch on their last hook after a long day of hauling gear. I hope they ate it. We were pleased with our prank.

Last winter I wrote a column about canned seafood. I thought it was brave of me, an apostle of fresh fish. Well, fresh fish are often not available, and even the "fresh" fish found in supermarkets and fish markets are no fresher than last week's news. When I was a kid, fish were often wrapped in newspaper when purchased – last week's fish in last week's news, it seemed somehow appropriate. When fresh fish is not available and nothing but seafood will do, do not despair, for canned fish or shellfish may be used to assuage seafood yearnings.

Everybody, or almost everybody, likes the American classic, seafood and noodle casserole, made with cream of mushroom soup. (We should have provided the Japanese longliners with some!) This casserole is good, not great, but as good and comforting as a lullaby. The possibilities for delight do not end here for there are many more options for delectable dishes based on tinned fish. Canned creatures range from anchovies to octopi, from abalone (frightfully expensive) to Asian mudfish (frightening and cheap). There is probably a can of fish lurking in your pantry right now. Why not use it?

TUNA ROCKEFELLER *(for 6)*

1 lb. fresh spinach (frozen can be used)
1/2 lb. sliced bacon
1 cup sour cream
1/2 cup bread crumbs
1 tsp. salt
1/2 tsp. pepper
Juice of 1 lemon
2 cans of tuna (drained)
4 TBS Parmesan cheese, grated

Steam and chop, or purée, the spinach. Fry the bacon until it's crisp, and crumble it. Combine all the ingredients, except 2 tablespoons of Parmesan cheese, and put the mixture into a buttered 8-inch casserole or cake pan. Sprinkle the remaining Parmesan on top, and bake in a preheated 350-degree oven for about 20 minutes or until bubbly and slightly brown on top.

It is not the Oyster Bar's best, but it is very good!

The following recipes, altered by me, are based on the fine book Tin Fish Gourmet by Barbara-Jo McIntosh, West Wind Press, 1998. I am an advocate of fish cakes, and I especially enjoy the next two recipes. They are even low in fat, and kids will eat them.

SALMON BURGERS *(for 4)*

(2) 7.5-ounce tins of salmon, drained
1 egg, beaten
1/2 cup onion, chopped
1/2 cup sweet pepper, chopped
2 TBS parsley, chopped
1/2 cup bread crumbs
1 TBS lemon juice
1 tsp. lemon zest (optional, but good)
1/2 tsp. ground rosemary or thyme

Mix all the ingredients well, and form into 4 patties. Heat some oil in a sauté pan, and lightly brown the patties ("burgers" sell better to kids) on both sides. Serve on hamburger rolls with all the fixings available – nice!

CRAB CAKES WITH CAYENNE MAYONNAISE
(for 4)

(3) 4-ounce tins crabmeat, drained
2 TBS tomato paste
1/4 tsp. cayenne pepper
1 tsp. lemon juice
2 scallions, chopped, include green part
1 tsp. fresh cilantro (or parsley)
1 egg, beaten
2 tsps. grated Parmesan cheese
3 TBS cornmeal
1 TBS butter
1 TBS olive oil

MAYONNAISE
1/4 cup mayonnaise
1/2 tsp. cayenne pepper
Lemon wedges

Melt the butter and olive oil in a frying pan over medium heat. Mix all the ingredients listed, except for half the cornmeal, and form into 4 cakes (patties). Dredge the cakes in the remaining cornmeal, and cook until nicely browned and heated through – about 4 minutes per side.

Mix the mayonnaise with the cayenne pepper, and serve with the crab cakes, along with lemon wedges. Oh boy! Creamy mashed potatoes and tiny peas would go well here.

Here is an easy, "hurry up" dish that seems more complex than it is.

SPANISH RICE WITH SHRIMP
(for 2)

(1) 4-ounce tin shrimp, drained
1/2 cup spicy prepared salsa
3/4 cup rice (Arborio is best, but any will do)
2 cups vegetable broth (use cubes)
2 scallions, chopped, with green part

Heat the rice and salsa in a medium saucepan. Add the broth and bring to a boil, reduce to a simmer and cook for 20 minutes or until the rice is done. Remove pan from heat, and stir in the shrimp and scallions. Voila! Serve with salad and crusty bread – a little cold white wine . . . mmmmm.

TUNA AND CANNELLINI BEANS IN PITA POCKETS *(for 6)*

(1) 6-ounce tin tuna, drained
1/2 cup canned cannellini beans, drained
1/4 cup celery, diced
1/4 cup scallion, diced with green part
1/4 cup sweet pepper, diced (red is pretty)
6 mini pita breads

DRESSING
1/2 tsp. (or more) cumin
1 TBS lemon juice
2 TBS olive oil
Salt and pepper, to taste

For an easy, delicious lunch, try this.

Stir dressing ingredients in a bowl, add all the other ingredients, and mix well. Serve in pita pockets. A beer and some potato chips will really do it up, I promise.

Frozen Fishing And Frozen Fish

Midwinter and no fish, or at least damn few to catch from the sea in my neighborhood. I would like to have some truly fresh fish; fried yellow perch, the fish of my boyhood in Michigan, come to mind. I loved them!

Coincidentally, a couple of days after my bout of culinary nostalgia, my neighbor Win Maclane, a native of Vermont's Northeast Kingdom, suggested that when things freeze up I should go ice-fishing with him. This might get me some yellow perch. He said it would, but that means ice fishing, a far less attractive activity than it was when I was a boy or in my early adulthood when I was still drinking hard liquor. I have since been to the Florida Keys in pursuit of permit and tarpon, the Bahamas to hunt the bonefish, and Tobago for wahoo, mahi-mahi and tuna. I have pursued salmon in Quebec and Ireland, and the striped bass on the Monomoy Flats in summer – all magnificent fishing experiences!

I have not caught all of the species I have sought, but I intend to. I have, however, cooked and eaten all of them, with the exception of the tarpon, which I do not intend to eat. Not one of them was better tasting or more delicious than the yellow perch of my youth in Michigan, so I guess I will go ice-fishing with my neighbor. I asked him if he used the perch eyes for bait.

"Of course," he said. "They are the best perch bait of all."

We shared this opinion in Michigan, so I guess he knows what he is doing. We will probably get perch and this is how I will cook them.

PAN-FRIED YELLOW PERCH
Four 8-inch perch per person (scaled and gutted)
Seasoned flour
Olive oil, butter or peanut oil for frying
Seasoned coating (see below)

Make a seasoned coating using one part flour to a half part fine cornmeal, for example: 1 cup flour, 1/2 cup cornmeal, 2 teaspoons salt, 1 teaspoon black pepper (1 teaspoon Creole seasoning or 1 teaspoon adobo optional).

In a skillet big enough to hold your fish, heat oil, butter and oil, or plain butter to a medium cooking temperature. Dip your fish in milk, then in seasoned flour, and fry gently until richly browned on both sides, about 4 minutes per side. Drain on brown paper bags or paper towels. Keep them warm in the oven until all the fish are cooked.

In Michigan we ate these with German potato salad and wilted dandelion greens.

If you cannot get any perch, you could use the same recipe with smelt from the supermarket and not be disappointed. Smelt, along with farm-raised catfish and salmon, are three fish that are usually good from supermarket cases. I have strong opinions about some of the fish sold by large markets. My opinions are as strong as some of their fish.

For now, do up some smelt like this:

FRIED SMELT COCKTAIL (for 4)
1 lb. medium or small smelt
1 cup cornstarch
1 tsp. salt
1/2 tsp. ground pepper

Smelts

Mix the cornstarch with the salt and pepper, and place in a bag. Shake up the smelt with the seasoned cornstarch until well coated.

Heat 1/4 inch of oil in a skillet until quite hot, about 350 degrees. Fry the smelt in the hot oil, turning once, until crisp. They will not, and should not, brown much at all. Drain on paper towels or brown bag paper and keep warm in a 200-degree oven until all the smelt are cooked. Serve with cocktail sauce. These are outstanding!

I will now give you a recipe using "tinned," or canned, anchovies as part of a flat bread. Baking bread is a serious hobby for me, so I am happy to pass this simple recipe on to you. Even if you have never made bread before, try this — you will not be sorry.

FOCACCIA (FLAT BREAD)

2 cups lukewarm water
1 package dried yeast
4 cups unbleached flour
2 tsps. salt
2 or 3 tsps. olive oil
1 can anchovies with capers
1 bunch scallions

Put water and yeast in a large bowl, and stir to dissolve yeast. Add the salt and 2 cups of flour; mix thoroughly until smooth. Add 2 more cups of flour, and stir with a heavy spoon until incorporated into dough. This dough should pull away from the sides of the bowl but remain sticky. Cover with plastic wrap, and allow to rise for about an hour.

Turn on oven to 500 degrees. While oven is heating, oil a 13x18-inch baking sheet. Pour the dough onto the sheet, using a spatula to help it out of the bowl. Spread the dough over the entire sheet, making indentations and holes with your fingers. Brush the dough with 2 teaspoons olive oil. Now chop the anchovies and capers along with the scallions. Spread these over the oiled dough, pushing them down with your fingertips. Pour the oil from the anchovy can over all.

Put the bread into the hot oven, turn the heat down to 450 degrees, and bake for 15 to 20 minutes, until nicely browned on the edges. This stuff is delicious; your friends will rave about it and you.

If you hate anchovies, sprinkle the bread with rosemary or thyme, and sprinkle on sea salt. This can be served with almost anything.

Remember: Man does not live by fish alone, so let's make bread with fish. Even Jesus thought this to be a good idea. I would love to have his recipes!

The recipe I have given you is based on the writing of Suzanne Dunaway in her fine book *No Need to Knead*, published by Hyperion.

One of my heroes, Al McClane, wrote in his Encyclopedia of Fish Cookery that "Few mortals would deny that a yellow perch taken from a clear, cold pond is a supreme taste experience."
After reading that, I must go ice-fishing with my neighbor.

Defeating The Doldrums

February, March and early April are my least favorite times here on Cape Cod. The charm of the first snows and the beauty they bring is past; days are short, damp and gray; the air is chill. This is the time of the "winter blues," and I do not mean fish. In fact, there are almost no fish to be caught by anyone but the most intrepid angler who is willing to brave the dank and cold.

My New Oxford Shorter English Dictionary defines the doldrums as "a condition of dullness or drowsiness; low spirits, despondency." This sounds about right. Doldrums are also defined as "The condition of a ship which makes no headway," or "A region of calms, sudden storms, and light unpredictable winds near the Equator," and finally, "A state or period of little activity or progress in affairs." All the definitions seem too true, though I would rather be experiencing the one that's "near the Equator" – at least there would be fish to try for with minimal suffering. So we must beat our way out of the doldrums right here, where the winds of winter are predictable, stiff and cold, by forcing ourselves into activity and heading for the kitchen to find something interesting to cook and eat.

Gourmets will frown at the following recipes using canned fish, though I think their frowns would turn to smiles if they would but deign to try them.

The first recipe is a favorite of fisherman and design manager of On The Water magazine, Andy Nabreski. He calls these simple delicious morsels crabmeat appetizers.

CRABMEAT APPETIZERS NABRESKI

1 small can (6-oz.) crabmeat
(1) 8-oz. jar Old English cheese
1/2 stick of butter
English muffins (split), 1 package

Melt butter and cheese over medium heat in a saucepan. Stir in the well-drained crabmeat. Spread the mixture on the English muffins, and bake them in a 350-degree oven for about 10 minutes or until bubbly. Cut in quarters and serve. They will vanish!

You can make this with tuna, canned shrimp or lobster without suffering. I like to add 1/2 teaspoon of Tabasco to the mix and sometimes 1 tablespoon of Worcestershire sauce.

Try it Andy's way first, and then get creative. This is an easy recipe for kids to make. If you worry about small kids and the stove, just bring the butter and cheese to room temperature and have the kids mash them together with a fork, mix in the chosen canned seafood, spread on muffins, and pop in the oven. The kids will be delighted both with themselves and their creations. Do it!

This next dish can be made quickly out of stuff most of us have on hand. Someday I am going to prepare a suggested list of supplies to keep on hand for making good meals on short notice should unexpected guests arrive, or for when you have been unable to plan and prepare a meal in advance. The following dish could be included using such materials.

SIMPLE TUNA SAUCE FOR PASTA
(for 4)

1/2 lb. of mushrooms sliced (or 6-oz. can)
(1) 6-oz. can of tuna
2 TBS olive oil
2 cloves garlic, minced
2 cups tomato sauce

Heat the olive oil over medium heat. Sauté the mushrooms until heated through. Add the minced garlic, sauté briefly. Add the tomato sauce, and Bob's your uncle! Enough for four if you have boiled 1 pound of pasta. Serve with a green salad, crusty bread or toast, and grated cheese. I like some pepper flakes on mine.

EASY TOMATO SAUCE

(1) 18-oz. can crushed tomatoes
1 tsp. dried basil
1 bay leaf
1 medium chopped onion
Lump (2 TBS) of butter
1/2 tsp. pepper
1/2 tsp. salt

Simmer all ingredients over low heat for half an hour. You want it to reduce by about one third. Taste for salt, and stir in the butter. This is better than canned sauce and can be used in any dish calling for tomato sauce.

I like this tuna sauce over linguine, and I bet you will, too. This will also work with canned clams, shrimp or crabmeat. It's quick, easy and good. Add 1/2 cup of chopped linguica and 1/4 cup of chopped black olives, and suddenly it is Portuguese. I add 1 teaspoon of sugar to the tomato sauce when I make it. You are on your own.

Now we will try something almost as easy and more sophisticated to satisfy our gourmet readers.

PASTA WITH ANCHOVY SAUCE
(for 2 to 4)

1/2 lb. egg or green noodles
2 TBS olive oil
2 TBS butter or margarine
2 garlic cloves, chopped
1/4 tsp. dried basil
1/4 tsp. dried red pepper flakes
6 black, Sicilian, dry-cured olives, pitted and halved (optional, but delicious)
(1) 2-oz. can anchovy fillets
2 TBS freshly grated Parmesan cheese
Freshly ground black pepper, to taste
Chopped fresh parsley (for garnish, I like at least 1/4 cup)

Cook the noodles in boiling water until al dente (almost soft, but not quite). While the noodles are boiling, heat the butter and olive oil with the chopped garlic until garlic is golden brown (no darker!). Add the basil, red pepper, olives and anchovies. Stir with a wooden spoon, crushing the anchovies to make a sauce.

Drain the pasta and return it to the saucepan. Toss with the anchovy sauce and the grated cheese.

Put it all on a heated platter; grind a lot of black pepper on top, sprinkle with parsley, and go for it.

Get your share? There will be no leftovers. Try this even if you think you don't like anchovies. You may experience an epiphany. My wife is nearly an anchovy sauce and pasta addict. We may need a culinary 12-step program soon.

I adapted the anchovy sauce recipe from *The North End Italian Cookbook* by Marguerite DiMino Buonopane. With a name like that, she must be a cook!

Now we will leave the pantry and buy some yellowfin tuna steaks to pan sear. This can be marvelous and will surely be good.

SESAME-CRUSTED TUNA
(for 4)

3/4 cup sesame seeds
(4) 1/2-lb. tuna steaks (1 inch thick)
2 to 4 TBS vegetable oil
Salt and pepper

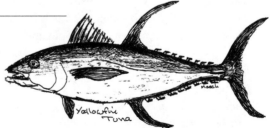

Pat the steaks dry with a paper towel. Use 1 tablespoon of oil to rub both sides of each steak; sprinkle with salt and pepper, and press into sesame seeds (which you have poured on a plate) to coat both sides. Set aside.

Heat 1 tablespoon oil in a 12-inch nonstick skillet over high heat until just beginning to smoke; swirl to coat pan. Add tuna steaks, and cook 30 seconds without moving them. Lower heat to medium and cook 90 seconds. Turn steaks carefully using tongs (the seeds should be golden brown); cook for 1½ minutes for rare (the best) or 3 minutes for medium rare. Remove from pan, and slice in 1/4-inch slices. If you do not slice them right away, they will continue to cook from residual heat. Serve with a salsa, or lemon wedges. Or a soy-based sauce.

Frozen tuna works here, especially if you make the soy-ginger sauce. I urge you to try this tuna; you will come out of the doldrums!

"Gourmet Anathema"

•••

I often talk about the danger of overcooking fish, something that Americans, even professional chefs, often do. How long to cook a given piece of fish is a dilemma for most cooks, especially beginners. I often quote the "Canadian Rule" for fish cooking, "Cook fish for ten minutes per inch of thickness in a preheated 425-degree oven, a hot frying pan or on a grill." This general rule applies to fillets, steaks or fish in the round. It is also a good general rule for poaching. This rule is not foolproof, but it is generally accurate and a good place to start. It is often difficult to estimate (not a good idea) or measure (not always easy) the thickness of a given piece of fish. I recently found a gadget in a cookware shop that measures thickness precisely. This device is inexpensive and should be in every fish cook's toolbox. It measures steaks, fillets and whole fish.

Even though fish is best barely cooked, or even undercooked, I occasionally like to break the rule and fry the moisture almost totally out of thin fillets of fish, being careful not to burn the batter or breading, and eat them like fish-flavored potato chips. You must be careful not to have the oil too hot when you do this, or your coating will burn before you have cooked most of the moisture out of the fish. (I can hear the gourmets rustling in their graves.) You can do this with trimmings from large fillets, or fillet the tiny fish caught by your children or yourself. The kids will love them "destroyed" like this. Silversides and other small minnows are also good. I have bought farm-raised catfish to cut into pencil-size pieces in order to fry them this way. Try some barely browned and some cooked nearly dry. It is fun to sometimes break the rules.

NOT FISH AND CHIPS BUT FISH CHIPS
Whatever thin 1/8-inch slices of fish you can find
Flour seasoned with salt and pepper
Cornmeal (optional), add to flour or crumbs
Bread crumbs
1 egg
1/2 cup milk

I am not providing precise amounts in this recipe because you will eat these as fast as you make them – more of a snack than an entrée.

Shake damp fillets in bag containing seasoned flour, shake off excess, now dip floured fillets in bread crumbs (or crumbs mixed with cornmeal). Heat 1/8 inch of peanut oil in frying pan over medium heat. Put coated fillets in pan, and fry until rich brown on both sides, drain on paper towel, and eat. I like Tabasco-laced ketchup with mine.

Don't tell any gourmets I suggested this recipe. These can be delicious; use cheap fish, you won't be sorry.

While we are ignoring the groaning gourmets, here are a couple of recipes for old-fashioned and fancy tuna noodle casseroles. These are derived from old and new versions of Rombauer's classic *Joy of Cooking*.

TUNA, NOODLE AND MUSHROOM SOUP CASSEROLE
2 cups of pasta or noodles (I like elbows), cooked
(1) 10 ½-ounce can condensed mushroom soup
1 cup canned tuna (or salmon)
Cracker crumbs, bread crumbs or crushed cornflakes

Put cooked noodles in a greased ovenproof pan, layer or mix flaked tuna with noodles, then pour soup over all, and cover with buttered crumbs or whatever topping you choose. Bake in a 450-degree oven until brown on top and bubbly.

You may flavor the soup if you wish with sherry, curry powder, Worcestershire sauce or whatever you wish. This is easy and good and an American tradition that deserves to be preserved.

The next recipe is from the revised *Joy of Cooking,* and though a little more work, it is still easy; a gourmet might even decide to try it – he or she can buy expensive imported tuna.

FANCY TUNA NOODLE AND CHEESE CASSEROLE

4 TBS unsalted butter (1/2 stick salted O.K.)
3/4 cup thinly sliced mushrooms
1/4 cup diced red or green pepper
1/4 cup finely diced onion
1/4 cup flour
2 ½ cups milk
1 cup shredded cheddar
(2) 6-ounce cans tuna
2 cups cooked noodles
1/4 cup minced parsley
Salt and pepper
1/2 cup bread crumbs, cracker crumbs,
  or crushed corn flakes
2 TBS melted butter

Tuna Noodle Casserole

Melt butter over medium heat in a saucepan; add mushrooms, peppers and onions. Cook about 5 minutes, stirring occasionally until soft. Stir in 1/4 cup flour and cook, stirring for 1 or 2 minutes. I prefer the latter time. Remove from heat and whisk in 2 ½ cups milk. Return to heat, and bring to a boil, stirring frequently. Sauce should thicken in about 10 minutes. Remove from heat and stir in cheese until melted. Drain tuna, and flake, add this gently to hot sauce, along with parsley and salt and pepper. Now add noodles, and pour into a 1 ½- or 2-quart baking dish. Top with chosen crumbs mixed with melted butter. Bake in a 375-degree oven for about 25 to 30 minutes or until bubbly and brown on top. Good enough for grandma though she may not admit it.

NON-GOURMET TUNA SHORTCAKE

1 can cream of chicken soup
1/4 cup milk
(1) 7-ounce can of tuna
1 cup cooked peas (frozen, more gourmet)
1 TBS chopped pimento

Heat, stirring frequently in a saucepan until bubbly and warm. Serve over cornbread, English muffins or biscuits, even toasted white bread. You can "fancy" this up with a little wine, slivered almonds or canned mushrooms, but why bother? Kids often love this, especially if given a choice of what to eat it on – rice, noodles, bread, whatever. Try it.

Now for the kicker. I have had squid cooked on a fishing-boat muffler and fish fried on a garden shovel over an outdoor fire but have only recently come across this modern method.

POACHED FISH A LA MAYTAG

Take any fish you wish to poach, and cut into 1/2-pound servings. Put each serving on a large piece of foil, season with peppers, onions, bay leaves, lemon, parsley, garlic or whatever you like, remember the salt and pepper. Seal individual packets carefully. Place packets on top rack of dishwasher, and turn on to long cycle. If you seal your packages well enough, you can even wash dishes at the same time, probably best without soap. This works! I am told you can poach a whole 5-pound bluefish in two cycles. I haven't tried it, but I will. I think you should, too.

Limited Wintertime Options

Here we are in the dead of winter in the Northeast, and most of us are not fishing, except for a few intrepid ice fishermen, so most of the seafood we eat is from the fish market or even from a can. This is not necessarily a totally bad thing. If you are not intrepid enough or lucky enough to get some yellow perch – wonderful fish indeed – caught through the ice, you too may have to resort to a can. Here are a couple of recipes for either circumstance.

I have a generous, cold-proof neighbor, Win MacLane, who gives me beautifully dressed yellow perch every winter. He comes from northern Vermont and thinks our winters here on Cape Cod are balmy.

FRIED YELLOW PERCH
(for the fortunate few)

1/2 lb. perch per person (at least), scaled or skinned
Flour to coat
1 egg
1/2 cup milk
Salt and pepper
Cayenne pepper or Tabasco (optional)
1 cup or more bread crumbs (or fine cornmeal or a mixture of both)
Oil (I like peanut) for frying

Mix flour and salt and pepper in a bag. Coat each fish by shaking in the bag of seasoned flour. Dip the floured fish in the milk in which you have beaten an egg, and roll in bread crumbs to coat. Shake off excess and put aside on plate to dry a bit as you repeat the process with the remaining fish. Allow the last fish coating to sit for at least 10 minutes for the coating to "set up" before frying.

Heat 1/4 inch of oil in a skillet placed over medium-high heat until quite hot but not smoking. When the oil is hot enough to cause a bit of bread to foam when you drop it in, it is ready.

Now add fish to oil, do not crowd, and cook until nicely colored on first side. Turn carefully so you don't knock off the breading, and repeat on second side – a total of about 5 minutes in the pan is usually right. Drain on paper towels and keep warm in a 175-degree oven as you fry the remaining fish. Serve with lemon, tartar sauce and, for me, "a gormey," some ketchup laced with Tabasco.

This is fine eating, as good or better than smelt prepared the same way. That is high praise from me, a smelt lover!

When neighbor Win finds it too balmy for ice fishing, he cools down by going "quahogging," and he often gives me the big "chowder" clams. I like to stuff them in many ways but especially in the classic Cape Cod manner, which is less fancy than using the usual more Mediterranean-style clams commonly available and uses only ingredients found in authentic clam chowder.

STUFFED CAPE COD QUAHOGS
(for a dozen stuffed clams)

24 chowder clams
1 large sweet onion, chopped
1/4 lb. salt pork (cubed small)
1/2 tsp. ground black pepper
1 cup crushed Saltines
A pinch of thyme (optional)

Stuffed Clam

Put an inch of water in a pot large enough to hold the clams. Steam over high heat until the clams open. Drain, save the broth, and remove clam meats from shells. Chop or grind in a food processor (do not purée). Measure an amount of cracker crumbs to equal the chopped clams in volume.

Sauté the cubed salt pork over medium heat until it is lightly browned, tan colored. Remove pork pieces from the rendered fat and set aside. Sauté the onions in the fat until they are soft and transparent.

It is sometimes hard to find fat salt pork because modern pigs are much leaner than they were in the "good old days," so if it seems you have too little fat for cooking the onions, add some butter.

When the onion is soft, return clams and pork bits to pan, put in cracker crumbs and mix. Moisten with reserved broth until you get a clammy mush that will just hold together and fill a dozen reserved sets of shells, and you are finished except for heating and serving. The most persnickety old Yankee may even compliment you for your purity of preparation.

I hope global warming does not force generous Win back to the Northeast Kingdom.

I am going to jump now from the frozen North to sunny Italy for a quick easy recipe for a winter's night using canned fish, tuna, in fact.